Flawed Genius

Flawed Genius

Scottish Football's Self-Destructive
MAVERICKS

Stephen McGowan

BIRLINN

First published in 2009 by
Birlinn Limited
West Newington House
10 Newington Road
Edinburgh
EH9 1QS

www.birlinn.co.uk

Images of Jim Baxter, Chic Charnley, George Connelly, Hughie Gallacher, Paul
Gascoigne, Andy Goram, Frank McAvennie and Andy Ritchie © Press Association
Image of George Best © ProSport
Image of Willie Hamilton © Scran
Image of Paolo Di Canio, Jorge Cadete and Pierre van Hooijdonk© SNS Pix
Image of Steve Paterson © Aberdeen Journals Limited

ISBN: 978 1 84158 842 1

British Library Cataloguing-in-Publication Data
A catalogue record for this book is available from the British Library

Typeset by Iolaire Typesetting, Newtonmore
Printed and bound by MPG Books Ltd, Bodmin

For Anne, Catriona and Jill

Contents

Acknowledgments

I'd like to thank the following people, without whose contributions this book would never have been possible:

Andy Ritchie, Willie Henderson, Walter Smith, Rodger Baillie, Pat Crerand, Jim McArthur, Jackie McNamara, Tony Higgins, Craig Paterson, Milan Mandaric, Frank McAvennie, Gerry Britton, Jim Duffy, John Lambie, David Hay, Bryan Cooney, Jim Black, Archie Macpherson, Hughie Gallacher, Brian Laudrup, Pierre van Hooijdonk, Pat Bonner, Tom Boyd, Richard Gough, John Brown, Craig Brown, Alan Hodgkinson, Ian Ferguson, Mike Aitken, Alan Gordon, Pat Stanton, Jimmy O'Rourke, Tom Purdie, David Speed, Marion Jones, Jock Brown, Billy Stark, Malky Mackay, Andreas Thom, Peter McLean, Jorge Cadete, Gabriele Marcotti, Andrew H. Smith, David Pleat, Faye MacLeod, Keith Wyness, Kenny Strang of the Scottish Football Museum, Peter Kay of the Sporting Chance Clinic, Jimmy Calderwood, Andy McInnes and Stephen Ritchie. Also, Neville Moir and Richard Wilson.

Apologies to any unwitting omissions . . .

Prologue

'There was never a genius without a tincture of madness.'

– Aristotle

As the straggling foot battalions of the Tartan Army trudged doggedly through the streets of Glasgow's south side on a November evening in 2008, the autumnal gloom was lifted briefly by a thundering commotion. Scotland v Argentina had never threatened to be the standard, soporific fare of the typical international friendly match. The presence of a bona fide wayward superstar ensured as much. The clamour to be in the same stratosphere as such a man occupied the minds of those traipsing past the boarded up shops on Cathcart Road, Tam O'Shanters perched precariously on their heads.

Suddenly, a police motorcycle, lights flashing urgently, commanded the attention. Squinting their eyes at the plush coach trailing close behind, supporters craned their necks to seek out the source of the persistent thumping that was discernible above a blaring siren.

In a rush to reach the sanctity of Scotland's National Stadium, the bus driver granted little time for sightseeing. Those with the best vantage points would testify later, however, to the bizarre spectacle of Diego Armando Maradona banging the roof and the windows of the vehicle as he led his players and backroom staff in an impromptu rendering of the Argentine National Anthem.

For three days, this maverick maestro of world football had held court in a city centre hotel. A media scrum had accompanied his arrival at Glasgow Airport as the most unlikely coach since Cherie Lunghi decorated our television screens in *The Manageress*. The headlines and recounted tales of excess went on for a week, dominating sports pages. Hardened old hacks who normally reserve little more than scorn for Scottish football were suddenly booking business-class seats on the British Airways shuttle from Heathrow. When Maradona indulged in some England-baiting in his pre-match press conference, it was clear he knew how to play an audience. Shameless barely covers it.

That Scotland and Hampden adopted a starring role in the coaching induction of one of the twentieth century's greatest, most contentious and divisive players was entirely fitting.

It had been here in another friendly match, on an unforgivingly hot June afternoon in 1979, that Maradona announced his arrival on the international stage.

Before 61,918 well-refreshed Scots on the hottest day Glasgow had witnessed in 30 years, Maradona sizzled as he claimed his first goal for his country at the tender age of 18. A Scotland team featuring European Cup winners such as Kenny Dalglish and Alan Hansen, as well as future national coach George Burley, was left tracking shadows in a breathless exercise in futility. To this day, Paul Hegarty, then a Dundee United defender, remains almost scarred by the experience.

'It was the first time Europe had seen Maradona,' he recalls. 'Straight away, you knew he'd very soon be mentioned in the same breath as Pele, Franz Beckenbauer and Johan Cruyff. He was just head and shoulders above everyone else.'

His balance and strength on the ball peerless, Maradona scored the third goal in a 3–1 triumph, flummoxing Scotland's substitute goalkeeper George Wood with an audacious dummy. Not since the European Cup final of 1960, when Real Madrid outclassed Eintracht Frankfurt in winning 7–3, had the old arena witnessed the likes.

The standing ovation afterwards was deserved, the hype predictable and drawn out.

What came next, as word spread, serves as a cursory tale of the dangers of fame and fortune for the impressionable footballer from the wrong side of the tracks. A life begun in the shanty town of Villa Fiorito spiralled from triumph to turmoil at a dizzying pace.

In the years which followed, Maradona's fame created a monster. He would go on to win the World Cup almost single-handedly in 1986, suffer the ignominy of being expelled from the greatest show on earth when he was sent home from the 1994 World Cup in the USA after being caught using the banned substance ephedrine (adrenaline), overcome a cocaine addiction, swap cigars with Fidel Castro and utilise the 'hand of God' to the collective anger of the English nation, when he punched the ball into the England goal during Argentina's 2–1 win in the 1986 World Cup quarter-final. All of which was guaranteed to bring a warm welcome from the Scottish nation when he was appointed the coach of Argentina the month before the friendly at Hampden.

The reason for that was simple. In this country, sports fans adhere to an old truth: brilliance and individual application may be admirable, but a sportsman often garners greater appeal when he reveals his darker side. Sir Chris Hoy and Andy Murray might one day sit comparing honours from the queen, reflecting on the glories earned from a life of selfless dedication and commitment. The contrast between these men and Maradona could hardly be starker. Give a child in Wester Hailes, Easterhouse, Lochee or Torry the choice between emulating Murray by lifting a racket at Flushing Meadows, or Hoy by donning latex cycle shorts or becoming a maverick World Cup winner, however, and the chances are they will opt for the Argentine every time. In this country, we like our heroes to come with a health warning.

Our football, like our boxing, has thrown up some tragic figures. In Scotland, we have witnessed all too many footballers who, allowed half an opportunity, will find the most contrived method by which to waste their privileged lifestyles. When the gods of sport bestow greatness upon footballers like Jim Baxter, George Best and Hughie Gallacher, they also hand them great fame and responsibility. The headlines, the adulation, the champagne, the sponsorship deals and the glory suddenly find them, rather than the reverse. And some soon become the victims rather than victors.

Deciding who to omit from any list of Scottish football's self-destructive mavericks will always be a difficult task. To this observer, there is no shortage of bad boys in a sport with a magnetic attraction for working-class kids on the make, or of players who felt everything was fine even as their lives slowly unravelled.

Those featured here are magicians who under-achieved in some way, either on a short-term basis or by failing to win the honours they might have achieved had they been blessed with the professionalism of Sir Bobby Charlton or Billy McNeill.

There is, for example, no place for the incomparable Jimmy Johnstone. The Celtic winger was as errant as they come, yet you have to draw the line somewhere and one European Cup, nine Scottish League championships, four Scottish Cups and five League Cups hardly represented a career in freefall for the most part, even if Jinky owed his longevity to the firm hand of Jock Stein. Towards the end of his career, at Sheffield United, the drink may have taken a firm grip, but he had already proven himself Celtic's greatest ever player. The statue standing outside the main stand at Parkhead in his honour hardly hints at a talent cast down a man-hole.

On those grounds Hughie Gallacher, the prolific Wembley Wizard, might also have been omitted. The last man to captain Newcastle to the English Division One Championship was unquestionably a legendary footballer with a love of the good life. But his infamy extended beyond a taste for liquor. In a contentious career, Gallacher pushed Newcastle to the limit with his quick temper and found himself implicated in allegations of accepting illegal payments at Derby. All this before he tragically took his own life.

Amongst other considerations came the thought of including only those born in Scotland. At a time when alcohol abuse is a live political issue, the examples of Barry Ferguson and Allan McGregor, who were banned from playing for Scotland in the aftermath of an extended drinking session while on international duty, prompted the question of whether Scots are particularly prone to stray off the rails.

And yet to omit some of the notorious figures who passed through our game, such as Paul Gascoigne, George Best, Paolo Di Canio and Pierre van Hooijdonk, would have been a great shame. Not all of them were boozers, but they were most certainly frayed at the edges.

The mavericks of Scotland's national game have come in many shapes and nationalities, and with many temperamental make-ups.

Amongst the Scots featured, the chapters on Andy Goram and Chic Charnley encountered unfortunate timing. Both men were working on their autobiographies when I approached them and politely indicated an understandable inability to assist with this book as a result. Where George Connelly was concerned, the reasons for non-cooperation will be clear enough to those familiar with the man's long-standing problems.

To those I did meet, I explained that the aim is not to find fault or pass judgment. The English, Scottish, Northern Irish, Dutch, Portuguese and Italian superstars featured in this book illuminated Scottish football in their own unique ways, whilst displaying a frightening capacity for self-destruction. Each was blessed with brilliant ability, a genius for the unexpected and the kind of charisma which divides the leg men from the legends. Some, like Best and Celtic's Three Amigos, were merely passing through. Others rose on a bed of adulation from their kitchen sink estates to become very real heroes. And, very occasionally, villains. Most were loved – or loathed – as much for their failings as their flair.

As this book will seek to demonstrate, aspiring football superstars should be careful what they wish for. Fame and fortune can be fickle mistresses.

1

Slim Jim

JIM BAXTER

'I shall cherish for a long time the memory of Baxter slowing the game down to almost walking pace, insouciantly juggling the ball with instep, forehead and knees while Stiles, no more than a couple of yards away, bobbed up and down, unsure whether to make his challenge at knee or head level.'

– Glyn Edwards, *Glasgow Herald*

It remains an iconic image; a grainy snapshot of a gloriously black and white past.

On Saturday, 15 April 1967, Scotland's national team overcame the world champions, England, under the shadow of Wembley's old Twin Towers. They did so playing beautiful, inventive football. And, in the gleeful words of the late James Curran Baxter, midfielder extraordinaire, by 'extracting the urine'.

As Baxter observed before his death at the age of 61 in April 2001, victory in itself was never enough. 'I wanted to show the English how easily we could beat them,' he said. 'The manner of winning meant a lot to me.'

Recorded in his many obituaries was the suggestion that the hero of the hour sat reading the *Sporting Post* in the dressing room until 10 minutes before kick-off. Invited by the team's management to do some warm-up exercises, the wayward star stretched out his right leg and then his left, all the while his eyes remaining fixed on the newspaper.

'That's me warmed up,' he announced.

Here was a man with the capacity to make a day become one hell of a long night. Every moment, be it with a ball at his feet, a drink in hand, tearing up a betting slip or holding court in the St Enoch Hotel, was for the living. And the less effort required to live it, the more rewarding the moment.

On the pitch, he brimmed with industrial quantities of vision and imagination, if not defensive graft. The instant Baxter juggled the ball in the air, socks around the ankles and shirt half hanging out in trademark fashion that fateful 1967 day, he created a memory which has acquired a legend of its own in the Scots psyche.

What few realise, however, is that Wembley was akin to a last stand, the football death throes of a fading emperor. The drinking and socialising had spiralled out of control, exacting a heavy price in physical terms.

The outline of greatness was diminishing amid a lifestyle of hedonistic chaos. In the home of Scotland's Auld Enemy, fortified by a pre-match nip of whisky, his feet danced their last great waltz. The demise had already begun.

'Jim was between Sunderland and Nottingham Forest when he played at Wembley and his reputation went before him,' recalls Rodger Baillie, the ghost-writer of Baxter's lucrative 1960s *Sunday Mirror* column and best man at his wedding. 'Wembley was his last great hoorah.'

For some, Wembley 1967 remains the national team's finest hour-and-a-half. England had been 4/7 odds on favourites, Scotland no shorter than 4/1. Baxter's showboating appealed to a land where little-country syndrome is a national condition. With a chip on both shoulders and a frustrated desire to match a southern neighbour's size and world influence, ridicule and taking the piss has become Scotland's default setting. Even if not everyone shared in the joie de vivre of Scotland's number six.

'Jim wanted to play to the crowd at 3–1 when we might have scored five or six,' Denis Law recalls. 'When I screamed, "Let's give them a doing!" Jim would smile that infuriating smile of his and reply, "Naw, let's take the piss out of them . . ." But he was magnificent that day, and you could never stay angry with him for long.'

Sir Alf Ramsay's England team had captured the Jules Rimet trophy in sterile fashion in the summer of 1966. The team's lack of wingers and the dearth of any great flourish stood in stark contrast to Baxter's fast and loose concept of how football should be played. Like Law, the Manchester United striker who had suffered 11 months of triumphalist coverage in the media, this was some form of payback; a victory for style over pragmatism.

The epitome of the '60s in a Scottish context, Baxter was the forerunner of George Best. The only Caledonian celebrity with the profile and status to match Twiggy or the Kray Twins, pork-pie hats and snazzy ties were his calling card as the staid 1950s came to an end. He celebrated the Wembley victory by swaggering into Piccadilly's Café Royale in the company of Law.

'[That] was almost as much fun as playing England off the park,' he would later recall. 'There was this big, round table in the middle with 12 hairy-legged Highlanders sitting round it in kilts. Instead of a tablecloth, the table was covered in this huge swatch of lush Wembley turf. They had the kitty in the middle and their drinks all lined up on top.'

The son of a Fife miner, Jim Baxter started out earning £7 a week working underground, but had always marked himself out as distinct from the rest. Before joining Raith Rovers in 1957, he regularly travelled to Edinburgh to spend his earnings on the kind of clothes which added colour to a grimy spit and coal dust community.

Baxter's football ability did likewise, covering a multitude of sins. Yet as a teenager he had been a slow burner. Moving from Halbeath Boys' Club to junior side Crossgates Primrose, Baxter played left-half and believed he was heading for a free transfer until Crossgates Secretary Bill Butchart decided his future lay on the left flank of midfield and switched him. Six games later, Raith were impressed enough to make their move.

As Christmas 1959 twinkled on the horizon, his glittering star was in the ascendancy. The young Fifer had witnessed a £12,000 move to Rangers flounder as the Kirkcaldy club held firm in their desire to elicit a higher price from their more illustrious Glasgow rivals. Yet within the pages of a local newspaper, the 20-year-old protégé confidently plotted out his future in an interview.

'I hate to hear, "Boot the ball! Get rid of it!"' he revealed. 'There are times when there's no alternative, but when there is no emergency it's silly to do so.' No one would ever accuse Baxter of breaking from his personal manifesto.

Revealing that his favoured post-match meal was soup, grilled steak, egg and chips, rounded off with peach Melba, and that Hibs were his boyhood idols, Hill of Beath's prodigal son also divulged his address at the time to be 93 Sinclair Drive, Cowdenbeath. This was a different, more innocent age of player interrogation. Few of the pampered, high-profile footballers of the current era, cosseted behind high security electronic gates, would dare to divulge that kind of detail.

Neither would they expect to be asked how long they might last in the professional game. Baxter's interviewer had inadvertently stumbled upon the million-dollar question where this particular player was concerned.

'If I get 10 more seasons out of the game, I'll be satisfied,' he responded. 'But I like to think that I'll be able to play a bit longer than that. With my build, I should manage to keep pretty fit, even after 30.'

How poignant those words would prove. Baxter made his final appearance as a Rangers player on 29 December 1969 in a 3–2 triumph over Aberdeen at Pittodrie – 10 years and two weeks after the *Sporting Post* interview appeared. As predicted, he had indeed made it to 30 as a professional footballer – but only just.

An unsatisfactory spell of National Service in June 1960 had already hinted at an incompatibility with discipline. Baxter flouted convention by socialising with Celtic players – rather than his own teammates. Reared on Scotland's east coast, where bigotry was in remission, the Fifer saw nothing wrong with his choice of afternoon companions. As Paddy Crerand recalls, however, there were raised eyebrows elsewhere.

'Myself, Billy McNeill, Mick Jackson and John Colrain would all hang out at Ferrari's restaurant at the top of Buchanan Street every day,' recalls Crerand. 'We would have a nice lunch and Jimmy would travel up from Ibrox and join us. Was that unusual in the Glasgow of those days? It was worse than that, it was crazy. But Jimmy was from Fife, where the bigotry was more remote than it is in Glasgow. He didn't care a damn what people thought.

'There was no drinking culture amongst our wee group at that time. We would spend most of the day together, just hanging out. Then, at night, Jim would go his separate way and we'd go ours.

'The fact was that there was nowhere else to go. It was our equivalent of hanging about the streets. And if we did have somewhere to go we had no money to go there; footballers were maybe paid a bit more than the ordinary working man in the yards, but not much.'

Crerand and Baxter had become friends through serving their country on Scotland duty. Their kinship reached across Glasgow's great divide to a degree where rumours persisted that Baxter had begun dating Crerand's (Catholic) sister. With Rangers being a club where outdated traditions meant everything, and marrying Roman Catholics was taboo, this was another early sign of the rebellious streak which could not be tamed.

That Baxter was creating leeway for himself through outstanding performances on the field helped substantially. His arrival transformed a functional team into a great one; with three league championships, three Scottish Cups and four League Cups in a startling five-year spell. A European final defeat to Fiorentina over two legs and two quarter-final appearances added to the team's aura of greatness.

To supporters, he was a figure of mythical quality. Walter Smith, a Rangers fan who later managed the club, became entranced by his brilliance at a young age:

'When I was a supporter growing up, Jim Baxter was, without a doubt, the man. On a personal basis, Jimmy Millar was my favourite Rangers player,' Smith smiles, 'but Baxter was the best player ability-wise in a team which had so much of it. He stood out as one who had a kind of arrogance about him – but in a good way. It was all, "I'm the best player on the pitch, like it or lump it." That was the first time I ever became aware of a player with that kind of persona.'

Dubbed Slim Jim, Baxter's contribution to Symon's side in this spell was full-bodied. 'You would have thought his legs had no flesh on them at all,' smiles former teammate Davie Wilson. 'He came in a slim boy from a miner's village in Fife, but Jimmy Baxter was the ingredient we needed at that time.'

Scott Symon was a manager of the old school, his distant approach being exposed in clinical fashion by Jock Stein's arrival at Celtic in 1965. Yet for all that he would warn younger players such as Willie Johnston to stay away from the devil incarnate in the corner, he himself had been hypnotised by Baxter's brilliance, prompting a degree of tolerance and indulgence few could conceive of.

Baxter would turn up for training hungover and down a pack of Alka Seltzer before regaling teammates with tales of his carousing in the St Enoch Hotel – the venue which would become his own personal nightclub.

'Jimmy didn't give a damn,' concedes Crerand. 'He was George Best before George Best arrived on the scene. He began to like a drink and a laugh, but he was so likeable with it. He was carefree. If he couldn't do you any good then he certainly wouldn't do you any harm, that's how I'd describe Jim.

'We respected each other's ability and he had that devil-may-care approach to his life until the day he died. What harm was he doing anyone other than himself? But I'm not so sure the Rangers directors saw it that way. Bob Kelly, the Celtic chairman, loved the fact that he came and ate with us rather than his own teammates. It was good, old-fashioned one-upmanship Old Firm style. I don't think the Rangers board knew what to do with him – or about him.'

That was how Baxter liked it. Rodger Baillie quickly identified a trait in Baxter's make-up which would explain at least some of the controversies which would blight the great man's career. Not least when the midfielder had a friend drive him up and down Edmiston Drive, in full public view of the elegant main stand at Ibrox, whilst engaging in amorous activities with a female journalist in the back seat of the car.

'Jim was fond of gestures against figures in authority. Gestures always appealed to him. Right to the end, he had a devotion towards Scott Symon because he was granted so much latitude. Others didn't impress him so much.'

Rangers chairman Baillie Wilson provoked grunts of derision from this talismanic man-child, yet the greatest contempt was invariably reserved for SFA secretary Willie Allan, a man Baxter regarded as the epitome of pompous, self-regarding bureaucracy. Their mutual loathing would come to a head twice in the course of 1963, most notably after Rangers, in their Baxter-inspired pomp, destroyed a hapless Celtic 3–0 in a Scottish Cup final replay to secure a domestic double.

An increasingly nocturnal animal, Baxter had been up all night playing roulette in a Fife gambling club before returning to the parental home at 9.30 a.m. with £1,700 burning a hole in his back pocket – a quite phenomenal sum at the time. With a feeling of invincibility based on league results over Celtic that season – and his flawless night at the tables – the playmaker had the Parkhead team chasing shadows, easing off the gas to take the mickey when others in the ranks favoured a more direct approach to avenge the 7–1 hammering sustained in the 1957 League Cup final.

Triumphant at time up, Baxter claimed the match ball and stuffed it up his shirt to adopt the appearance of a heavily pregnant woman. The ball in question was earmarked as a gift for Ian McMillan, the man known reverentially in the Rangers changing room as the Wee Prime Minister. When match referee Tom Wharton approached him to request the return of the ball, the response was in the negative. Hearing of this, Willie Allan, spoiling for a fight with Scottish football's *enfant terrible*, took matters into his own hands – marching to the Rangers dressing room to demand the ball's return. He was informed in no uncertain terms that the ball was a souvenir for Ian McMillan and would remain that way.

The SFA had their revenge of sorts when they sent Baxter a bill for the ball. Whether he paid it or not remains unrecorded. Few would bet on it.

Cheek, rebellion, defiance and sheer bloody-mindedness were

becoming a way of life. As Baxter evolved into a Scots celebrity and the integral component of a dominant Rangers team, however, his earnings were steadfastly failing to keep pace with his profile or with players of a similar stature down south.

With Rangers unwilling to significantly up the ante – despite grudging annual concessions of a sort – the rising star of Ibrox accepted the offer of a newspaper column with the *Sunday Mirror*, which would effectively double his earnings.

Rodger Baillie had already forged a relationship with Baxter on Scotland international trips and took care of ghost-writing the column on a weekly basis. The two men had become acquainted on a trip to Norway in 1963, which also saw Baxter's first run-in with the officious Willie Allan. Returning to the team hotel inebriated, Baxter marched over to where the SFA blazers sat and threatened to walk out on the team. Already scandalised by this behaviour, the Park Gardens officials were further outraged the next day when a hungover Baxter vomited violently out of an open window on the team coach. Regrettably, the wind did the rest, blowing much of the debris in the direction of SFA selector Bob Thyne.

'That was quite an impression,' smiles Baillie in understated fashion. 'But while Jim could be a desperado in all kinds of ways, he had two sides to him. When we signed him up to do the *Sunday Mirror* column it raised eyebrows, but he was intensely professional and serious about it.

'We would run a competition whereby one lucky reader would win the prize of a lunchtime meal with the great man himself. It didn't matter who won, Jim would be incredibly charming company. They would bring their children or brothers and sisters along and he would go out of his way to pose for pictures and accommodate them. He really was fantastic that way.

'Jim would turn up for our meetings full of ideas and snippets, because he was the manager Scott Symon's golden child and he could get away with saying and doing things others wouldn't have dreamed of.'

His growing reputation was also attracting new friends, some of the superstar variety. Sean Connery, a former Edinburgh milkman, had played Ian Fleming's James Bond for the first time in *Dr No* in 1963. His star was rising at a similar rate to Baxter's and when Rangers faced Red Star Belgrade in a Cup Winners' Cup play-off at Arsenal's Highbury Stadium, the two men arranged to meet at the main entrance to the old arena, after Connery had sent a telegram signed simply '007'. The *Sunday Mirror* was delighted when the telegram found its way onto their pages as a showbiz exclusive.

Like Connery, Baxter had emerged from humble, working-class beginnings on the east coast of Scotland. As the movie star earned exorbitant sums from his acting career, however, Baxter was living on an income more in keeping with his Fife roots. Nevertheless, he went to great lengths to look the part of the minted celebrity in the way he dressed.

At Rangers, a collar and tie was the minimum standard required, even for training. For Baxter, however, it was important to set trends rather than follow them. In the working-class environs of the west of Scotland, male fashion was an alien concept in the 1960s. And yet colleagues would enter the Rangers dressing room and find themselves admiring Baxter's attire.

To teammates, the cut and style of Baxter's suits were invariably superior to their own high street fashions. The ties, in particular, would be that bit louder than the rest. On away trips in Europe, he was fastidious in the lengths to which he would go to find the trendiest clothing store in town, and the more fashionable and outlandish the garments, the better.

'It was a statement to him,' states Henderson, 'a way of spelling out his personality.'

Discretion was never a word likely to be attached to the extrovert Baxter. In his dress sense, he was asserting his individuality to the world, firmly in keeping with his football swagger.

'Let's just say he never suffered from anything resembling an inferiority complex,' laughs Baillie. 'He had a remarkable level of self-belief, which never left him.'

The lot of so many modern-day top-flight footballers is to retreat into a world of aloof unreality, exchanging normal life and conversation for a sullen demeanour and an obsessive attention to materialism. Yet Baxter never surrendered his sense of humour or humanity. On a distant, grainy video of a victorious Ibrox side recording a version of the Rangers Song in the early '60s – a rendering reminiscent, it should be said, of the heather and whisky offerings of New Year television – Baxter can be seen centre screen, laughing almost uncontrollably into the microphone at the sheer absurdity of it all.

On the field, he was more comfortable, enjoying the kind of *Top of the Pops* billing he preferred. And yet behind the scenes, team-mates became disillusioned and concerned by the level of indiscipline being flaunted off it. Symon was reluctant to call the bluff of his star man so long as he was being courted to play for a star-studded Rest of the World team against England at Wembley. Or serving as the fulcrum of the team which stormed to a domestic treble in 1963/64. In the end, Baxter would be cut down to size, not by Symon, but by a combination of swaggering arrogance and an incensed Austrian defender.

In December 1964, Scotland's champions and treble winners had overcome Red Star Belgrade in the aforementioned Highbury play-off to earn a third-round meeting with Rapid Vienna. Baxter's assist teed up the only goal of the first leg at Ibrox and, travelling to a snow-bound Austrian capital, Rangers believed they were on their way to the last eight.

Storming to a 2–0 lead, 3–0 on aggregate, Baxter played what most – though not the man himself – believed to be his finest game in a light blue jersey. Right-back Walter Skocik endured a truly miserable evening, lunging bullishly into forlorn tackles and wasteful challenges against his imperious left-sided matador all evening. In the dying stages of the match, Rapid supporters had begun lobbing snowballs at their own team in derision when Baxter beat Skocik once, twice, but not a third time. Tired of the Rangers star man's grandstanding, the defender lost his composure; the crack could be heard by Baxter's teammates, including Davie Wilson.

'In the last minute of the game he was being arrogant,' Wilson states. 'I remember shouting to him, "Give it to me, I'll go to the byline with the ball." The game was finished, we were winning 2–0. But, no, Jimmy decides to nutmeg him – and the boy clobbered him.'

As Baxter's right leg was encased in plaster and the Rangers team had their flight diverted to Salzburg, the true implications of the break were slow to dawn. Typically, Baxter marked the evening by organising a party with two friends and some hired female company in his hotel room, cleaning out the minibar in the process. The bill, needless to say, went to Rangers.

'That broken leg was a real disaster for Rangers Football Club and for Jimmy Baxter,' claims Henderson. 'He was a huge presence in the team; he was playing superbly at that point. For me, that season had been his best in a Rangers jersey and this was a huge setback. I know others have said it and I believe it – he was never quite the same player again.

'I don't know the reasons for that. There were lots of players who broke legs at that time and recovered well. Dave Mackay, if memory serves, broke his three times and played on at the top level. Willie Ormond and Gordon Smith also overcame it to bounce back – maybe they were better trainers throughout their career. But what happened in Vienna damaged Jimmy psychologically as well as physically.'

Baxter had hitherto regarded himself as almost untouchable to defenders and Rodger Baillie agrees with Henderson's assessment of the impact the fracture had on Baxter's air of gliding, aerodynamic invincibility.

'I was in Vienna that night and his display was as good as you will ever see – especially when you consider the icy conditions. He admitted himself that he had taunted the defender and that, by and large, the tackle was his own fault. He was never quite the same player afterwards. Oh, he produced the flashes of course – most obviously for Scotland at Wembley.

'But [Rangers] rushed him back from that injury as quickly as they could. He must have worked harder than anyone gave him credit for because he returned to action within four months.'

When he came back in March 1965, Baxter would play only another eight games for Rangers before his annual cash tango with the Ibrox board. This time, the men at the top of the marble staircase decided enough was enough. Earning £45 a week plus a further £42 from his *Sunday Mirror* column, Baxter had a forthcoming wedding to Jean Ferguson to pay for and believed he should have parity with the top players in England. Scott Symon and Rangers had frowned upon newspaper tie-ups as a rule, but had been happy to make an exception in order to keep the club's star player content. And yet such tactics could only delay the final reckoning so long. The order came from the Rangers chairman, Baillie Wilson, to sell their prize asset, with the caveat that the blame be shifted onto the 'disloyal' agitator Baxter.

If teammates sensed there was always one disciplinary book for the errant Fifer and another for them, most accepted his right to be paid top dollar. When Baxter told them as much on a near daily basis, it was difficult to think otherwise – and yet his conceit was well founded.

'One of my best memories was when Jimmy and I were picked to play in a Rest of Europe XI against a Great Britain XI in Stoke in Stanley Matthews' last game in April 1965,' recalls Henderson. 'We were at a hotel before the game and in the company of Lev Yashin, the legendary Russian keeper, Ferenc Puskas, one of the finest players ever, and Alfredo Di Stefano. These were the best players in Europe.

'I was only 19, I was a young kid and I was so excited. We were going to get on the bus to go to the game when Jimmy shouted to me, "Willie, you go on ahead, keep a seat for us, I'm hanging back because Puskas and Di Stefano want my autograph." Not many folk have the self-belief to even joke about that.'

That Baxter was mixing in such company as he prepared for his final showdown with the Rangers board merely strengthened his resolve to seek a spectacular deal. At Ibrox, however, players were expected to be seen and not heard.

'One thing football clubs and other walks of life have in common is that people don't like you rocking the boat,' adds Henderson, 'that's the case throughout society. It unsettles them. Jimmy Baxter and myself were being asked to play beside the best players in the world. So why wouldn't we ask for a pay-rise? Now, that didn't make us very popular with the directors of Rangers or with some supporters, because the club were very good at playing the loyalty card. It was frowned upon to ask for a pay rise, it was very uncommon. The reaction when you went up the marble staircase would be along the lines of, "What about the cheek of him?" But there were other clubs who were willing to pay us the money, so why shouldn't we ask?'

Sunderland were a wealthy, if unfashionable, English club with big ambitions. Baxter's former Scotland manager, Ian McColl, himself a one-time Rangers player, believed that luring his fellow countryman to Roker Park would send a message of intent well beyond the north-east.

That Baxter's nocturnal activities had become an open secret in football circles was effectively confirmed by his choice of new club. McColl himself could have been under no illusions after witnessing Baxter's antics at close range as manager of Scotland.

'Sadly, there's no doubt that Jimmy's reputation went before him in England,' states Crerand. 'He had a reputation all right, but it wasn't a great one. As a footballer, yes, but not as a professional.

'There were a lot of managers put off by his drinking. Ian McColl knew Jimmy from Ibrox and he probably felt he could change him. You do, don't you? For years we all tried at Man United to change George Best, and we couldn't do it. I even took him into my family home.

'But I knew George and Jimmy well and they were similar in one respect. They would listen to your well-meaning advice for sure, but then they would ignore it. You were banging your head off a brick wall.'

The bigger English clubs had been made aware of Baxter's talent in 1963 when he first destroyed their national team at Wembley in a virtuoso performance. Yet few were willing to gamble money on a loose cannon with dubious vices.

Even one capable of attracting thousands to Glasgow city centre for a glimpse of the wedding of the year.

'Jim asked me to be his best man and I asked him, why me?' Rodger Baillie recalls. 'I knew Jim on a superficial, professional level and had been in his company in the St Enoch lair once or twice, but I wouldn't say I was one of his circle as such. His answer was to the point: "You're the only one I know who can write a f******* speech."

'There were hundreds of people at the wedding itself in Jean's native Coatbridge and hundreds, maybe even thousands, outside the St Enoch Hotel for the reception. It really was like having the Beatles in town.

'The St Enoch stood on the site of the shopping centre today and there was an incline which allowed people to crowd up to the doors. In that era, Jim was a symbol of the '60s in Scotland. Reo Stakis, the hotelier and entrepreneur, who had a huge presence at the time in Scotland, wanted to set him up with his own place with Jim's name above the door. But for all that he was always on the lookout for more money from Rangers, he had a strangely cavalier attitude to making it. He could have earned absolute fortunes at that time from endorsements and so on, but he never took them up.'

Signing for Sunderland in the North British Hotel in Edinburgh, there were plenty who felt Baxter had reached another cavalier decision at the age of 26, when he accepted an £11,000 signing-on fee and a weekly wage of £80 a week – whilst still retaining his *Sunday Mirror* column earnings. Friends and colleagues held severe reservations about the move.

'People definitely felt Jimmy could have done better than Sunderland,' Willie Henderson admits. 'But you have to remember that Sunderland paid him a huge signing-on fee. Even so, at that stage of his career, you might have thought that a bigger club would come in. The fact is that Sunderland were spending a lot of money then and Ian McColl being the manager was a big influence for Jimmy.'

For some, the move was a source of near funereal mourning. When Baxter scored a wonder goal against Sheffield United in his first home game at Roker Park, a raft of Rangers supporters had made the journey to the north-east of England for the occasion, ignoring the fact that there was a game at Ibrox the same day.

One of the spectators was a young Jimmy Calderwood, who went on to manage Dunfermline and Aberdeen.

'My father thought Jim Baxter was everything and I agreed. When Jim was at Rangers, my old man took me everywhere to the games. So when he went to Sunderland, we did our usual and followed him. We weren't alone – there were a load of Rangers supporters there that day. I would say as many as four figures, and the atmosphere was fantastic.

'The fans just wanted to pay tribute to an absolute legend of his day. After the game, it was like mass hysteria as people crowded him for autographs. In retrospect, they were probably too small a club for his talents.'

The warm welcome was short-lived. A bitter feud with Roker Park legend Charlie Hurley came close to blows being exchanged when Baxter inexplicably arrived on a mission to challenge the defender's position as club king-pin. 'There's only room for one king here, and it's not going to be you', was the Scot's opening gambit. In time, Hurley was far from the only player to be put out by Baxter's high-profile arrival – or his flagrant disregard for the defensive or disciplinary side of the game.

Len Ashurst played 458 times for the club and would later go on to serve as manager, but retains a sense of grievance at the level of managerial protection afforded to Baxter.

'I'd have got 550 or maybe 600 (appearances) but for McColl,' he insists. 'He bombed me out. It all dated back to him signing Baxter, who was well over the hill when he joined us. He scored twice on his Sunderland debut – but the winger I was marking also scored two and I'd never had that done to me in my career.

'I went to see McColl afterwards and told him the way Baxter played I was being left with two players bearing down on me. I couldn't see how the team could survive with Baxter's non-existent defensive cover. McColl just looked up and said: "Baxter stays in the team – isn't that right Jim?" And out came Baxter from behind the filing cabinets. I was doomed as long as McColl remained.'

McColl served as Baxter's champion and protector. He had been prepared to overlook the midfielder's foibles at a time when others wouldn't touch him.

'Sunderland were a big club at that time,' recalls Crerand, by then already at the start of a hugely successful career with Sir Matt Busby's Manchester United. 'Whether they were the club for Jimmy or not is another matter. The truly big clubs were Man United, Liverpool, Tottenham and Arsenal. Once Jim Baxter left Rangers for the first time, it was over as far as I was concerned. I still ask myself, why did he go?

'I know the answer is probably money, that's always been the case, but some things are more important that that. He was God Almighty at Rangers, the Messiah. He might have doubled his pay at Sunderland, but was he happy? I don't think so. In fact, I don't think he was ever happy during his time in England.'

Whether things might have been any different for Baxter or not in a team where colleagues were more tuned in to his creative abilities is a moot point.

'It might have been better at Man United,' argues Crerand. 'There is more pressure on you at Old Trafford, you had to perform or else, Sir Matt demanded it.

'I actually remember Jim coming to Old Trafford for a game and absolutely dominating the first 45 minutes, he ran the show. He was nothing less than brilliant. But in the second half he faded because he didn't keep himself as fit as he should have done. That was the story of his career so far as I could see.'

The reasons for that were familiar; a ready-made replacement for the St Enoch Hotel had quickly emerged. Rodger Baillie no longer took care of Baxter's newspaper interests, yet kept in touch from time to time.

'I went down to stay with him once or twice when he was down there and he introduced me to a club called Weatheralls,' Baillie recalls. 'He was the king in there all right, whatever was happening at the football club. He took to that aspect of the move fine. But there were better clubs for his talents on the field. Dave Mackay, the legendary midfielder, once told me that Bill Nicholson at Spurs had toyed with the idea of signing Jim, but was scared away in the end.'

Most were. At Roker Park, Baxter's club career finally reached breaking point during a close season venture in North America, just weeks after his Indian summer at Wembley, his demise triggered by an arrest in another ignominious episode.

In an ill-fated and mildly bizarre venture, the FIFA-backed United States Soccer Association imported 12 overseas clubs to lend some short-term glamour by temporarily adopting the mantle of a stateside franchise. Sunderland became the Vancouver Royal Canadians for the summer, with Scottish clubs Hibernian (Toronto City), Dundee United (Dallas Tornado) and Aberdeen (Washington Whips) also paid $250,000 to grab a slice of the action. In tow with his teammate and cousin Bobby Kinnell, Baxter embarked upon a kamikaze regime of wild living during his stay in Canada.

Along the way there was the occasional football match, providing a young Walter Smith with the biggest thrill of his early career. Smith had ventured from his Carmyle home to watch Baxter's halcyon days and now, at the age of 18, was presented with the chance to take to the same field as him, when Dundee United – or Dallas Tornado – faced Sunderland – Vancouver – in the round robin competition.

'I had been aware at the age of 14 or 15 that Jim was a bit of a lad – but then he moved to another club,' states Smith. 'And here I was on the same pitch as him in North America. Not only the same pitch, but the same hotel, and it was a bit surreal. Even on a close season tour, playing against United, he still had that arrogance about him. I watched him carefully in that game and the supreme confidence was there. But then it occurred to me that he was purely a brilliant football player, so much better than everyone else. The arrogance maybe wasn't a contrived or a conscious thing. That was just the way he played his football – it just came to him. I was only 18 and came on as a substitute, and to be playing against this fella who had produced the kind of football I had never seen before was quite something for me.

'Later on, I played with my heroes Jimmy Millar and Davie Wilson when they came to Dundee United.They used to tell me that Jim would sit on the bench and say to his teammates, "I'm not going out there with you lot, you're not good enough for me". I suppose you can be happy to say things like that when you have the knowledge you truly are the best player in the team.'

At Sunderland, however, they were tiring of the hubris and disruptive mayhem. In Canada, where the touring footballers were expected to spread the word and serve as football missionaries, Baxter managed to get himself charged with fighting, alongside Northern Irish teammate John Parke. For Sunderland, it was the final straw.

McColl had done all he could to indulge Baxter, yet like Scott Symon before him, could do no more. The problem was this: when it came time to approach potential purchasers, Baxter's rabble-rousing reputation preceded him.

Most of the maestro's episodes involved fellow footballers; and footballers, like any other profession, gossip. Word was spreading.

Many of the calls Sunderland manager Ian McColl made to contacts, fellow managers and potential buyers for Baxter went unreturned. Manchester City's Joe Mercer was rumoured to be interested, but told McColl there was 'no way he wanted Baxter near [his] club'.

Eventually, Nottingham Forest took the bait. This was Forest long before the rein of the maverick Brian Clough at the Midlands club that brokered two European Cups. In Clough, Baxter might have discovered a kindred spirit. Yet at this point, Forest was another ill-fitting stage for his talents; a fact Baxter was willing to overlook as soon as a five-figure signing-on fee became available.

A player who had performed beside Ferenc Puskás and Alfredo Di Stefano, a man who had only a few weeks earlier single-handedly terrorised the world champions on their own territory, had now been deemed too hot to handle by England's top clubs.

Rampant indiscipline reached its apex at Forest, where his stay might diplomatically be described as ill-starred. Manager Johnny Carey, it was said, never wanted Baxter but was overruled by his chairman Tony Wood. The experiment was short-lived.

And so, as a result, a decade of ever-declining performances and uncontainable laddishness, Baxter ended up back at Ibrox, where a lie-in would effectively cost him his career, manager Davie White his job and Scottish football its greatest entertainer.

The Slim Jim of yore had begun to be replaced by a bloated and faded figure on the downward spiral. Released on a free transfer by

Forest, Baxter wanted £10,000 up front as a signing-on fee – but was offered a house in Bearsden to the same value. Such were the concerns Rangers harboured over his rampant gambling addiction, there was no appetite for paying cash in a lump sum.

Given this kind of advance knowledge of Baxter's life of vice, it surprised some that the Ibrox club were willing to gamble their own reputation on an increasingly erratic individual. That Rangers might come back had been beyond a not-so slim Jim's wildest expectation. And yet, as Rodger Baillie insists: 'There was no surprise for me that he went back to Rangers. Davie White had taken over as manager from Scott Symon and was looking for a totem figure, someone to stimulate and unite the fans behind the team at a time when Jock Stein's Celtic were running riot and dominating the scene. It was just unfortunate that it didn't work. It was a gamble which backfired spectacularly.'

Baxter promised to turn over a new leaf, at the urgings of his closest friends, all of whom knew he was drinking in the last chance saloon after a condensed lifetime of boozy nights.

'I remember when he went back to Rangers in 1969, I was playing golf up at Newton Mearns with Tony Queen, the bookmaker who was friends with Jock Stein,' recalls Pat Crerand. 'Jimmy came to join us and I said to him, "You have a great second chance at Ibrox, get yourself fit and take it." But as always, he would listen then take no notice. He always knew better, Jimmy.

'At his peak, Jimmy was fantastic, a one-off. But in football you have to keep yourself fit and he was never good at that part of the game.'

Baxter was even less fit than Rangers had hoped on his return. Nor was he capable of turning over a new leaf as promised. On his first day back at Ibrox, the midfielder had offered manager Davie White, Scott Symon's former assistant, a promise to grasp the chance afforded to him with both hands, despite reservations within the Rangers boardroom over his return. When the phone rang in the manager's office and a senior police officer reported an incident in Fife, it was a personal let-down for a manager who had put his relatively inexperienced neck on the block.

'He was arrested hours after returning for drink driving,' recalls Baillie. 'And that set the tone for what was to follow.' Baxter was, by now, on a final warning. He had come close to blowing the second coming and promised to avoid any future disciplinary faux pas.

Baxter's playing comeback started brightly enough when he inspired his team to a League Cup section win over Celtic, yet the man now performing in light blue was a pale imitation of his former self. If he was as mentally sharp as ever, physically his faculties had deserted him. A rotund midriff was evident and training could no longer atone for the years of self-harm.

'If I'm being honest, there was a difference in Jimmy second time around,' says Willie Henderson. 'It wasn't the Jimmy Baxter we all knew and loved. He was maybe playing out time by then. It's hard to explain that, other than by saying that it's always difficult to go back to a former club. You are inevitably going to be compared to the way you were the first time, but Jimmy was a bit older by the time he came back. And when you get older you're not quite the same, so you can't always turn back the clock.'

Drawn against Polish club Gornik in the second round of the European Cup Winners' Cup, a minor storm arose when Baxter and Henderson, sharing a room, slept in at the team's Largs hotel and missed training, a fact reported back to the newspapers by an unusually sharp photographer. In typical Glasgow fashion, wild rumours of an all-night drinking session became statements of fact within hours. A 3–1 home defeat to the Poles witnessed the sleep-in elevated to a greater prominence than it deserved and, judged to have lost the dressing room, White was dismissed. Almost four decades later, Henderson remains adamant that it was a non-story.

'Nothing happened. We were fined, but if it had been as serious as folk said then Jimmy and me would have been hauled over the coals, and we weren't.'

Taking up the tale, Rodger Baillie recalls: 'It was felt the board were looking for an excuse to act against Davie White and that was it. They felt he was never truly in control of the players. More than that, though, he never truly got on top of Jock Stein or results, and that was the real problem.'

The relatively inexperienced White had signed Baxter as a faintly desperate throw of the dice. Against Jock Stein, however, precious few threw a double six.

'Celtic were going really, really well at the time,' states Henderson. 'It was an era when they were nothing less than superb under big Jock. When you manage Rangers you have to be winning, there is nothing else for it. Davie got the sack because we were not winning things, not least the title. You can't go any length of time at Rangers in that situation without paying a price.'

Willie Waddell's elevation to the Ibrox hot-seat would mark a fruitful enough chapter, yet a grim ending for Baxter after just 22 appearances in his second spell. His final release from Ibrox would be delayed another four months, but a bitingly cold December day in the North-east, when Aberdeen were narrowly beaten, was the final swansong for Baxter in the aftermath of one scandal too many.

There were attempts to enter management at his first club, Raith Rovers, and then Queen of the South. Offered Baxter the player, both clubs would have swooned; offered Baxter the potential manager, they ran a mile.

For 13 years, there was a life as a publican near Ibrox, a grimly inappropriate profession for a man by now drinking three bottles of Bacardi a day and gambling uncontrollably on horses, card games and even impromptu pub pool challenges. For five years the good times rolled, yet when Rangers entered a desperate slump under John Greig and Jock Wallace, prior to the Graeme Souness revolution, takings went the same way and the bar closed.

These days, Baxter would be a natural and forthright pundit or the co-host of a radio phone-in. In the '70s such opportunities were scarce. 'Jim was unfortunate that there was little in the way of ex-players in the media in his day,' says Rodger Baillie. 'These days you can hardly avoid them, but back then I think he was held back by that sing-song Fife accent of his. That was a pity because he had very strong views and was never backward about coming forward with them. He could be absolutely scathing about those with less ability than himself, and these days that's what broadcasters look for.'

Unsurprisingly, Baxter's marriage to Jean floundered. And yet that break-up paved the way for Baxter to meet Norma, his ever-present companion in the last great fight for fitness which followed the onset of liver damage in 1994.

Popping 25 to 30 pills a day, his pallor increased to the point where he was sent for assessment to the Liver Transplant Unit at Edinburgh Royal Infirmary. The operation which followed had never been requested by Baxter, who sought neither pity nor assistance in his 61 years. Given a second chance and granted permission by a specialist to have the odd glass of wine, he stayed on the wagon for 15 months before a spectacular return to drink became front-page news and the topic of discussion for every columnist in the land. Baxter had become a prime example of NHS waste and was cast in the role of the undeserving sick. And yet the reality, according to friends and former colleagues, was one of a man spending the years before his death trying desperately hard to look after himself, restricting his intake to two glasses of wine with a meal.

The public opprobrium had abated by the time Baxter was welcomed into a suite at Hampden in December 2000 as a member of the best-ever Scotland team, Denis Law just edging him out for the vote as the greatest player to wear a dark blue jersey.

That most of those cheering Baxter to the rafters had never seen him play did nothing to deter his legend. The black and white images of a Wembley juggling act have received many an airing for the benefit of younger generations. Those who cannot fully savour the magnitude of the man can still marvel at the cheek.

When doctors conducted a regular test on Baxter's replacement liver, they discovered a cancerous growth the size of a 20 pence piece on his pancreas. In Edinburgh Royal Infirmary, they tolerated the final acts of rebellion, black pudding suppers regularly being smuggled into the dying patient's ward.

On 14 April 2001, 11 weeks after being told nothing more could be done, Baxter passed away. The outpouring of grief united Glasgow and, for once, dissipated the petty bitterness of sectarian-fuelled bickering. The funeral cortège passed Ibrox Stadium before joining 400 mourners, including the future prime minister Gordon Brown MP, Lord MacFarlane and Glasgow's Lord Provost Alex Mosson, at the city's Linn Crematorium. The streets en route were lined with respectful mourners, their memories of a wayward football magician intact following a life lived to the full.

'I went to see Jim a fortnight before he died,' says Rodger Baillie. 'And whatever faults he had, he owned up to in full. He knew he was dying and there were no attempts to justify himself. Just a man who had no regrets and who was willing to accept his role in his own demise. Self-pity was of no interest to him.'

In the years which followed, Crerand would also attend the football equivalent of a state funeral in England when another of football's great hedonists took his leave.

'If you look at Jim and poor George Best then maybe you come to the conclusion that there are some free spirits out there you simply can't tame.'

And yet there are others who believe it inappropriate to dwell on the downsides of a life such as Baxter's. The man himself rarely did.

As Willie Henderson puts it: 'Listen, if you play for Glasgow Rangers as the star player, play for your country and win the right to play beside some of the greatest players in the world in representative games, you can't do much more, can you? How many players in Scotland achieve all that? There are not too many real Scottish football legends left – and he was a legend.'

2

Jinglin' Geordie

GEORGE BEST

'Watching George was like being a witness to a car accident taking place in slow motion.'

— Former Hibernian manager Eddie Turnbull

Eyes shimmering brightly in the reflection of a dozen drained glasses, the extent of George Best's deep-lying problems were exposed to the Scottish public by a black and white picture in a tabloid newspaper.

Halfway up one of Edinburgh's oldest alleyways, the Jinglin' Geordie pub remains one of Auld Reekie's hidden treasures. In the shadows of Fleshmarket Close, yards from the old North Bridge home of the *Scotsman*, this popular drinking howff is a welcoming old inn; the kind of bar where a lone drinker will always be found scanning a copy of the *Racing Post*.

And it was here, one afternoon in 1979, that Best was surreptitiously snapped by a shadowy member of the paparazzi; surrounded by empties, he seemed a man alone in a state of drink-addled paralysis.

As with so many images viewed through an empty pint glass or 12, however, all was not entirely as it seemed.

The orchestrators of this optical illusion were Best's own Hibernian teammates, who leaned back, out of sight when the flashbulb started popping. The empties were largely theirs. With a national newspaper building just yards away, prying eyes were never far. There must, then, have been better places for the Hibernian players to introduce their new world-famous teammate to a spot of team bonding Easter Road style.

The sessions were a practice tolerated, if not exactly encouraged, by the manager Eddie Turnbull – a scowling presence at the club, unhappy with the decision of his chairman Tom Hart to recruit football's most fêted playboy at a rate of £2,000 a game.

The late *Edinburgh Evening News* sportswriter Stewart Brown had the ear of Jock Stein and many of Scottish football's big names. It was he who first suggested to Hart that Best might be available. It was, for this chairman with an eye for the grand gesture, tantamount to a Klondike moment.

The struggling Leith squad had won one and drawn three of their opening 14 games and desperately required some form of divine inspiration. Turnbull believed the days of a 33-year-old Best walking on water had, however, long since passed.

This wily old manager would, in time, be fully vindicated. The arrival of this globally recognised celebrity footballer in Scotland's capital was occasionally as farcical as it was sensational. Not least the day the pictures were taken, which seemed to show Best on a solo drinking binge, with empty glasses scattered in front of him and not a teammate in sight.

'I think one of the snaps appeared in the *Daily Record* a day or two later,' recalls former goalkeeper Jim McArthur. 'They cropped the picture and all you saw was George Best with a load of empties around him. He looked like he was the only one there.'

On the face of it, this was an open and shut case hardly worthy of challenging Hercule Poirot; a photographer had taken advantage of some footballer horseplay to stitch up his stranded victim. And yet, the eyewitness testimony of then Hibs captain and active protagonist, Jackie McNamara, thickens the plot.

'The magazine *World Soccer* was due to do an interview with George and the journalist had been chasing him all over Edinburgh trying to get his words,' he recalls. 'I know a bit about how papers work because my father was with the *Daily Express*. Anyway, the photographer found us fine, but when the writer turned up he started berating George for not meeting him at the agreed time in the old North British Hotel on Princes Street, now the Balmoral. George had already pocketed a cheque for £500 and when this fella started laying into him, he took it out and ripped it up – he now wasn't doing the interview.

'When all this was going on the photographer, who was dependent on this interview for his payment, nipped to the toilet. Unbeknown to him Bobby Hutchison, my big pal and a Hibs striker, picked up the camera and started taking pics. It was only when the photographer left us and developed the pictures that he realised he suddenly had gold dust on his hands.'

The arrival of Best at the foot of Leith Walk for a weighty appearance fee had already raised eyebrows amongst teammates earning an average wage of £110 a week.

'We were intrigued by the arrival of George I suppose,' says McArthur. 'Everybody knew he was getting two grand a week, paid for by Tom Hart, and we wanted to see what we'd get for that money. George Best was earning almost 20 times what his teammates were on. The reason for that was obvious – the crowds went up. And that's what paid for him. Before his home debut against Partick Thistle, I said out loud, "Why's George Best on £2,000 a game?" Tom Hart overheard me and invited me to take a look outside. "What do you see?" he asked. I said I saw a big crowd. There were 22,000 fans where there would be normally be 8,000 or 9,000 max.

'I laughed and he laughed at the same time. "Well, there's your answer", he said and walked away. We both knew the score. We all did.'

Hibs moved quickly to double the squad's win bonus scheme and quelled the unrest. What transpired in the Jinglin' Geordie, then, was no act of espionage. Far from resenting their new teammate, indeed, Hibs players warmed quickly to Best's laddish, mildly shy demeanour. His arrival had been to everyone's benefit. On days such as this, however, protecting an apparently glassy-eyed teammate from himself was a bridge too far.

'I had said to George that the pub might not be a good idea,' recalls Tony Higgins, the midfielder who would become an unofficial minder for the Northern Ireland and Manchester United legend.

'But the ironic thing for me is that I'm not entirely sure George even had a drink that day. We were mainly sticking to shandies and most of us had a maximum of two or three. I couldn't say for certain that George even had one, let alone two.'

The resulting pics suggested otherwise and appeared to confirm what most already knew, George Best had a chronic problem with drink. That, in any case, was Eddie Turnbull's take on the matter. Long enough in the tooth to suspect a dressing room cover-up, a phone call from the Jinglin' Geordie landlord had allegedly reported Best to be drunk as a skunk. To this day, however, Best's former teammates hold true to their story. What few realised was that the poster boy for wayward footballers was already taking Antabuse tablets – a drug designed to make the drinker violently sick following even modest alcohol consumption.

'It was common knowledge amongst the boys that George was on the tablets,' claims McArthur. 'I'm not so sure the punters knew about it. Three or four pints could have killed him so far as we were concerned. We would say to him, "Another drink and you'll die Bestie", and we'd ask him if he'd taken his pills. It became a running joke.'

The fractured 11 months George Best spent as a Hibernian player still rank as one of the more eccentric marriages in Scottish football's chequered history. Black humour was a natural response when laughs were thin on the ground. Until Best, no one had hitherto succeeded in importing a touch of world-class glamour to the staid environs of Scotland's domestic scene.

In 1964 Celtic had tried, failing to capture the fading talents of Real Madrid legend Alfredo Di Stefano after dispatching manager Jimmy McGrory and defender John Cushley on a fruitless quest to Spain.

Dumbarton, too, had dabbled with greatness – audaciously attempting to lure the Dutch master Johan Cruyff to the delights of football at the old Boghead stadium.

For the Scottish game, then, this appeared to be third time lucky. Here was a cultural and sporting phenomenon. At his peak, a Portuguese paper had dubbed Best the Fifth Beatle. Prior to his death in 2005, there would be those who would come to know the man for reasons other than football. He had, at the age of 59, become a tabloid newspaper staple, Britain's best-known alcoholic. And the long goodbye had already commenced by the time of his arrival in Edinburgh.

An impressionable teenage defender when Best was invited to earn his corn at Easter Road, defender Craig Paterson had been steeped in the Easter Road traditions. Paterson's father John had played with the championship-winning Hibs sides of the 1950s, which gave prominence to the legendary Famous Five, featuring his manager at the time of the Best sideshow – Eddie Turnbull.

'Hibs greats like Gordon Smith, Lawrie Reilly and Eddie were always around when I was growing up. To me they were just my father's mates,' he recalls. 'But from my point of view it was something special when, as an 18-year-old breaking into the Hibs first team, I walked into the ground one day and there was one of the planet's most famous footballers standing there. That was an incredible thrill for me.

'I was driving about in an old Mark Three Ford Cortina at the time and on his very first day, George pitched up in a shining new Saab Turbo Convertible laid on for his use by Eastern Motors of Edinburgh. And I remember thinking to myself, "That's where I want to be in football."'

To some, the capture of a living legend was a stroke of genius. And yet it was, by any stretch, a bold and risky venture. As celebrity Hibernian fan and Scots literary icon Irvine Welsh once observed, Best was the 'patron saint' of the undisciplined footballer. And Eddie Turnbull, an avid admirer of the younger Best, feared the consequences of importing a dressing room rabble rouser on the wane. This, after all, was no longer the snake-hipped young protégé who sprang to attention in the aftermath of a dazzling proclamation of talent on the European stage in a 5–1 thrashing of Benfica in Lisbon in March 1966.

'The fans at Easter Road got to see a different side of George compared to those at Man United, who saw him in his pomp,' recalls Tony Higgins. 'George still had the skills, but he could not go past people as he used to. His pace had gone, so he developed the passing side of his game.'

Bewildering feints and darts, stops and starts, twists and turns had once made him Europe's most hypnotic footballer. In October 1967, Best had turned Celtic's European Cup-winning full-back Tommy Gemmell inside out in a mesmerising display for Northern Ireland in a 1–0 triumph over Scotland in Belfast. British Footballer of the Year and the continent's star player in the period which followed, Best would also score for Matt Busby's Manchester United in the 1968 European Cup final, which went some way to assuaging the pain of the Munich Disaster, when the Busby Babes were stolen in their prime.

By his 30s, however, this son of the Cregagh Estate in Belfast had become a circus act, a travelling cavalcade certain to attract headlines and controversy in equal measure wherever he ventured. His break-up with Manchester United had been protracted and messy, his downward spiral inexorable. In a two-week spell in November 1972 alone, he was fined for missing two training sessions, axed from the team, banned for three games by FIFA and accused of assaulting a nightclub waitress. Under the management of gruff Glaswegian Tommy Docherty, such passages would become the norm rather than the exception for Best at Old Trafford.

His final appearance for Manchester United on New Year's Day 1974 preceded spells in England's Division Four with Stockport, Cork Celtic in the League of Ireland, Los Angeles Aztecs and Fort Lauderdale in the North American Soccer League and Fulham in England's Division Two. Then came Hibernian.

For a player of his incredible talent and prodigious ability, there must have been an element of humiliation in embarking upon a cook's tour of the world's football outposts. In the throes of uncontainable alcoholism, however, pride never entered the equation when £2,000 a week was on offer.

'You don't have to live up in Scotland,' Tom Hart had implored, as part of a compelling sales pitch. 'Fly up on Thursday, train with the lads on Friday and fly back after the game on Saturday.'

If the notion of a soccer mercenary was a relatively novel concept, for clubs mired in various states of desperation it was nevertheless an attractive one. Best was a man capable of drawing crowds in much the same way as the Elephant Man once enlivened Victorian freak shows.

'What always struck me was the sackfuls of mail he would receive on a daily basis,' Paterson remembers. 'He was being asked to open shops, pubs, appear here, there and everywhere. It seemed to me that if he charged for these appearances then he would never need to kick a ball again. He was sitting on a fortune just by being George Best. But this was before the days when the David Beckhams of this world became savvy concerning the value of their image rights.'

The son of an alcoholic mother, Annie, Best's arrival in Scotland dovetailed with relationship problems and an urgent need to propel his life back onto the straight and narrow. His mother had died in October 1978, a year prior to his arrival in Scotland. In an emotional interview at his sister Barbara's French villa years later, Best wept as he admitted to feeling overwhelming guilt at the failure to be there for his mother in her hour of desperate need. His damaged conscience plagued his waking hours, but the truth was that his own needs had become too pressing for him to be concerned with anyone else.

After Best left Hibs to return to San Jose, he was ordered to write a letter to his late mother as part of his alcoholism treatment. The message he wrote was simple, heartfelt and could be summed up in one word: sorry.

His younger sister would also succumb to alcoholism, reinforcing the family's belief that some form of hereditary defect was at work. Against this backdrop, Hibs never stood a chance of helping, or witnessing, the real George Best.

'We were savvy to the problems George had,' admits Higgins. 'I enjoyed a bevvy or two like the other players, but for most players there is a limit they won't go beyond. We knew booze was running his life by the time he arrived at Hibs.'

For Higgins, a night out with Best in Edinburgh was never a simple affair. Knowing when to let him make his own mistakes and when to intervene was a perennial judgement call. There were those in the Hibs dressing room only too willing to bask in the great man's fame; to accept the scraps from the table, as it were.

'If the truth be told, there was no real resentment of George or his money, because he really was a lovely fella,' insists Jim McArthur. 'For all the public image, he was one of the good guys. That Hibs team was full of good lads. We had built a decent camaraderie and there weren't many shy guys in there. The season before, we had made it to the Scottish Cup final and we had a good spirit. So George fitted in well.'

Best made his debut against St Mirren in Paisley, Scotland's largest town, where home crowds rarely rose beyond the mediocre. As Best opened his account with a late goal in a 2–1 defeat, however, there were 13,670 in Love Street on Saturday, 24 November – a significant increase on the norm.

Despite the defeat, Best granted the Sunday newspapers a ready-made picture and headline opportunity. By the time of his home debut against Thistle, excitement was palpable.

'George paid off his wages for the whole time he was with us in that one night when Partick Thistle came to town,' says Craig Paterson. 'He brought out people who would never normally watch Hibs, or a football match for that matter. My dad had never watched a single game I had played in because he never felt modern football was worth watching. He felt football had changed beyond all recognition. But then one of his neighbours wanted to go to a game involving George Best and my dad decided to join him. I thought to myself, God Almighty, he never comes to watch me, his own son, but he's coming to watch George Best.'

If first-team regulars were earning just over £100 a week, then for the novices of the Hibs side the money Best was making at Easter Road was stratospheric.

'I was probably only on about £45 a week at that time,' says Paterson. 'I had signed as a teenager and if you were lucky, you made £50 as your top whack at that point in your career at Hibs. But it never concerned us what George was earning. Just the fact he was there in our midst was the main thing.

'There was a small gym under the main stand at that time and after training, myself, Gordon Rae and Colin Campbell would go and play three-a-sides or whatever, putting a school PE bench on its side as a goal.

'George would often come down and join us after training. Now, this clearly wasn't the George Best of 1968 with the pace and guile of yore, but the footwork and skill were still mind-boggling. We couldn't get near him. 'We were happy just to listen to him, never mind play with him. He had already lived the kind of life half of us could only dream about.

'I had never seen a footballer with his own toiletries bag before. He had a bottle of aftershave in there worth £100 an ounce, he told us. So one day he went for a shower and we went into his bag and pinched the bottle. By the time he emerged to dry off we must have whacked about £45-worth of the stuff onto ourselves. He was a lovely fellow so he just laughed and started telling us about the Miss Worlds he had known in his time. "You need to do more than smell nice to get to that level", he told us.'

There were, however, less desirable aspects to the Best sideshow. For years, he had been an object of suffocating curiosity. Although the Beatles look of dazzling blue eyes under a rock star's impeccably glossy dark hair had faded by the time of his arrival in Edinburgh, and the facial frame was a little pudgier, his intrinsic stardom had been dulled only marginally by the effects of excessive boozing and a tempestuous relationship with first wife, Angela McDonald, or Angie as she would more commonly be known.

'George would fly up to train with us on a Friday generally, but sometimes he would be in Edinburgh a bit longer,' fellow socialiser McArthur recalls. 'The striker Bobby Hutchison and me became his mates at the club. We would go up the town with him for a few drinks. We would go into a bar, stand there beside him and be aware of women gravitating towards him. They would just touch him. It was crazy, like nothing you'd ever seen. We would say daft things like, "How do you put up with this?" And he'd just shrug and say it was always like this. I was married at the time, but for any single guy he was a good shadow to follow. I just liked the guy's company, to be honest.'

Before joining Hibs, and tortured by his mother's passing, the former Old Trafford idol was hitting the bottle in the States harder than ever and his relationship with wife Angie was suffering accordingly. In a desperate quest to win back his glamorous wife's affections, Best returned to London from the States to prove he could change. Regular work and a solid income would provide a measure of stability. Here was where Hibernian came into the equation.

'George was now moving onto a stage in his career where he was hired to play per game,' recalls his Fort Lauderdale coach Ron Newman. 'He was prostituting himself and it was a shame because we had all enjoyed some of the great stuff he could do.'

Best himself was under no illusions in Edinburgh. This was a marriage born both of despair and convenience. It was, from the start, doomed to end in separation. By his own admission, the Northern Irishman never truly garnered an understanding of what made his teammates tick, and never truly cared. For their part, the other Hibs players tried hard to get under the skin of one of the world's sporting superstars and make him welcome.

After the Jinglin' Geordie picture storm, Hibs players closed ranks around their troubled teammate. Higgins, a highly intelligent and articulate figure, was aware that Best was trying to patch up a fractured marriage and tried to protect the great man from himself where possible.

After one friendly match with Leicester City, the Hibs players retreated to the Fifty Club, a bar at the ground, while the crowd dispersed. As was so often the case, the night moved on to a city-centre nightclub, where photographers got wind of a gilt-edged picture opportunity. Thronged by females with a lust to kiss and tell, Best was implored to leave the club by Higgins, mindful of the permanent damage an indiscreet picture could do to his already shaky marriage. Best quickly made his escape from a back exit.

Set against all of this, the football was in danger of becoming a sideshow. Hibs had signed Best to dig them from a trench and yet here was a man struggling to keep himself from the gutter.

Used to operating in the upper echelons of the game, Scottish football's less illustrious venues appeared to be of limited appeal, as evidenced by his performances against the big guns in his first spell at the club.

'There were some highlights,' Craig Paterson points out. 'There was a 1–1 draw against Celtic when he scored his first goal at Easter Road, cutting in and hitting a screamer. He also starred before that in a 2–1 win over Rangers when we were fighting a losing battle against relegation. The pitch that day was really slippy and hard to negotiate. There was no value in having pace in those conditions, it was all about having great balance and ability and that was made for a 33-year-old George Best. He glided past players as if they weren't there and ran the show. He still had something and the big games brought it out.'

The game against Rangers provided a personal highlight for Higgins.

'George loved the big games against Rangers and Celtic. That excited him and he rose to the challenge,' Higgins says. 'We really needed to win against Rangers because we were in relegation trouble. George hit a 40-yard pass, threading it through the Rangers defence to Ally McLeod, who came inside to hit this 25-yard shot into the net. It was the way George weighted the pass that I really remember.'

There was humour that day also. As violence flared on the terraces, and with the ban on alcohol in Scottish grounds yet to be imposed, Rangers supporters began throwing cans of beer at the superstar as he ran to take a corner.

'George picked one up, pretended he was taking a sip from it and put it back down by the touchline,' Higgins smiles. 'It defused the situation and the Rangers fans started applauding him.'

A week after the first goal against Celtic at Easter Road came the third round of the Scottish Cup. Best was uninspiring in a 1–0 win over Meadowbank Thistle and the cracks were beginning to show.

Following a non-appearance for a league game against Morton in February, Tom Hart was left with little option but to discipline his personal vanity project. A suspension from the club was renounced following an apology, but words and good intentions were no match for the ravages of rampant alcoholism. The worst was yet to come.

'Our fourth round Scottish Cup game with Ayr had been postponed to the Sunday because of worries over a clash with the Five Nations Rugby international between France and Scotland at Murrayfield,' recalls Craig Paterson. 'Before kick-off, it was clear George wasn't turning up and they found him drunk following a lengthy session with the French rugby team the night before.'

The whereabouts of Best were quickly established when Hibs chairman Hart received a call from a waiter at the old North British Hotel. The French players had been granted carte blanche to socialise despite an Andy Irvine-inspired 22–14 defeat to the Scots hours before. Best, on the other hand, should have been preparing for an important cup game. Instead, the master of the round ball game was out scrumming with some new Gallic friends – most built like a brick outhouse and in excess of six foot – with his fearsome capacity for booze.

Hart arrived at the hotel in a panic to find Best in a sorry state. An SOS call was quickly placed to Turnbull who, preparing for the game, was of no mind to assist, sending club officials instead.

When Hart first knocked on the room door of his star signing, there had been no response. In his own account of the affair, Best recalled a polite approach from the Hibs officials handed the sorry task of rousing their comatose patient.

'Do you think you'll be all right to play today George?'

'It might be best if I gave this game a miss, I'm pissed,' was reported to have been the extent of the great man's contribution to the debate. This time there could be no escaping the inevitable.

'The marriage between Hibs and George Best is over,' said Hart later in the Easter Road gymnasium that served as a media room. 'The divorce took place at 3 o'clock.'

The tone was statesmanlike, but the effect was dramatically diluted when the chairman stepped back from the table at which he was standing and tripped over a stash of whisky boxes.

Within a week, Hart – if not the vanquished villain of the piece – had endured a sobering experience. Without Best, Hibernian were plummeting towards the financial black canyon of the First Division.

Best was once more reinstated. And Turnbull was once again furious. Best was putting on weight and making the astute calculation that if he had survived wild indiscipline at Hibernian once or twice then he could do so again and again. In that assumption, he was correct.

Victory over Ayr – minus Best – in the fourth round of the Scottish Cup was a joyless experience, as Craig Paterson attests:

'There was another regrettable side to that because I felt terribly for the little winger Willie Murray, a young lad who had to stand in for George. There were 20,000 people there, most of whom had come to see George Best, and the man who had to take his place had to put up with boos and everything. There was a chorus of them when folk discovered George wouldn't play and it was so unfair on the lad.'

Again, Best was forgiven and that, in turn, led to a murky, gloomy March afternoon in Berwick, down the A1 from Scotland's capital, in the last eight.

'George was hooked at half-time,' recalls Paterson. 'It was a waste of time and talent for him, that kind of game. We beat them 1–0 in a replay but George effectively sat that one out.'

Best would score his third and final Hibs goal in his tenth appearance for the club, a 2–0 home win over Dundee on 25 March. Three successive defeats to Celtic, Dundee United and St Mirren witnessed precious little impact from Scotland's highest paid player, as the Leith club lost eight goals, scoring none in the process. Hibs were sliding – and the fate of the manager, Turnbull, was becoming increasingly forlorn.

'I suppose the bottom line is that George didn't really help us,' concedes Jim McArthur. 'We made the semi-final of the Scottish Cup and we hadn't lost a goal up until that point. We fancied our chances of getting back to the final. George was on our side and Bobby Lennox was the old boy in the Celtic side from the same era. If memory serves me, wee Lennox got a hat-trick and at one point consoled George. Bestie barely got a look in and we lost 5-0.'

Turnbull would later complain bitterly of Best failing to find teammates in that Hampden showpiece with 'pass after pass'. Three days after the humiliation, on Tuesday, 15 April 1980, this legendary member of the Famous Five was invited to a meeting in the Easter Road boardroom.

'There had been a fall-out between Tom Hart and Eddie in 1978,' recalls Jackie McNamara. 'The relationship between the two suffered after that. This was a time when it was a manager's prerogative to decide who the club were buying and selling. Ultimately, he was far from happy that George had been brought in above his head.'

In Turnbull's eyes, George Best had been none of his doing – but cost him his job.

Craig Paterson, whose own father could still describe the sacked manager as a friend, watched this latest turn of events with a sense of unease.

'It was an awkward situation for me as a player, that. But whatever he came to think after the event, Eddie was always eulogising George in the confines of the dressing room, saying how good he was. He still admired George as a player.

'If you had to change your boots at half-time to adapt to the conditions, it would be all, "Why you doing that? George isn't changing his." He never gave the impression to the players that he resented the way George was signed or that he didn't want him there. The talk was always of how lucky we were to have him playing with us. The instruction was usually the same: "Give the ball to George and let him play." Maybe he was just maintaining an air of professionalism – publicly at least.'

McNamara also harbours little recollection of Turnbull speaking out against Best within the hearing range of players.

'I suppose there is a contradiction between what Eddie says now and what he said to the team. From what I witnessed, George was always a hard trainer when he was with us – even at 33. He was fit.

'Sure, the drink had taken its toll on his speed of movement, but he never lacked the basic fitness to perform. He would still be on the pitch after training, with ourselves or some of the young players, practising his crossing or finishing and teaching the kids good habits. It's a tragic fact that when guys like George and Paul Gascoigne leave the football pitch, something goes wrong.'

If Best felt frustration with the obvious limits of a team destined for the drop, then he obscured his feelings from colleagues. In turn, they declined to apportion blame for the fact that the man hailed as a new messiah was failing miserably to lead his disciples to the promised land.

'We were already in relegation trouble by the time George first arrived and that never really changed,' McArthur recalls. 'Near the end of his first spell, we played Aberdeen up at Pittodrie and him and

Willie Miller had a bit of a run-in. Aberdeen were behind in the title race and he was saying things like, "Ah, you've no chance of winning the league."

'Willie didn't seem to be taking it too well and had a go at George for passing the ball back to me at one point, but he had the last laugh because Aberdeen did win the league – at Easter Road. George had already gone off back to America by then and we didn't really expect to see him again.'

Best played for what most expected to be the final time in a Hibs jersey in a 2–0 home defeat to a rising Dundee United team.

The Easter Road club still had three league games remaining, but with relegation already a certainty, paying Best £6,000 for the remaining games would be an exercise in financial folly. He made 13 league appearances and three starts in the Scottish Cup when Milan Mandaric, owner of San Jose Earthquake, travelled to Edinburgh in a quest to take Best back to the North American Soccer League.

Mandaric, a Serbian-born business tycoon from the city of Novi Sad, would become a key figure in the final 25 years of Best's life, passing a platoon of media men to visit the legend in hospital during his final days.

'I miss George so much even now,' says the Leicester City owner. 'Every day actually, he was a wonderful man. I came to Scotland with the aim of bringing him back to America and I have to tell you he did not need much persuading – his heart was still in California, where his wife Angie was.'

And yet for all the sunshine which followed his initial spell in Auld Reekie, Best would come to regard San Jose as the bleakest period of his career. Reunited with Angie, moves to integrate more native American players into the professional leagues led to a decline in standards – and in the star player's morale. Injury problems were beginning to bite as he doubled his earnings by simultaneously playing in the Indoor Soccer League. Overcommitted and placing his joints under strain, his right knee was by now a liquidised mess. Drawing only misery from the experience, Best reverted to traditional methods of consolation in spite of the best efforts of his new friend.

'He was such an exciting player for us – the kind I wanted in San Jose,' says Mandaric. 'I had also taken another player from the Scottish League in the great Jimmy Johnstone three or four years earlier and it would have been my dream to have them in the same team together. They were the kind of players who did nothing for my blood pressure, but they were wonderful to watch. I will never forget when the Earthquakes went to play Fort Lauderdale and my coach phoned me before kick-off to say, "Boss, George Best is not here. I have to score him from the team sheet." I appealed to him not to do it, begged him, but 10 minutes before kick-off, when he handed in a sheet without George's name, he arrived on cue.

'I had to go personally to the referee's room to appeal to let George play. I was so upset and I told him that, but George could be very contrite and for the first time, he called me Boss and said, "I will make it up to you."

'Well, that was the game when he scored the MLS goal of the season, beating player after player and taking everybody on before dispatching the ball beyond the goalkeeper. And then he turned around and ran towards my box and gave me a thumbs up. What can you say to that?'

Temporary situations were, by now, becoming the norm for a worn-out Best. Exhausted and unenthused, he returned to Edinburgh in September 1980 to make some more cash, against all expectations, five games into the new season.

'George had a very good relationship with Tom Hart,' explains Tony Higgins, who by now had left the club for Partick Thistle. 'Tom must have gone to George and asked him to have another go at it. There was a strong bond there and Eddie Turnbull and his distaste for the situation had gone by then.'

Before returning to Scotland, Best had learned that he was to be a father – to Calum, his only son. With a renewed determination to support his family, Best spoke to teammates about settling down in Edinburgh and making a go of life at Hibs. How this might be possible on the back of signing a new deal with San Jose was never entirely clear. Most took such talk with a large pinch of salt. Best would confess years later in his autobiography, *Blessed*, that he never took playing for Hibs seriously. The main concern in his life at this point was where the next drink was coming from.

On one occasion, Andy McInnes, a *Daily Express* sports writer, drove to Edinburgh to interview Best in the North British Hotel – his adopted home from home. Offering to get the drinks in, McInnes headed for the bar with instructions from Best to order his 'usual'. Nodding, the bar man returned seconds later with a beer for the journalist and what appeared to be a large Coke for the superstar footballer.

'Only when I went to pay the bill and studied the receipt,' McInnes recalls, 'did I notice that he had had four vodkas poured into the coke. No wonder it looked so large. And this was his usual . . .'

No one ever doubted that the arrangement with Hibs depended entirely on economics. And with the team now playing in Scotland's second tier, the box-office takings came without any future guarantees.

'We'd be playing at places like Dunfermline, close to Halbeath, where I came from,' says Jim McArthur. 'I never lost there, as I recall, and neither did George because he wasn't around for long after that. He drew the crowds even then, but in the First Division the novelty was wearing off a bit.'

That game, on 4 October 1980 at East End Park, remains this observer's only sighting in the flesh of George Best.

A 2–0 win for Hibs was mundane enough and meant significantly less than the chance to see an increasingly bloated Best in the flesh. Like others who had paid out pocket money for the experience, younger fans never truly quite appreciated why Best was the name he was. We were by now witnessing a reputation rather than the reality of Best's younger self. Even in the First Division, the crowds came because a new group of people had never seen the incomparable George Best play in the flesh and they still wanted to say, 'I've done it, I've seen him'.

Minus fixtures against Rangers and Celtic, however, Best was akin to a Rolls Royce in a league full of Skodas. His exorbitant talents were unsuited to the rigours and demands of a division where old-fashioned Scottish grit invariably holds the key to promotion. As the skipper that season, Jackie McNamara enjoyed a healthy relationship with his teammate but acknowledged that Best was 'not what was needed'.

By now, the inevitable parting of the ways was less about no-shows and drinking bouts than it was about the onset of apathy. With his wife four months away from giving birth to Calum in California, Best played his final game for Hibs in a 2–0 home win over Falkirk on 11 October 1980. He had picked up £12,000 for six further appearances at the club and his final game was only the second at home. So far as the club was concerned, he was no longer paying his way in a meaningful fashion.

'We all grew to like George and I think he liked us,' says Tony Higgins. 'We were average players sharing a dressing room with someone who had assumed the mantle of a superstar. If he thought we were rubbish, he never said so.'

On 2 March 1981, five months after leaving Scotland, one of the world's greatest ever footballers checked into the Vesper Hospital alcohol rehabilitation unit at the expense of San Jose's insurance company. It would be the first in a series of fruitless attempts to stop the rot. By 1982, Best was bankrupt, and by 1983 Bournemouth had become the new Hibs, providing a final English platform for his talents.

On 5 August 1984, there would be one final swansong in a green-and-white jersey, Best returning to Easter Road to play in his former captain Jackie McNamara's testimonial against Newcastle United.

'During that game, George and Dave McCreery were having a go at each other despite having been teammates for Northern Ireland,' McNamara recalls with a smile. 'George Smith, the referee, called George to him for a word. George pointed to the stand and said, "They haven't come to see you, they've come to see me." He then spotted me out the corner of his eye and quickly added, "Oh, and Jackie as well."'

Through his subsequent work with the PFA Scotland and the forerunner union, the SPFA, McNamara, a publican by trade, has helped many footballers unable to help themselves.

'Alcoholism is an illness,' he says. 'Having worked in the pub trade for 18 years, I know that much. What George had was an illness, beyond doubt. And it was exacerbated by his lifestyle. I was a bread-and-butter football player and I can only imagine what it must have been like to receive the kind of adulation that was constantly thrust onto George.

'Personally, I always thought he was a lovely guy. I'm lucky to be able to say I played with him and that he came back to Edinburgh to play in my testimonial game when he didn't need to.'

An infamous, slurring and almost incoherent appearance on the *Wogan* show in 1990 propelled the wayward genius back onto the front pages.

Marriage to second wife Alex Pursey seemed to provide some impetus for change, while a column in the *Mail on Sunday* finally revealed the thoughtful, articulate and intelligent depths which lay below the public image. Television work with Sky Sports then followed the national debate which commenced when a new liver was obtained through the National Health Service. Like the Manchester United and Irish FA officials who felt an alcoholic with an image problem was unworthy of a testimonial, there were those who felt that a new liver would be wasted on a hopelessly depressed alcoholic.

Relapsing into drink, Best died on 25 November 2005 of multiple organ failure in London's Cromwell Hospital. In the inevitable tributes, Hibernian barely merited a mention. Yet all of those who met, played with and witnessed Best in Scotland remember their brief brush with greatness.

'We were just average players, most of us, journeymen I suppose,' adds Tony Higgins. 'His days of being one of the top 10 footballers on the planet had long gone, but when the big crowds came in you would see the sparkle in the eyes come back. Even now, when I go to Hibernian supporters' clubs, there is a picture of George on the wall. He is up there with Lawrie Reilly, the great legend of the title winning teams of the 1950s, Joe Baker, who went to Italy, and Pat Stanton, who captained the side for a decade until 1976. He may not have had the longevity of the other players, but he is remembered because he was a great player who brought excitement to Hibernian at a time when glamour was in short supply.'

3

Samurai Warrior

CHIC CHARNLEY

'A lot o' managers had a problem with Chic, but that suited me
because I kept getting him for nothing.'

– Partick Thistle legend John Lambie

From the spot they call the Flagpole in Ruchill Park, it is possible to
see for miles on that rarest of Glasgow phenomena: the clear day. A
360-degree panorama offers unrivalled views of the dear green place
plus a few of its darker nooks. In the distance, the peaks of the
Erskine Bridge direct the eye as far as Dumbarton Rock on the banks
of the Clyde.

Much clearer to the naked eye is a nearby oasis of football
tranquility: Partick Thistle's Firhill Stadium. In the early 1990s,
Thistle players training in the park could be found simply by following the smoky plume cast up by their unconventional, cigar-chomping
manager John Lambie. Or by taking up a useful vantage point at the
Flagpole, known locally as Ben Whitton.

It is a spot from where you might also have once witnessed a group
of sprinting footballers giving chase to a retreating maniac recklessly
wielding a Samurai sword.

At the head of the chasing pack was James Callaghan Charnley,
armed only with a traffic cone for protection, who was, at the
time, emerging as the midfield fulcrum of Lambie's reshaped
Partick Thistle team. Hailing from Possil, a district in the north
of Glasgow where the closure of the old Saracen Foundry had
created streets of poverty and hardship, Charnley had learned
never to turn a deaf ear to even the subtlest insult. From an early

age, the infamous reputation of a Partick Thistle legend was almost pre-ordained.

As part of their training regime, Thistle players would be required to scale the hills of the park while attached to worn-out car tyres tied to their waist. Local wags suggested the tyres often returned first, in significantly better shape. Better condition, at least, than those ill-advised assailants who decided to interrupt the serious business of a Partick Thistle training session.

It is with something approaching pique – possibly shame – that the captain of that team, Jim Duffy, recalls his own role in the incident. In a list of British football's 50 hardest men, Charnley slid in, at a disappointingly modest forty-ninth position, by virtue of what will now be known as Sword-gate.

Duffy, an excellent defender in his day, would go on to become an integral managerial figure in Charnley's career – signing him twice, for Dundee and Hibernian. The working relationship was founded on a deep-rooted respect forged in the Firhill dressing room. A place where, in the code of footballers' honour, a friend always lends a hand to a colleague in need.

'It's always said it was just Chic, Gerry [Collins] and Gordon Rae that day and it was, but I was chasing up the rear as well,' claims Duffy. 'As I recall, it was three guys who had come along and one of them had a dog which Chic bent down to pat, as you do. In the background, meanwhile, one of them starts shouting along the lines of "Charnley ya knob", and so on. Of course, Chic being Chic, he tells him he'll see him after training. The three of them went away before appearing back minutes later. One of them had the Samurai sword and another had a knife or something.

'Chic went after them, with Gordon and Gerry, and I'm chasing as well. I don't think I ever saw Chic run as fast, but he caught up with them, traffic cone in hand. The guy with the sword slipped and it cut Chic's hand. Gordon Rae was a massive big guy and he picked the sword up and bent it over his knee as Chic leathered the boy. What was bizarre was that we went back to get Chic's hand bandaged up as if nothing had happened. He thought nothing of it. Honestly, folk don't believe me when I tell them this, but Chic never mentioned it afterwards. We had to go to the police station to give statements and so on, but to Chic it was the kind of thing you encountered every day in Possil. He didn't talk about it.'

Others were less comfortable with the surreal turn of events.

'The minute I saw that sword I was away like the shot of a gun down to the dressing room,' smiles Charnley's long-term father figure, Lambie. 'I'll argue with a player all right, but I'm not arguing with some f****** nutter with a sword.'

In the next Thistle home game, Charnley emerged with a heavily bandaged right hand, lifting his battle scars in acknowledgment before kick-off to a band of supporters desperate to acclaim their very own have-a-go vigilante. 'Should have seen the other guy', seemed to be the message. On the scarred streets of working-class Possil, it was said often enough that there was only one person Chic Charnley feared – his mother Isa. Mrs Charnley reared both a formidable and a gifted son.

It is Charnley's misfortune by a quirk of the alphabet to follow Baxter and Best in this account of the flawed greats. Some will wonder what business he has in such company, perhaps even the man himself does.

And yet those who recall Charnley scoring spectacular free-kicks, nutmegging Eric Cantona at Old Trafford, embarrassing Henrik Larsson on his Celtic debut and forcing his way to the edges of a Scotland World Cup squad at the age of 34, will attest to his underrated abilities. Put simply, Charnley, a possible victim of his hard-bitten upbringing, under-achieved to a ludicrous degree. The red cards outweighed the flashes of colour in his play.

'Chic has always been an emotional guy,' states Jim Duffy. 'If you know him and you know where his head is at, you'll be fine with him. As long as he doesn't lose control of those emotions he's a terrific guy. I was always honest with Chic and he was honest with me, and because of that we got along fine as player and manager. It was the same for him and John Lambie.

'But the reason you took it all on was quite simply because of his ability. I don't say this lightly, but Chic was one of the best I ever saw in my career. Anywhere. And I've worked at Celtic, Norwich,

Portsmouth and Chelsea. I've played with and managed a number of very good players, and none were better than Chic.

'Unfortunately, he never reached the profile of the truly great player and when he did have a profile, it was often negative. But I saw the guy score direct from corners and at least three times from his own half.

'You can't do all that unless you have exceptional technique. He could also play a diagonal pass better than anyone I ever saw. There were great Rangers players like Terry Butcher, Jorg Albertz, Gazza and Brian Laudrup when he was playing and I'm not suggesting Chic was more skilful than them. But in terms of his range of passing, he was magnificent.'

Charnley's 17 red cards in competitive football remains a perpetual source of embarrassment to him. Albeit one capable of raising an indulgent smile or two.

He puts the litany of shame down to the streets he walked as a child. Not so much how he was brought up, as where. Talking the talk was never enough in Possil, it was also necessary to walk the walk. Hence the reason he came to be regarded as the nemesis of the refereeing fraternity.

At a dinner one evening he sat side by side at the top table with former Liverpool star Ronnie Whelan, winner of two European Cups, three League Championships, one FA Cup and one League Cup. As the announcer moved down the table, he reached Charnley, 'the guy with 17 sending-offs and absolutely no medals . . .'

As always, the Glaswegian laughed off the joke. Yet the underlying truth was unmistakable. Were it not for a reputation for persistent bad behaviour, Charnley might have been granted chances handed to lesser players.

Some might say the affection which has flowed freely in his direction by dint of his erratic lifestyle was ample compensation for the wasted opportunities. Charnley himself disagrees emphatically, insisting he would readily trade the love and laughter for medals.

By the time he began training the Thistle youths at the end of his career, the penny had dropped. He would point to the example of

Paul Lambert as a midfielder of medium ability who applied himself wholeheartedly to improving his football education.

The two were teammates at St Mirren. Few would dispute that Charnley was the more skilful. But the difference? As Charnley would tell the kids frankly, it lay in the levels of dedication. Lambert grabbed the chance to go on trial at Borussia Dortmund in Germany, transforming himself from a decent SPL-standard attacking midfielder to a Champions League-winning holding player in 12 months. All of this under the astute guidance of Ottmar Hitzfeld. A £2.3 million move to Celtic at the tail-end of 1997 was his reward.

For Charnley, the perennial discipline problems were rooted in a number of causes. As well as an inability to turn the other cheek, he was also cursed with no great pace and a deficiency in the art of tackling.

Referees across the land came to loathe his backchat and, as the headlines piled up, gave the appearance of marking him out for particular attention.

'I played with Chic at Thistle twice and once at Dundee,' says Gerry Britton. 'He was passionate and competitive, ultra-competitive. But he was unfortunate that he was branded with this reputation by referees. They were always quick to clamp down on him – it's just human nature. If you have a reputation, people are going to pigeonhole you. But he never received a red card for being a dirty player. I know that because he never tackled anything more than a fish supper. There was nothing malicious about him. He was just competitive and enthusiastic, probably over-enthusiastic.'

Duffy had more hands-on experience of the problem than anyone except Lambie and believes nurture, rather than nature, explained an atrocious record for dismissals and bookings.

'Possil is the kind of place where, from a young age, you are almost roped in to having to prove you are tough,' he says. 'If you get into something there, you don't back away. Of course, anywhere else you would, but by the time Chic finally realised he had nothing to prove to anybody, he was almost out of the game.

'At Easter Road in 1997, he had a three-month spell where he was outstanding. People were seriously talking about him as a Scotland player, at the age of 34. The World Cup was in France in 1998 and some folk were even talking about him for that. He had calmed down by then, but unfortunately it was close to the tail-end of his career before that happened. In his younger days, Chic was living by the rules of an area where you couldn't show weakness – and he took that attitude onto the pitch.'

When someone confronted him, he had to fight back, he was almost programmed that way. But as he got older, he slowly realised that wasn't necessarily the case. That was probably his biggest career downfall. He grew up with close friends from Possil who lived a bit on the edge. When Chic went out on a football pitch, he went out with an edge as well. From a distance, Charnley can laugh about it now. He always could, if truth be told. He still maintains that five of his sending-offs were unwarranted. Duffy agreed more than once – deciding against implementing a fine. And the rest?

'I probably deserved them . . .' Charnley will admit with a chuckle.

Born in Glasgow on 11 June 1963, Chic's early career was a harum-scarum affair. A tentative beginning as a 19-year-old teenager at St Mirren flitted quickly onwards to Ayr United. In the early 1980s, however, the riches of today's professional footballers remained a distant prospect.

The chairman of the now defunct Clydebank, Jack Steedman, took pride in producing gifted players – his greatest prize to the game being the late Davie Cooper, the richly talented and impulsively skilful Rangers winger. In 1987 Steedman, a wily football wheeler and dealer of the old school, became aware that a young Charnley was now working on the oil rigs in the North Sea, where the cash was more generous than that paid to a lower league footballer. Hankering for another crack at the game he loved, Chic took the bait when Steedman offered a route back.

'A blind man could see Charnley's talent,' Steedman once observed. 'Other than Davie Cooper, he was the most gifted footballer we handled. Yet he never took anything seriously. He would miss training every Monday because he felt it was his duty to visit certain friends who were being detained as guests of Her Majesty in Perth. But that was Chic; these things are more important to him and he remains an irrepressible character.'

Charnley played 31 times for the Bankies in season 1987/88, scoring 11 goals, and Steedman, who always had an eye for a sale, accepted an offer from Hamilton. The Douglas Park experience, like so many, was a short-lived source of frustrated potential. A dismissal in a bounce game against Falkirk resulted in Charnley's being shown the door.

Where others were beginning to see only madness and mayhem in this particular player, one manager in Glasgow's West End saw only the maestro within. John Lambie had signed Charnley for Accies before moving to Partick Thistle for the first of three remarkable spells at the helm at Firhill. His unmistakable influence in Charnley's rollercoaster career was about to commence.

By the player's own admission, Lambie was a 'major part' of his success. The two had a regard for each other which, in the rough, macho world of Scottish football, is difficult to quantify. At heart, Charnley appreciated that here was a man who never picked on him indiscriminately and who accepted his faults.

There were occasions when the two came close to blows, particularly when Lambie pointed the finger at Charnley for tomfoolery on a team-bonding trip to Blackpool – when he hadn't even been there.

The midfielder flew for the manager, assistant boss Gerry Collins placing himself strategically between the two to prevent a scrap Charnley would regret for the remainder of his career. Fearing the worst, Charnley was summoned to the manager's office afterwards for what he suspected might be the final time. Fixing his stare steadily upon his errant player, Lambie beckoned to a chair and said:

'For f***'s sake, Chic, sit down, calm down and join me in a wee cup of tea.'

Lambie, notorious for an Anglo-Saxon turn of phrase, spent the following years yo-yoing between Hamilton and Maryhill in a restless state of apparent indecision. Like Charnley, the renowned pigeon-fancier with a love of a fine cigar – now traded for cigarettes –

would leave Thistle more than once before returning like a bad penny.

'Chic always had a smile on his face,' Lambie states with understated warmth. 'He was different class. The referees were always a bit sore on him. But the old ref Brian McGinlay was brilliant with him. He would be the type to say to him, "Just get f****** on with the game." You know what I mean? Chic appreciated that kind of thing. Ach, he was his own worst man at times, but I don't think his disciplinary record was that bad under me. He knew the score with me, every player did. If they arsed around then they were hit where it hurt – in their pockets. They accepted that.'

But it wasn't all cracking the whip. 'He hit me on the back of the head with a golf ball once. I didn't say it to him at the time, but I thought to myself, "I'll get that b****** back." So I stood on a chair behind a door a few days later and I had this big medicine ball in my hands. When he came in, I brought it crashing down on top of his nut.'

Reminded this was one of his star players we were discussing, Lambie responds: 'That didn't matter. I dropped it on his heid and he deserved it.'

Charnley left Firhill for the first time after a productive return of 22 goals in 73 midfield appearances. Joining St Mirren, where his boyhood Celtic hero David Hay was the manager, the Glaswegian again failed to control his rampant disciplinary problems. Charnley arrived in a £250,000 double deal alongside David Elliot, with the popular striker Georgie Shaw moving in the other direction. Charnley was dismissed three times in forty-two starts, and the placid Hay found it difficult to comprehend the player's volatile temperament, which was making the transfer begin to look disastrous.

At this point, the mesmeric midfielder was offered his first crack at the big time, when Bolton Wanderers manager Phil Neal signed him on loan. Three appearances followed, but no permanent deal was forthcoming.

'I didn't know what to think,' reported a bewildered Neal. 'I'd never seen anything like it before.' In Scotland, the comment drew knowing nods.

There was respite of a sort in the unlikely environs of Sweden. Yet the status of his employers, Djurgardens, was as volatile as the nature of this highly turbulent, redheaded Scotsman, with the club being relegated from the Allsvenskan no fewer than three times in the 1990s, whilst flirting with bankruptcy. This, then, was far from the kind of stable environment Charnley required in which to thrive.

At the age of thirty, and with the bulk of his career already gone, Charnley had played for nine clubs.

Tail fixed firmly between his legs, it was to John Lambie he again turned. In a Firhill dressing room containing the likes of Alan Dinnie – jailed for cocaine dealing in 2002 – and the uncompromising Steve Pittman, Charnley added craft to a combustible and unruly crew.

Towards the end of the 1993/94 season, however, came his gravest disappointment after a second tantalising brush with the big time. Charnley grew up dreaming of wearing the green-and-white of Celtic. And a highly unlikely opportunity to do so arose when he was invited to guest for the Hoops by manager Lou Macari in a testimonial for Manchester United legend Mark Hughes at Old Trafford. Pulling the Celtic jersey over his head for the first time, there were said to be tears in the eyes of this emotional figure. There was, however, no hint of inferiority.

An improbable 3–1 win over a side featuring Eric Cantona and Ryan Giggs contained a typically gallus display from the trialist. Afterwards, a £200,000 switch from Thistle was discussed. Common folklore has it that the midfielder blew his chance by rejecting the chance to tour Canada with the Parkhead side – going on holiday with Thistle teammates instead. Charnley claims now that was an over-simplistic distortion of the matter, stating that Macari granted him the choice of going to Canada – or awaiting his return and holding signing talks then.

Believing he was heading for Celtic come what may, he opted against the tour and headed to the Algarve with his Thistle teammates instead. On his return, Charnley received a call saying he had put drink before the advancement of his career. The move to Parkhead was off. To this day, he regrets what happened, yet also suspects Macari had undergone a change of mind and simply wanted an escape clause.

That Charnley had opted against playing more games for Celtic seems incredible in retrospect. If Macari had set him a test of his professionalism and desire then he had failed it – miserably. There will be those who believe the willingness to consider such a player was an indication of Celtic's desperate straits at the time. Charnley's entire approach to his Old Trafford try-out had been off the wall from the start.

'I remember when he played that game,' says Jim Duffy. 'I was talking to him about it afterwards and he was telling me he had won man of the match and managed to get the jersey of Ryan Giggs for his wee boy. I was asking him what his preparation for such a massive game had been. Did he go down early? Check into a hotel? And he told me quick as a flash, "Nah, I just went down with my pals on a minibus. They were going to the game anyway." That just summed him up for me. Here's a guy given the chance to win the move of his dreams to Celtic by playing at the most famous ground in world football against Cantona, Giggs and co. And he's travelled down there in a bus with his mates!

'But for me that says it all about the ability the guy had. If you can go to Old Trafford and play without so much as a single training session with the team and be the pick of the bunch, then you can obviously play. Celtic didn't have a bad team either, obviously. So, yes, he under-achieved. Because in terms of his natural ability, Chic was phenomenal.'

How Charnley might have fared had he tried to slug from a can of McEwan's pale ale while puffing on a half-time cigar at Celtic is a grizzly thing to contemplate. In any case, the chance had gone and here he was, back at Thistle. Broken, yet not entirely bowed.

Cursed by the belief that a player over the age of thirty is on a downward spiral, Charnley lasted just two years in the Premier Division, before drifting on to Dumbarton at the age of thirty-two. His time in the game looked to be rattling to an unsatisfactory end.

All of this reckoned, however, without another of his career saviours. Like a guardian angel on the left shoulder, with Lambie perched on the right, Jim Duffy decided Charnley could do a job at Dundee, paying £10,000 to salvage the football equivalent of Rocky Balboa.

'I remembered he had scored a goal against Dundee when he was with Dumbarton,' Duffy explains. 'It was one of those days when nothing was going right. And Chic got a free kick so far out you expected him just to howff it into the box. It was a good 40 yards out – and he just placed it right into the postage stamp corner. Our keeper was completely dumbstruck.'

Eyebrows were raised in the Dens Park dressing room at the signing, the players turning to Gerry Britton – Charnley's former Partick Thistle teammate – for reassurance as much as a character reference.

'Chic's legend went before him,' laughs Britton. 'So they were all asking me what he was like. I was trying to play it down, obviously, telling them everything about Chic was blown completely out of proportion. But we were due to play a game at Dens Park – I can't remember who against – and that was to be his first involvement. He had signed on the Friday and it got to 1.30 p.m. on the Saturday, with the game kicking off at 3 p.m. and he still hadn't turned up.

'Of course, I'm sticking to my guns defending Chic, still telling folk it'll be all right, when Jim starts his pre-match team-talk. Sure enough, the door bursts open and in walks Chic – 10 minutes late and complete with a massive big black eye. And he says to us, "The only place I know how to get to in Dundee is the casino – so I got lost." I'm aware that all these eyes are looking at me quizzically – the guy who'd told them he was straight up and that his reputation was overplayed.'

Charnley overcame that unfortunate introduction by going out and scoring a trademark 35-yard strike on his debut. In as neat a summary of the wayward hero's career trajectory as it's possible to find, he was dismissed in the next game. With Chic Charnley, it was always one step forward, two steps back.

But Duffy also remembers some highlights:

'There was a Dundee and Dundee United derby where Chic took one of those free kicks from about seven yards out you see every now and then. The defenders were all in a line on the goal line. You hardly ever see anyone get the ball past the wall in that situation. But Chic ran up as if to blast the ball and, as the wall jumped up in anticipation, he fooled them and just side-footed it under them and into the net. How often do you see that? Hardly ever.'

In his final game for the Dark Blues came another dismissal – once again in a Tayside derby. This time, there would be no fine or disciplinary action from the player-manager Duffy. He was sent off as well.

There was, then, always empathy between the two Glaswegians based, states Duffy, on a warmth to the Charnley character which, like Best and Paul Gascoigne, made him a difficult man to dislike. And so it was that Duffy signed Charnley once again – this time for Hibs. What began in razzmatazz, with the new manager arriving on the Easter Road pitch in a helicopter ended, however, in a savage crash-and-burn exercise.

Over the course of 29 games, Charnley enjoyed what many suspect to have been his finest hour. At 34, this was an Indian summer that, on his debut, began with a long-range winner over Wim Jansen's new-look Celtic team. Charnley famously received the ball from a loose pass by new Parkhead signing Henrik Larsson. It was an inauspicious start for the Swede, but one from which he would recover admirably – claiming a place among the Celtic greats with 174 goals in 221 appearances.

'I'm the man who made Chic Charnley famous,' said the Parkhead legend later with a rueful smile.

To counter Charnley's wilder streak at Hibs, Duffy used a carrot and stick approach to disciplinary matters.

'I employed Chic on a three-strike rule – three disciplinary strikes and he was out. By the end of his three months he had probably comfortably reached two. But in fairness, he had arrived on a very basic salary. He had fallen out with John McCormack, the Dundee manager, which was ironic – because he and John were good pals for years. So I took him on at £200 a week basic, rising to £400 if he played and £600 if he played and we won. It was probably a lower minimum wage than was legally permissible, I suspect, but it seemed to do the trick, because the Hibs fans loved him. It didn't matter where he went – the fans always loved him.'

The reasons for that were clear enough: Charnley was touched at times by heavenly instincts. He was a player who could switch from magic to madness with all the unpredictability of Mount Etna. Even his own colleagues approached the midfielder with something akin to wariness. In one of the more public blemishes of his time at Hibs, Charnley picked up a red card against Dundee United for an altercation with Joe McLaughlin – his own teammate.

'Chic's three favourite words never altered,' states Duffy. ' "F****** geez it", was all he shouted, whether he was in training or a game. He would demand the ball from teammates wherever he was. He wanted it in areas no one should ever want the ball – on the edge of his own box, the lot. As a manager I loved that, any manager would.

'He was infectious. But if someone didn't give him it, he could lose the rag in a split second. I remember bringing in a French trialist and the guy being terrified by the aggression in Chic's voice when he demanded the ball. He'd never experienced that before.'

Post-Hibs, Charnley's career frittered out in unremarkable fashion. Games here and there for non-league Tarff Rovers, Portadown in Northern Ireland and junior club, Kirkintilloch Rob Roy, culminated in a prodigal return to Thistle for a third spell at the club.

'His last involvement in football was probably here,' says Gerry Britton. 'We took the reserves together and it was great. Probably the only negative I would offer on Chic is something common to many of the great players. They get frustrated with lesser players because they can't do what they themselves find easy.'

Charnley made some substitute appearances for Thistle at the age of 39 – the last one just a month before he turned 40. By the end, he had served some 16 clubs – with just the one 90-minute run-out for Celtic. Few doubt that a dream move to wear the green-and-white hoops might have been a more fitting stage for his talents. Even at a time when the mediocrity of Wayne Biggins, Carl Muggleton et al stalked the corridors of Parkhead.

'I always felt that playing with some really top players by his side might have been what he needed,' adds Duffy, 'because they would have complemented his style and he would have risen to the challenge. For all his faults, Chic was one of the best trainers I ever managed. We went once to Paisley to train at an indoor facility with treadmills and all the rest. The fitness instructor told us you could only run at the maximum speed on the treadmill for 10 minutes, no more.

'Of course, Chic said he'd do it for 15 and the boy said, "No, can't be done." So Chic bets him £100, the guy accepts with a smug grin and then has to watch as he loses his cash by five minutes. Chic was never the quickest, but he never lacked fitness. I would give him the odd Monday off at Hibs because I knew he would be out socialising hard over the weekend. But he would be back sharp on the Tuesday and train like a beast.

'It wasn't just Chic's ability that made guys like John Lambie and me go back for him. He'll tell you himself that his social habits were never those of a professional athlete. But no matter what he was getting up to away from the park, he was always up at the front in training. And he was a tremendous guy to have in a dressing room. That was why managers kept signing him. That, and the fact he was a fantastic player.'

Ultimately, those who came to know Charnley saw charm and likeability behind his fearsome outward demeanour. Appearances were always deceptive where the midfielder was concerned. Beneath the temper and the explosive tendencies lay a man with a heart, both on and off the field.

On a blustery February afternoon in a hospitality lounge at Firhill Stadium, Chic Charnley is holding court. The temperature in the room is such that every word creates a breath of condensation in the chilled air. Yet the warmth surrounding the local hero is unmistakable.

Here to launch a charity game for the under-threat St Margaret's Hospice in Glasgow, a new side to a renowned bad boy of Scottish football is on show. It's entirely apt, then, that Charnley should be found in the middle of the Alan Rough Lounge, a room dedicated to

Thistle's erstwhile Scotland international goalkeeper. Over the years, both men proved useful with their hands. Albeit in different ways.

If this erratic Firhill legend had merely been about thuggery and lashing out at opponents, he would have no place in this book. Yet Charnley is perfect flawed genius material: a mercurial footballer with magic in his boots and a loose connection in his brain. Rather than cause alarm, his beaming smile and wide boy persona charms those who come into his company. Most important of all, he could play the game of football with a joyous level of off-the-cuff brilliance.

Who else in British football can boast of making Larsson look an idiot at Celtic before scoring against Alloa from fully 60 yards in his very next game? Since retiring from football after his fourth stint at Thistle in 2002–03, Charnley has shown a softer side to his nature. By his own admission, maturity came late to this chameleon of the Scottish game. His reinvention as a charitable figure will never change his reputation as one of the madmen of the sport. It may convince potential employers, however, that the 45-year-old man standing before a group of journalists in a pink shirt and dark pin-stripped suit – as lean as he ever was as a player – has turned over a new leaf.

These days, private charitable donations are the norm for Chic. The more private the better. The charity work, he admits, clears the conscience and cleanses the soul.

If the need exists to sell his soul to the devil to secure the cash, then so be it; various stories in newspapers and media outlets have provided the means to become a better person. Other times, he admits, fiscal shortages have forced him to be less generous. When it comes to Yorkhill Sick Children's Hospital in Glasgow, he is always available. His own son underwent treatment there and Charnley has never forgotten his debt of gratitude.

With broadcaster Chic Young, the former midfielder has participated in a raft of charity football games and is now a member of the Dukla Pumpherston celebrity team. By his own admission, the games fulfil a double mission. They help the needy and they quell his need to feel involved once more in football. After two decades at the coalface, Charnley never expected to miss it all, but admits that he does.

At the end of Charnley's playing career, John Lambie – only ever called 'the gaffer' by the man himself – took him on as a coach. The idea of Chic as some kind of dressing room figure of authority is not unlike placing Keith Richards in charge of the Rolling Stones' mini-bar. Working beside Gerry Collins and Bobby McCully, however, he thrived.

When Collins was dismissed in the aftermath of a 40-minute board meeting and just 16 games in charge after succeeding Lambie, there was no pressure on Charnley to leave. The chief executive, Alan Dick, he insists, said his job was safe. The honour system of professional football dictated that he fall on his sword, however, Samurai or otherwise. Morally, he saw no other option.

At first-team level, the offers have been scarce. Currently, Charnley does some youth coaching for Coca-Cola, with former Celtic star Murdo MacLeod and Hearts legend Gary Mackay, building upon the experience he gained with Thistle's youths. Like all old pros, however, he yearns for the real deal, for the language and ribaldry of a first-team dressing room.

He suspects that his reputation goes before him. Granted the opportunity, Charnley would turn the clock back. He would keep 5 per cent of the mayhem and swap the other 95 per cent for a life of early nights and sombre professionalism.

'I would listen to people more,' he admits. 'I know hindsight is a great thing, but I would listen to the people who actually know what's best for me. We've all done it – not listening to the people who are right. But I was always too stubborn. I thought I knew more than I did.'

He spends his time these days making amends for the sins of his past. Even if he was never as bad as his reputation would have it.

'Chic has always given a lot of his time for charity,' states Gerry Britton. 'It is a side to him people don't really see. He's a warm, generous guy. His daughter Danielle used to have a Sunday news-paper round when she was younger. But one day the rain was torrential. So rather than get her up out of bed, he decided to deliver the papers himself in the car. So he was putting a paper through one of the letter boxes when this woman opened the door. Chic said to me later, "She wasn't sure if I was delivering it or stealing it!" '

An NHS decision to stop funding 30 of the beds provided in the St Margaret's Hospice posed a threat to its very existence. As the MSPs talked, it fell to Chic Charnley to galvanise his football friends in search of a solution. Lambie, Neil Lennon and Ally McCoist were just some of those who responded. History shows that, with a posse of football friends behind him, Chic Charnley can take on all comers. Sword or no sword.

4

The Kaiser of Kincardine
GEORGE CONNELLY

'I looked out the car window and glimpsed this guy standing
beside a pub. I wanted to be that man who seemed completely
without a care or a responsibility.'

– from *Celtic's Lost Legend*, by George Connelly

It was a night when Celtic's European past and present married in
perfect symmetry.

On 3 October 2007, a modern-day enigma returned to Celtic Park
following a 32-year absence. When George Connelly accepted an
invitation to make the half-time draw at a major European game, the
significance extended far beyond the £8,000 cheque pocketed by the
night's Paradise Windfall winner. The main event was Celtic versus
AC Milan, a pulsating throwback to the days when the aristocrats of
European football were regular visitors to the old arena and the man
himself performed with grace and no little style. In showbiz circles,
they say you should always leave them gasping for more. When
Connelly quit football at the age of 27, he certainly did that.

When he was just 16, the Fifer was sent out by Jock Stein to
entertain the Celtic Park crowd by playing keepie-uppie during the
half-time interval of a European Cup Winners' Cup quarter-final
first-leg against Dynamo Kiev. Balancing and juggling the ball with
every limb, estimates placed his tally at around 2,000 unbroken
touches. Now, at the age of 57, and a Fife taxi driver by trade, his
capacity for making a ball dance had dimmed following dark
passages of alcohol abuse. For most of the 60,000 crowd, however,
his return to the main stage after a lengthy absence was a moment of

immense curiosity. Here, in their midst, was a genuine man of mystery. His feet, they knew, should never have skipped away in the first place.

Scott McDonald and Milan's Brazilian goalkeeper, Nelson Dida, would steal most of the headlines. Celtic's Australian striker slid a close-range shot into the net, after the keeper's fumble, to spark scenes of mass jubilation, an advertising hoarding being ripped from its foundations amid the celebratory frenzy. On nights such as this, Celtic Park represents a throbbing, thumping assault on the human senses. Dida's theatrical tumble to the ground following an idiotic walk-on part by a Parkhead supporter eventually became an international incident, earning the supporter a lifetime ban and the keeper a two-match UEFA suspension. But, as he would himself attest, the role of the walk-on cameo always suited Connelly's temperament better than that of the leading man.

This icon of the club's halcyon days made the journey over the Kincardine Bridge to Glasgow's East End for the Milan game in a blacked-out people carrier, with his second wife Helen and friends Andrew and Linda Connor. He was invited to the Celtic boardroom, where Peter Lawwell, the club's chief executive, fulfilled a personal ambition by greeting one of his heroes.

Then, at half-time, came the long walk down the Celtic tunnel which culminated in a gargantuan roar to accompany the return of a legend, Celtic scarf draped loosely around his neck. By his own admission, Connelly had a variety of deep-rooted issues to sift through his mind as he battled valiantly to fend off the onset of tears. Why had he done it? Why had he walked? Why had he stayed away so long?

For Celtic supporters, the answers to those questions eluded a generation. For every child of the '70s and '80s with a green-and-white perspective, indoctrination in the whys and wherefores of Connelly's squandered genius were akin to a rite of passage.

His was the kind of talent to have grown men gnashing and wailing at the waste of it all. He was Franz Beckenbauer in a Scotsman's skin, a player of the year, an international, a man for all tastes. He announced his arrival by tearing Rangers asunder in the 1969 Scottish Cup Final, embarrassing the great John Greig in the process. He then took a set of shears to the pristine white shirts of Don Revie's all-conquering Leeds United team, his performance in the European Cup semi-final of 1970 pivotal to his legend. With Scotland, Connelly was equally potent, producing a distinguished display as the national team swept past Czechoslovakia at Hampden in 1973 to qualify for the World Cup finals.

And yet that very year had provided the most visible sign that Connelly was veering off the rails. He was voted player of the year but walked out on Scotland at the check-in desk as Willie Ormond's side prepared to fly to a qualifying game in Switzerland.

'It was a personal thing with George, that walk-out,' states close friend and Celtic legend David Hay, who was beside him at the airport desk when Connelly departed. 'There was never any mischief or contempt behind his actions, that wasn't his style. It was as if he just had to do it. We had been at a small hotel in Largs the night before and I sensed there was unease there. There were psychological and psychiatric reasons playing their part – nothing else.'

In all, this man of contradictions would walk out on Celtic a total of five times before the inevitable permanent parting of the ways.

In the years after his Parkhead contract was torn up, a compendium of half-baked theories would be offered by way of explanation. That the Fifer was a painfully shy, insular individual ill-suited to life in the city of Glasgow was the most accurate offering. Connelly, they said, yearned to be a long-distance lorry driver. He had been deeply upset by a prank played on him by teammates in New York. He drank too much and found alcohol to possess a compulsive grip. He heard uncontrollable voices in his head. Despite all the myths, the truth was much more prosaic.

The youngest of eight children – three girls and five boys – Connelly's parents had arrived in Fife from the west of Scotland, his father heading east in search of work down the mines.

Attending St Margaret's School in Dunfermline, the young man with the awkward manner was undistinguished. What vocational ability he had shone through only when he was juggling a ball in the air continuously. Most school kids are told they are dreaming when they talk of being a footballer; for Connelly, it was a pipedream to think he could be anything else.

He body-swerved his local club to accept a £20 signing-on fee at Parkhead, partly swayed no doubt by wages of £2 a week. But he hailed from a large family of Celtic supporters and even the inconvenience of meandering 7 a.m. bus journeys from the north side of the Kincardine Bridge to Glasgow's Alexandra Parade followed by a 10-minute walk to Celtic Park, failed to dampen a sense of excitement and awe. Yet this was allied, all the while, with acute feelings of inferiority and insecurity that were to undermine him.

There were, in fact, only two circumstances in which George Connelly found comfort and confidence. One was with a drink in his hand, the other with a ball at his feet. Stein had already dealt with such a player in Willie Hamilton during his formative years as a manager at Hibernian. Connelly was, however, a more challenging proposition. If only because he proved impervious to the big man's urgings and coaxing.

With a football at his feet, the teenage Connelly was engrossed, his troubled mind placed completely at ease by the artistry involved in his juggling skills. As Davie Hay points out, Connelly was essentially a painfully shy man who had to battle with himself to conquer the ailment.

'Nerves were never an issue for George when it came to 90 minutes against top-class opposition. It was the aspects of life off the pitch he could never come to terms with. He was never the sort to flaunt his status as a Celtic player, none of us were at that time. Under Jock Stein, you embraced a team ethos – you just wanted to do as well as you could for the team, not yourself.'

At Celtic, Connelly emerged as one of the famed Quality Street Kids, a band of players nursed by Stein as the natural successors to the Lisbon Lions. Kenny Dalglish, Hay, John Gorman, Vic Davidson and Lou Macari were marked out for future fame. As part of a rounded football education, Connelly played as a winger, striker, midfielder and even central defender. It was as a deep-lying, passing sweeper that he would eventually come to read the game best, however. A mark of his outstanding ability came in the fact that he made his Old Firm debut at Ibrox on the wing – in a League Cup clash with Rangers. He continued in that role in the game where his star rose to a different stratosphere – the 4–0 thrashing of the other half of the Old Firm in the 1969 Scottish Cup final. For a player of just 23, this was dazzling stuff.

The next season provided a summary of Connelly's unpredictable nature. Playing in midfield, the six-footer dazzled in the hyped-up Battle of Britain with Leeds United, in the semi-final of the European Cup. It was said that this was the final before the final. History dictates that Celtic – even Jock Stein – were seduced by such talk. In the final itself, Connelly was inexplicably overlooked as Stein switched from a 4–3–3 to a 4–2–4 – a decision David Hay still regards as a rare mistake from the fabled manager. The European champions of 1967 could not repeat the feat, taking the lead against Feyenoord in the San Siro Stadium before losing 2–1 in extra-time. Remarkably devoid of ego or preciousness, Connelly made no great fuss of his exclusion from the big occasion.

By the 1972/73 season, Connelly was in his prime. He slotted in alongside Billy McNeill as the spare man in defence and featured in another European Cup semi-final, against Inter Milan. Scotland, also, were attempting to utilise his talents. Tommy Docherty picked the Celtic man for a World Cup qualifier against Denmark in October 1972 – yet plagued by psychological problems and troubles at home, Connelly withdrew from the squad. It was to become a familiar pattern.

In June 1974, just weeks after being named player of the year, came the most infamous Scotland disappearing act. Another World Cup qualifier in Switzerland beckoned as his first wife, Christine, expected the second of the couple's two daughters. None of which explains why he bailed out with the briefest of explanations to Davie Hay at the airport check-in desk, buying two bottles of Cinzano to drink in bed as the entire Scottish media camped outside his Blantyre home.

'I phoned his wife Christine and told her to make sure he came up with a reason for his exit if he changed his mind and decided to come back. She told me he wouldn't – as she said, if I couldn't persuade him to go then there was nothing she could do.

'As George headed back to Blantyre in a taxi, we flew to London and no one on the plane knew there was no George. A journalist, Alex Cameron, had asked me where George was at the airport and I'd just given him a vague answer. It wasn't like now, where there are vast security checks and bags get hauled off if a passenger is missing. The assumption was that all the players were there. That was how footballers behaved. They didn't do what George did, and that was probably a sign of what was to come.'

Andy McInnes was a news reporter at the time of Connelly's walkout and was sent to doorstep the troubled maestro at his Blantyre home. After knocking repeatedly, McInnes and photographers received no answer and were retreating down the pathway when the door suddenly thundered open behind them, with a raucous cry of 'haw, you'.

Turning round startled, McInnes managed to duck the impact of a haymaker punch from a clearly inebriated Connelly. A photographer was less fortunate, however, having his equipment wrenched from his neck and smashed into pieces on the concrete path.

A disturbing incident ended with Connelly's wife Christine and an older woman shouting for calm from the doorway in tears. 'At that point,' McInnes recalls, 'George collapsed to his knees and burst into tears as well. He was inconsolable. It was an awful moment.'

Connelly's disappearing act brought mainly pity and concern. It was becoming apparent that this was a man with deep-rooted problems, not least in his growing regard for alcohol. These days, Connelly can go missing for weeks after saving taxi fares to fund benders, to the distress of his long-suffering second wife, Helen.

What, then, are the demons eating away at George Connelly's being? What prompted this gifted individual to cast his career into a chasm deeper than the Firth of Forth?

Connelly, frankly, has been trapped in a personal hell from which he is ill-equipped to escape. His first marriage had been a sham, and his gift for football a burden. None of this became apparent, however, until Bryan Cooney, a sports writer, succeeded where others had failed in persuading Connelly to break his monastic silence. Other journalists had long since given up trying.

As Cooney explains, his breakthrough was a combination of persistence and good fortune. It was, however, rooted primarily in a long-standing fascination with his subject.

'I returned to Scotland from London to work in 1974 and Connelly was established almost as a legend because he had come through the ranks of the Quality Street Gang to prominence in 1969 with that display against Rangers in the Scottish Cup final.

'I had only seen him play twice at that point, but I was absolutely thrilled by him, an imperious figure. He wasn't fast, but he didn't need to be. He looked so at home with everything he did. His passing, his gait, the lot. He just looked a great footballer, nothing seemed to faze him. It was all easy, the ball came to him and stuck. He could pass it with either foot, he could run with it, attack and rattle people. Here was your complete footballer.'

Jock Stein agreed. Perhaps as a by-product of his talent, he was a player capable of promoting a near paternal instinct in his manager. Where others were bullied or cajoled, Stein recognised that such psychological ploys would be counter-productive in such a sensitive soul. Yet there was one man George Connelly felt he could never hope to placate or please: himself.

The keys to the gates of heaven appeared to be his by the age of 23. Three cars, two homes – albeit of the modest rather than the electronically protected variety – a beautiful young wife and two daughters should have been the trappings of outward contentment. Later that year, he would also become Scotland's player of the year. Yet one day he peered at a solitary figure reading the racing pages of a newspaper outside a pub in Kincardine. Connelly saw the figure standing there as carefree, concerned only with the next winner at Newmarket, and entirely devoid of responsibility. He might have had tuppence ha'penny in his pocket and little in the way of career prospects, yet right there, in that instant, George Connelly wanted more than anything to be a free spirit, whose only worry was about the contents of his next glass. All this at a time when half of Scotland's football-loving population would have parted with their last penny to possess the talent of George Connelly.

These days, they would prescribe drugs for the symptoms displayed by such a man at the peak of his upward ascent. Connelly, it seemed, wanted to be invisible to the outside world, to draw the blankets over his head and be alone with his darkest thoughts and moods. He wanted more money than the rather pitiful contract on offer from Celtic, it's true. He also suffered separation anxiety as soon as his great friend and boyhood teammate David Hay left for Chelsea following a dispute with the club over cash. Yet most of the problems existed deep within the recesses of his complex brain.

He neither loved nor particularly liked his first wife, Christine. Theirs would be a silent, sullen union born in unhappiness and mired forever in negative emotions. Teenagers in Valleyfield, a mining community lodged between Dunfermline and the Kincardine Bridge, the pair had started dating in 1969, the year Connelly truly announced his arrival as a Celtic star of the future. In these times of teenage single mothers, it seems a difficult concept to grasp, but when Christine fell pregnant there was only one choice to make; hopelessly ill matched and ill at ease in each other's company, the couple married. Social mores demanded it.

By Connelly's definition, they were little more than 'village idiots'. The arrival of a child was as good a reason to get hitched as any. Other, that is, than the threat of death at knifepoint from Christine's formidable mother.

A £750 loan from Celtic facilitated the purchase of a room and kitchen in Kincardine, yet domestic bliss was never a given. The two had united in the interests of a child never born, a miscarriage bringing a desperately sad episode – if not the marriage – to an end.

A move to Blantyre, near Hamilton, ended the early morning journeys from Fife to Celtic Park. It would, they sensed, broaden their limited horizons. And yet by leaving Fife, the desperately introverted footballer removed his comfort blanket and exposed himself to the vagaries of a world he neither coveted nor revelled in. Socialising with teammates was out of the question for a man overawed by his more at-ease colleagues. Some felt Connelly was aloof and unfriendly. Towards the end, teammates came to resent the attention being lavished on their needy colleague.

At least some of the problems were financial. Celtic earned a reputation under the family dynasties who once owned the club for regarding every penny as a prisoner. It was a trait that manifested itself in high attendances and low wages for top-class performers. A key player in the drive for nine-in-a-row, Connelly earned just £65 a week and, with Hay, campaigned vigorously for an increase. It may be more accurate to say that the more savvy Hay did the campaigning while Connelly stood at a respectable distance to his rear. Whatever the negotiating stance, however, Connelly requested a transfer and was taking solace from his problems at home and in the workplace through alcohol. Hay knew their value and brokered for £100 a week. When chairman Desmond White turned the request down flat, Hay went on strike – and Connelly followed in sympathy.

Celtic agreed to the latter's transfer, yet when no takers came forth, he returned to action. An ankle injury in a European Cup quarter-final clash with Basle not only ruled the sweeper out of the World Cup finals in Germany – but proved a disaster for his bargaining power.

While Hay aggravated for a move and finally won a switch to Chelsea, Connelly caved in and signed a new contract. It was to prove a disastrous decision; the catalyst for the walk-outs which destroyed his career.

'My departure from Celtic was definitely a factor in what happened,' states Hay. 'George has acknowledged that himself. We were the same age, we did a lot together and we had a similar philosophy on how to play football. I'm not saying that George became dependent on me, I wouldn't want to put myself up on that pedestal. But George did look on me as his closest friend. It started from when we were talking to Celtic about contracts. I was effectively negotiating, not just for myself, but for George as well.

'George then sustained a bad injury against Basle and when he was in that state, he signed another contract without consulting me. When he told me, I just asked him, "Why have you done that?" It didn't make any difference to me personally. But he took what I felt quite hard and the issues just began to pile up after that.

'When I did leave for Chelsea, he phoned and told me he might have to leave Celtic. He regretted signing the contract and though he never told me so, he regretted me leaving as well. I told him if he was going to leave, to go somewhere that suited his game and his temperament.'

By now, Connelly's fragility was becoming apparent to friend and foe alike. That he needed help rather than bullying was clear enough.

'There was something that happened in New York when there was the kind of mickey-taking that goes on amongst football players,' Hay admits, 'but that had been away back in 1970. There was also a laugh and joke in Bermuda at a hypnotism show. But the impact of all these things was exaggerated. George did things which were never associated with football players.

'Initially, I put his exit from football down not only to my departure from Celtic, but also to the contract which he felt he shouldn't have signed. The biggest tragedy with George was that he was this exceptional talent playing for Celtic – and yet they never got the best years from him. No one did.'

Ironically, it was around this time that a young sports newshound was returning from Fleet Street with a developing interest in the flawed genius who had emerged as the finest player in the country. Bryan Cooney had taken up a post with the *Scottish Sun* and moved to the same locale as Connelly.

'I arrived back in Scotland and wanted to get to know him. Then came the first leg of the European Cup game against Basle, when he injured himself and effectively ended any chance he had of going to the World Cup finals. He went off the radar for a bit. I was probably a bit apprehensive over approaching him. A lot of people were.'

Even seasoned campaigners on the Scottish media scene had come to regard Connelly as something of an oddball. On the principle that rejection can often cause offence, most steered clear of a man the football writers themselves had dubbed the finest player in the country. Veteran broadcaster and journalist Archie Macpherson had the ear of most of the most influential men in the

Scottish game at one time or another, travelling the world with Jock Stein prior to the great man's death. Yet even his relationship with the enigmatic new star of the Scottish game was one maintained at arm's length.

'I remember going to the football writers' player of the year dinner when George won the award. I clearly recall it was May 1, because I had written off a car on the Fenwick Moors in heavy snow. This in May as well.

'Stein was there at the top table and I remember the compère being the Scottish actor of the time, Russell Hunter. I always remember him saying about Jock Stein that he was just sitting there looking at George Connelly as if he were his own wee boy.

'George was a controlled and disciplined player who would emerge as the Bobby Murdoch type of player rather than a more explosive sort. Oh, he could do the keepie-uppies and things, so he was a superbly skilled player as well. But there was so much to his game.

'When he quit, it was certainly a bit of a sensation. It was stunning and mysterious at the same time and the stories about his problems began to take root.'

Jim Black was a young sportswriter with the *Scottish Sun* when Connelly's walkouts became rife. He recalls a deeply wary individual – reluctant to play the media game.

'I would have interviewed George in the '70s, when he was in the midst of his problems. He was very careful with his words, you might even say very suspicious. The best description I can come up with is that he was a fish out of water.'

Connelly walked out on Celtic for a second – official – time in September 1974, shortly after David Hay's departure for London. He had missed five days of training and warned Jock Stein he had no intention of returning. In a rare newspaper address, he made his feelings clear.

'I'm sick fed up with football,' he told reporters. 'It just hasn't happened – the whole thing has been building up for a couple of years. During this time, I've never really been happy and I think the time has come to get out. I wish I hadn't inherited my football ability.

The club have been in touch with me, but there is no way I'm going back. I've made my mind up. Maybe it's something to do with me being from a village in Fife, but I just can't put up with the pressure and publicity of football. I don't like to be noticed and I want to be unknown again. The club have been good to me but I'm finished with the game.'

By now, Connelly had undergone six sessions with a psychiatrist at Celtic's expense – to no avail. He returned to the park, yet was merely whirling through the motions, a beaten hamster on an increasingly pointless wheel. His drinking escalated, divorce was becoming an inevitability and his life was in the kind of flux normally associated with a man hurtling towards 40 rather than the ludicrously young staging post of 26.

Relegated to the reserves, Connelly put on weight and was furiously attempting to sweat the pounds off on the running track when he decided enough was enough. After showering and changing, he walked out on the club in 1975. His last words? By his own recollection they amounted to, 'Oh f*** it, that's me, I'm off!'

Celtic cancelled his contract with immediate effect. A forlorn three-month spell with Falkirk followed by a low-pressure farewell with Sauchie Juniors failed to obscure the blunt truth. There was an offer to return with Manchester United, yet that held little appeal. George Connelly was finished.

'He simply chose to take the easiest route for himself,' says Davie Hay. 'He didn't give up on football, he simply gave up on the spotlight.'

And so it remained until Cooney reached something of a crossroads in his own journalistic career. Connelly, he concedes, was his own personal Everest.

'It was 1995 before I came back as sports editor of the *Scottish Daily Mail*. And I was sitting there one day rattling through some ideas and I'm thinking, "George Connelly, George Connelly."

'I asked the lads on the desk, "Did anyone ever get an interview with him?" It was all, "Oh no, George doesn't do interviews." So I found out where he lived and where he drank. I was thinking of going to do the piece myself, before sending a young lad instead. He went up to Fife then reported back that he had met George, he had agreed to a do a piece and he had bought him a couple of drinks of whatever.

'He brought back the piece and I sat and tinkered with it. This was the first interview with Connelly anywhere for over 20 years. I had been the instigator but still had no idea where it would lead.

'My next experience of George came when I left the *Daily Mail* and was doing interview features for the *Sunday Herald*. I went into Firhill and was cogitating when I saw Jimmy Bone, the Thistle coach. I asked him, "By the way, do you ever see George Connelly?"

'He told me George was in a terrible way. That he was an alcoholic and a taxi driver. Jimmy then explained George did his driving in stints for a couple of months to save up some money, then went on the booze again. He seemed to be a binge drinker and it occurred to me that it sounded like desperate stuff.

'I wrote to the BBC and asked if they fancied some radio programmes on an old idea I had about the pain of the game. I got a favourable response and one of the first people I thought of was George Connelly. Jimmy Bone had given me his number.

'I asked him to this Radio Scotland thing and it was all, "No, no, no, I couldn't do that. I might do a one-to-one with a newspaper one day, but I'm not ready for that."

'So the idea was implanted and on 30 November 2006, I phoned him and very reluctantly he agreed to do a piece. I went up and saw him and he was terrified. He was like an animal which had been locked up in captivity for years. He adopted a totally defensive posture and any question I asked got the same response.

' "Is this aff the ring?" he'd ask me, meaning off the record. It would be all, "You're not going to put that in the paper are you?" It was hard going, but we got something out of it and right at the end of the interview he asked me, "Do you think I've got a book in me?" A book? I told him he probably had a volume in him.

'But he was troubled by the stuff about his first marriage – the very heart of his problems. If we could keep off that then, largely, he would do it. I asked about the drink and he told me he'd talk about the drink as long as I liked. And the football? Well, he admitted he couldn't remember that much about the football. So it was never going to be a straightforward autobiography.

'This was ostensibly about a man withdrawing from society, running away from life and becoming a pariah of his own making.'

The makeover of George Connelly would, in time, prove far more than a job of work for the lifelong Aberdeen fan. Cooney would, in fact, uncover a friend, albeit one with the kind of problems that manifested in a disappearing act every few months. In an effort to broker a personal contribution to this chapter from Connelly himself, various efforts were made to make contact via go-betweens in the spring of 2009. As Cooney reports, the breakdown in communications during that spell suggested the portcullis had come down and that the drinking had resumed. I never would get the interview.

'He phones me every week, will tell me what he is doing, how far he has been walking, what his latest food fad is,' Cooney says. 'And then, of course, will come the period when I never hear from him. When that happens, he is usually in his other wee one-bedroom apartment in Alloa, where he goes when he has been naughty.

'You can actually hear from the tone in his voice when something is about to explode. But you know, for all that, he is the loveliest person. He is very solicitous and the moment you go and see him he leaps up and makes you a cup of tea.'

There was, he states, never anything personal in Connelly's let-downs or the walk-outs.

'George loved Willie Ormond [the former Scotland manager], really liked him. But he wouldn't have thought about whether he liked Ormond or not when he walked out on Scotland. It was all based on this marriage and he couldn't come to terms with what was happening. I expected some kind of backlash from Christine after the book, but didn't get it – at all. Without being disloyal to George, there are always two sides to the story, aren't there?'

As his career was collapsing around his ears, Connelly was fortunate enough to run into the woman who would become his second wife, in a Kincardine bar. Helen Connelly and their son

David became the first to hear the unexpurgated truth behind his tortuous life in an emotional late-night heart to heart.

'Helen is an incredible woman,' states Cooney. 'She is very intelligent and has had a regular commute to hell. All the stuff that came from Helen was spontaneous. She had just been waiting to tell someone about the life she had endured.

'But then, the converse of that is that George is such a nice person, like a son to her mother. She suffers from dementia and he runs errands and puts a note through her door to remind her what day it is. He also walks dogs for neighbours and so on. He is very accommodating and there are no delusions of grandeur about George. He has no conceit of himself. He won't watch himself on television and has never read the book.'

There were also lengthy contributions to Connelly's long-awaited tale from David Hay.

'If I had stayed, then George might have been all right. It would have led to more success for Celtic. When I left, they lost the league the next season and things started heading downhill. We had been on an incredible run of success, with two European Cup finals and two semi-finals in a seven-year period – it was phenomenal consistency.

'Though the Lisbon Lions were rightly immortalised by their achievements, I still felt the pinnacle might have been around the corner if players like me and Danny McGrain, Kenny Dalglish, George and wee Lou Macari had been kept together. We could have carried on their mantle as a great team. I honestly believe that to this day.'

In his own life, Hay has much to be thankful for. His family, his standing in football and his legacy as a bona fide Celtic great. For Connelly, there are long periods of healthy eating, power-walking and taxi driving followed by falls back to darker days and nights. The return to the public eye was enjoyable, yet brief. In George Connelly's life, the blanket comes up on a regular basis and shuts out the world around him. He prefers it that way.

5

Wembley Wizard
HUGHIE GALLACHER

'How a man so loved and so idolised could feel so alone,
I'll never know.'

– Newcastle great, Jackie Milburn

From the upstairs window of his Gateshead home, Hughie Gallacher junior gazes down upon a sweeping landscape.

The expanse of the Team Valley trading estate below is a scaled-down reminder of a proud industrial past. Ferrying traffic from the manufacturing units to the Durham Road at the top of Belle Vue Bank, meanwhile, is a railway bridge. Spanning the East Coast mainline, the sturdy crossing on Eastern Avenue is functional, yet soulless. In a lay-by on one side of the bridge, taxi drivers recline in their cars reading newspapers. On the other side, the forecourt of a decaying car showroom has long since shifted its last Nissan. When Gallacher looks down on this scene, the ghosts of the past are everywhere.

It was here, just after midday on 11 June 1957, that his famous father, flat-capped and anguished, emerged from a cloud of shame to creep down the embankment and take his own life. The guilt this proud son still feels at his wholly unintended role in a tragic episode 52 years after the event is palpable.

'I can see the bridge from my window every day,' he states, his 73 years now rendering the 'junior' tag largely obsolete. 'I can still see where my father walked down the side of the embankment.'

The words are spoken in a matter-of-fact fashion, yet do nothing to obscure the scars embedded in the psyche of Gallacher's eldest surviving offspring.

The morning Gallacher ended it all on the old Down Belle Vue Bank – as it was once called – a young boy and a girl watched, pencil and paper in hand, as this little man wrestled with an irresistible sense of despair and self-loathing.

Agitated and in some state of confusion, the former Scotland international walked back and forth, occasionally beating his fists on the railing before responding to the thundering onset of an approaching express train. Four hours before, Gallacher had failed to show up for work at a nearby factory. Hindsight is the only perfect science and those who met this local hero as he walked the streets would attest to his distant, uncharacteristically ill at ease, manner. At precisely 12.08 p.m., Gallacher scrambled down the embankment, pausing only to mouth 'sorry' to the dumbstruck young trainspotters, before launching himself into the path of the speeding express train. His decapitated body was discovered 100 yards from a spot known locally at the time as Dead Man's Crossing. He was 54 years old.

The last man to skipper Newcastle United to the English League Championship, Hughie senior had been a diminutive giant of the British game. His scoring exploits remain astonishing. Some 463 goals in 624 games in Scotland and England marks a ratio of one every 1.35 games. On Tyneside, the younger diehards talk wistfully of Shearer. Those of a certain age would contend that Hughie Gallacher was the greatest player ever to don the black and white jersey, or for that matter, the dark blue of Scotland.

All of which makes the story of his suicide so difficult to comprehend. That Gallacher was no angel is evident; his drinking, his temper, his human frailties were clear enough to the outside world during his life. Out of competitive football for the best part of two decades after ending his career with Gateshead FC, this proud little man had become disillusioned by the determination of the English

FA to block his path to a coaching post. Unproven allegations of the acceptance of illegal payments as a player dogged his standing for years.

Yet still one asks; how could a man decorated so widely throw himself in front of a York–Edinburgh Express train? How could a courageous personality, who wore the best suits and spats, and revelled in his celebrity, reach such a point; the point where thousands of weeping mourners took to the streets of Gateshead to mark his passing?

The answer lies in a poignant tale of parental love, human weakness and overwhelming shame as May 1957 rumbled on towards summer. Alcohol, as with so many of our flawed heroes, also played its part.

Hughie Gallacher had been tagged with the gravest label of all: that of a child abuser. His crime was of a physical, rather than sexual, nature. The father of four sons from two marriages, Gallacher had survived the death of his first child, countless suspensions, a bitter divorce, bankruptcy, corruption allegations and double pneumonia. When he lost his bedrock second wife, Hannah, to heart disease, however, his spirit was finally broken. Years of drifting desolation were accompanied by a surrender to drink. According to Hughie junior, the reports of alcoholism were exaggerated. He admits, however, that his father had been drinking the night that his youngest offspring, Matthew, then just 14, offered up some teenage backchat.

'Mattie couldn't have done much wrong,' states Gallacher wistfully. 'But he caught the quick temper of our father. He was cheeky, no doubt, and probably deserved scolding, but that was an everyday occurrence.'

This time, the older man lashed out – casting his ever-present ashtray, Woodbine ends and all, in the direction of Matthew.

Glancing off his youngest son's head, the missile drew blood. Leaving the house in a state of distress, the boy ran to where his older sibling – recently discharged from the RAF – was enjoying the hospitality of a friend in the same street.

The quick-fire events thereafter remain a bleak episode in Hughie junior's life.

'I could have done more to prevent my father's death,' he admits wistfully, reposing in a bar close to the vast Gateshead MetroCentre. 'When the incident with Mattie happened, I was out with friends of mine and went back to the house of this particular friend. It was just 150 yards from where we lived.

'There was a knock on the door and Matthew came in with blood around his ear. My friend's mother asked if she should phone the police.' Pausing to remove his glasses and choosing his words carefully, Gallacher adds in a near whisper: 'I said yes.'

The consequences of that split-second judgment were startling. Matthew was removed from his father's care by the NSPCC. Gallacher was charged with assault and neglect of his son and a summons arrived ordering his appearance before Gateshead magistrates on Wednesday, 12 June 1957.

By any standards this was a sensational development. The headlines, the column inches and the comment confirmed the status of the man as a bona fide Tyneside superstar. Suddenly, however, his 143 goals in 174 appearances for Newcastle were obscured by scandal. Hughie Gallacher loved and worshipped his sons. By killing himself 24 hours before the hearing, however, the fallen star confirmed his culpability in the eyes of the narrow-minded. Yet to others, his suicide on a barren railway track guaranteed his place among the football immortals.

'I was just 21,' explains Hughie junior, now a father of five himself. 'I suppose when I've had a drink now I wonder if I should have done something different. Events got out of control; I didn't think so much would come of that. I didn't speak to Dad for days after the incident with my brother. I was a bit upset. In fact, I didn't speak to him at all before what happened.'

What happened remains one of football's most sobering tales. Others might have done precisely the same in Hughie junior's position. Granted the choice now of silence and forgiveness or the suicide of his father, however, Hughie junior would do things differently.

'Oh aye,' he confirms, 'I should have said to Dad, "Look, let's me and you go to the courtroom and face this together." But I never felt he was short of friends to turn to at that time, in fact I know he wasn't. He was working in a factory, he knew people.'

In retrospect, many of those he knew were hangers-on; last-order stragglers when the most prolific footballer Scotland or the north-east ever witnessed was turning his pockets inside out in search of the price of a round. When the football career ended and the domestic troubles began, many of these so-called friends drifted away. Gallacher retained his celebrity, refereeing charity games and opening local events, but he wallowed in the loneliness of the forlorn widower as his eldest sons went off to serve their country.

'I didn't come home every time I had leave from the RAF,' recalls Hughie jnr. 'I would stay with this guy or see a girl, or hang about with good friends. So maybe I neglected him a bit towards the end.'

Older half-brother Jackie and younger sibling Thomas – or Tot as he was known – are now dead. Matthew, ensconced in a new life in South Africa for the last three decades, is a remote presence. Products of a typically tight-lipped working-class upbringing, the siblings did not discuss the awful events that culminated in their father's death.

'I never really spoke about it with my middle brother Thomas before he died, or Mattie,' says Hughie with a shake of the head. 'He was away all the time and from 1965 onwards I only saw him five or six times after he moved to South Africa to become a partner in a mining engineering company. It was all over the papers of course – they went bananas. They all wanted to get to me. But I would say to them, "You've got it all anyway."'

The voice tails away, as memories stream back. 'Ach, it still bothers me,' he admits. 'But you get on with it. I have family of my own now.'

*

Hugh Kilpatrick Gallacher was born in Bellshill, Lanarkshire in the early hours of 2 February 1903. Queen Victoria had died two years before, and George VII had ascended the throne. In the smoke-filled streets of post-industrial Lanarkshire, however, coal was king. No fewer than 20 mines peppered the area and, seeking a living wage, Gallacher's father Matthew had arrived from Northern Ireland and married a local girl, Margaret, the couple settling at 42 Cochrane Street. Active members of the Orange Lodge, the couple had two sons, John and Hughie. Boys too young to drink or gamble spent their free time on the streets playing with a two-penny ball instead. Gallacher's best friend was Alex James, a future Arsenal and Scotland teammate, while Sir Matt Busby and former Scotland internationals John Gilmour and John Plenderleith also hailed from Bellshill. Legendary Celtic defender and former manager Billy McNeill, ex-Scotland coach Craig Brown and Andy Ritchie can also lay claim to a background forged in a settlement more often overshadowed by neighbouring towns Hamilton and Motherwell.

That Sir Matt Busby and McNeill represented their country and lifted the European Cup and a raft of domestic titles makes them amongst the finest of all Scottish footballers. Judged purely on individual football achievement, however, Gallacher's record stands alongside any.

Those inclined to dismiss the pre-war era as a grainy, semi-professional dawn for football in Scotland would find it instructive to analyse some remarkable statistics. The record books state that Denis Law and Kenny Dalglish are Scotland's finest ever goalscorers, with 30 strikes apiece. A fuller study reveals, however, that Gallacher outshone both men in a proportional sense, scoring 23 goals in 20 games. He was only denied an unbeatable record by the dearth of international fixtures in the 1920s and 1930s and a four-year ban on Anglos imposed by the Scottish Football Association.

An ever-present cigarette in hand, coupled with a stocky frame and a taste for liquor, would suggest the Newcastle superstar had scope for improvement on the fitness front. The physicality of today's game would be a daunting challenge for a man of such diminutive stature. And yet he regularly flummoxed bigger, stronger defenders in his halcyon days.

His place in the Hampden lexicon was guaranteed by a key role in the 5–1 rout of England in 1928. The Wembley Wizards remain objects of fascination and awe to today's Scotsmen, reared as we are in an era of English dominance. It is remarkable, then, to consider that this was one of the few games for his country when Hughie Gallacher failed to hit the net.

He stood only 5 feet 5 inches in height, yet intimidated taller, fuller men. His talk was bigger than the mouth of the Tyne. He took ferocious punishment from defenders, gouged opponents in unarmed combat and knew every lowdown trick in the book. Growing up, he had a fitting partner in crime.

At Bellshill Academy, Gallacher established a ready-made rapport with Alex James. As James articulated it:

'Hugh and I hit it off right from the start. We scrapped together and dogged school together and we romped the streets together, the two of us would do anything for a game.'

Despite Gallacher's upbringing in a staunchly protestant household, he and James watched and admired the six-in-a-row Celtic team which dominated the Scottish game between 1905 and 1910.

That sectarian sensitivities meant nothing to Gallacher became clear when he married a local Catholic girl, Annie McIlvaney, at the age of just 17. By any reckoning, they were young and immature. Their first-born son died at just a year old, prompting a temporary separation, before they reconciled to have another boy, Jack. Like his father, he was born with football ability and would go on to play for Celtic during the war years.

Hughie junior remembers his half-brother fondly, as a centre-forward who played amateur football in Coatbridge before being spotted by Celtic manager Jimmy McStay playing for Armadale Juniors. Unlike his father, Jack had height and strength in his armoury.

'Jackie lived in Caledonian Avenue in Bellshill and I loved him dearly,' recalls Hughie. 'He used to call me the Golden Boy and we spoke at weekends. He was with Celtic and got badly injured playing in the Old Firm game and had an operation or two. They tried to fix him, but he served his time as an engineer so he had something to fall back on and went to work in Kettering, where he played some games.'

As grinding poverty proliferated amidst mass unemployment and inadequate housing, a determination to prolong a doomed marriage prompted a new resolve in Hughie Gallacher. Jack was not yet born, but his father's restless energy was already being channelled towards the future. Boxing was an early option, but the true break came when junior club Bellshill Athletic, who had earlier dismissed him as too small, found themselves a man short for a game against St Mirren Juniors. Recognising Gallacher in the 5,000 crowd, club officials offered the teenager a chance and he scored in a 1–1 draw.

Progress was swift. Soon, he signed professional terms with Queen of the South, back then a non-league club in existence for just a year. A wage of £5 a week was significantly better than the pay on offer down the pits.

'Playing for Queen of the South was money for nothing,' he would later admit. Yet his brief time at Palmerston became part of the Gallacher history, prompting Hughie junior to send a message of support to the Dumfries club before their unexpected appearance in the Scottish Cup Final of 2008 against Rangers. Eighteen goals in seven games had been an early indication of his father's prodigious capabilities and drew the attention of Airdrie.

A bout of double pneumonia threatened to stifle the interest of the Diamonds from the outset. St Mirren wanted to sign the striker regardless, but as Gallacher convalesced, Airdrie manager John Chapman took the trouble to venture to his home on a wet day. That was enough to convince the young forward that he should resist the allure of a switch to Paisley.

Airdrie were a middle of the road team in the old 22-team Scottish First Division. By the 1922/23 season, however, the Broomfield side was emerging as a genuine threat to the dominance of Rangers. Future Ibrox legend Bob McPhail came in to the team, forming a partnership with Gallacher. Airdrie, with a prolific forward line, triumphed in the Scottish Cup in 1924 and finished league runners-up three seasons in a row.

By then, however, Gallacher's marriage to Annie McIlvaney had floundered – creating a financial burden that would dog him in later years. His temper never far from the surface, the Airdrie forward was also acquiring a reputation for on-field entanglements, one altercation with a Partick Thistle defender resulting in a five-game ban. In English football, Gallacher would prove a regular visitor to the disciplinary chambers of the Football Association.

'He was a selfish wee fellow,' noted former Airdrie teammate McPhail. 'He thought of no one but himself. He had a vicious tongue and he used it on opponents. I learned swear words from Hughie I had never heard before. But he was a superb centre forward and he knew it.'

What some regarded as an attitude problem struck others as a major factor in this particular player's success. Had Gallacher allowed himself to be bullied or wrestled by more physical defenders, he might never have scaled the heights his stature denied him. Here was a footballer who made Little Man Syndrome a force for good.

By the end of his time at Airdrie, the Scotland caps were accumulating. Two goals against Wales in his second appearance were followed by one against Northern Ireland.

By 4 April 1925, at the age of just twenty-two, his first game against England would end with two goals in a 2–0 victory at Hampden. At various levels of international representation, Gallacher had now claimed eleven goals in five games.

That the Home Internationals were the only show in town effectively curtailed his Scotland appearances. These days, Hughie junior has one or two of the national team caps in his possession, while others are dotted around the globe. A greater prize to show for his father's feats in a Scotland jersey would have been a scoring record no one else could touch.

'Had he played as many games as Law or Dalglish, he could have smashed all records,' states his son in unequivocal fashion. 'People now say to me, "Ah, but he wouldn't have been any good in the modern game." If you have a nose for goal, you have a nose for goal.'

Naming the greatest players to have graced Scotland's colours will always be a subjective affair weighted in accordance with the bias of the judge.

Newcastle United had an equally high opinion of his worth. Five goals for the Scottish League in a 7–3 thrashing of Northern Ireland in Belfast came close to ending Gallacher's life when a bullet narrowly missed his head near the city's Queen's Bridge.

'I'll have to extend my stay,' an unperturbed Gallacher is alleged to have smiled afterwards. 'It seems I still haven't managed to teach the Irish how to shoot straight.'

Yet the Magpies were not about to miss their own prime target. Sunderland, Notts County and Everton were also interested in Scottish football's top scorer, but their Geordie rivals secured the prize. Gallacher played his final game for Airdrie on 5 December 1925 after scoring 100 goals in 129 appearances, leaving for a record British fee of around £7,000 three days later.

If Scottish league players are regarded with a derisory snort south of the border these days, then Gallacher drew nothing but gasps of admiration. His stature was slight, but his start was immense. Fifteen goals in his first nine games began a love affair with the Geordie race which survived until his dying day.

His second season at St James' Park retains a near mythical quality. Gallacher, a player who led by an example not to everyone's taste, was appointed captain at the beginning of the 1926/27 campaign. His first year at the club had summoned up a variety of spats and rows – most provoked by the flurry of insults which came from the mouth of this little man from Bellshill. Yet no one could deny that he also walked the walk.

Gallacher was keeping Celtic's prolific Jimmy McGrory from the Scotland team while establishing a name as the most feared striker in English football. Six successive wins carried Newcastle to the head of the old Division One as 1927 dawned, Huddersfield Town and Sunderland providing the unlikely rivalry by modern standards. On the final day of the season, Gallacher netted twice against Sheffield Wednesday as the new champions won the title. The captain scored 39 times in 41 games; it remains a Newcastle record.

In the aftermath of his greatest triumph, Gallacher became football aristocracy. He wore the best suits and white spats, opened fêtes, attended dances and cut bits of newspaper down to the size of a pound note before tucking them underneath real notes to give the impression of carrying around a wad of cash. Then, as now, female company was always available to a high-profile footballer. In Hannah Anderson, the 17-year-old daughter of a Gateshead hotelier, however, he had already met his second wife.

That the striker was still married to his first spouse caused an early rift with his new partner's family, none of whom were renowned for their shrinking qualities. Fighting with his future brother-in-law on a Tyneside bridge would bring the first court summons of Gallacher's tumultuous life.

His lack of discipline on the pitch was also causing problems. On New Year's Eve 1927, Newcastle faced Huddersfield on an icy pitch and, incensed by some dubious decisions from referee Bert Fogg, the irascible little Scot pushed the official into the bath after the game.

The amusement the incident provoked was limited to the streets outside the FA headquarters in London. Inside, the officials were sharpening their knives for a player who had long since acquired a maverick reputation. On 20 January 1928, Gallacher was hit with a savage two-month suspension. It came close to costing Gallacher a key role in the most fabled performance by a Scottish national team under the twin towers.

The Wembley Wizards remain the stuff of schoolboy dreams. To the modern generations, Baxter juggling the ball in 1967 is the ultimate image of two-fingered one-upmanship towards our southern neighbours.

How modern Scotland and our voracious media would respond to a 5–1 thrashing of the Auld Enemy is anybody's guess. And yet, a thumping victory over England in 1928 was less of a surprise than might have been expected. In 24 games since the end of the Great War of 1914–18, Scotland had won 17, drawn 3 and lost just 4. The Scots were, not to put too fine a point on it, the football kings of the British Empire. We may never see the likes again.

When the England game rolled around in March, Gallacher had no right to expect selection. Rusty, out of condition and with a reputation in intensive care, he was only just returning from his two-month ban. As such, the Newcastle skipper was expected to be overlooked for Celtic's Jimmy McGrory. When Huddersfield's Alec Jackson claimed a hat-trick, aided by two goals for Gallacher's old friend Alex James, however, any selection misgivings were silenced. It was a stunning triumph for the Scots. As the *Daily Mail* recorded at the time: 'Scotland's whole team played with a dominant mastery that was made to appear sheer effrontery.'

Unusually, Gallacher failed to score in the rout. His brother John's wife had died in the hours before the game. Mentally, also, the Newcastle star was struggling to overcome unease in the club boardroom at his role in the two-month suspension.

Stripped of the club captaincy, Gallacher was bound over to keep his nose clean, again finishing top scorer with 24 strikes in an otherwise forgettable season. Yet an end of season tour of eastern Europe came close to propelling the Scot into an international incident when he was red-carded against a Hungarian XI and accused of being drunk on the field of play. For once, the FA came down on his side, yet more damage had been done.

At international level Gallacher remained untouchable, striking twelve goals in his final five Scotland appearances. When he decided to play in a vital league game for relegation-threatened Newcastle rather than play for Scotland against England in 1930, however, the incident had repercussions. In the first recorded club v country dispute involving the SFA, the decision was made in Glasgow to choose only home-based played for internationals in future. On one of his final appearances in dark blue – against France in Paris – Gallacher's Newcastle career also rumbled to an end. After 140 goals in a black and white shirt, negotiations were taking place with Chelsea and, returning home to Bellshill, the little Scot was shocked to be told a bid had been accepted.

The departure for London hit him hard. As Hughie junior recalls, his fame in the north-east had been all-encompassing – his love of life all-embracing.

'He still holds the record at St James' Park for 36 league goals in a season, you know. Andy Cole pipped him for league and cup goals in one season, when he scored 41 to my dad's 39.

'He was top scorer every season at Newcastle. At Derby County and Chelsea, it was the same story.

'And he was doing it in London for Chelsea at a time when he was living the high life. He liked a drink or two and the whole celebrity side of things. Everything Dad did – and I mean everything – ended up in the papers. He liked a drink.

'Oh he got in trouble all right, on the pitch. And once or twice his temper got the better of him off the pitch as well, but I'm sure he felt justified in retaliating to some of the abuse.'

When Alan Shearer was hurtling towards his record of 206 goals in 10 years as a Newcastle player, there was a brief resurrection of the Gallacher legend on Tyneside.

Hughie Gallacher junior watched all the post-war worship with some bemusement. That Shearer was a spectacular striker no one would deny. The former England captain retired in 2006 and remains the club's all-time top scorer. Jackie Milburn, meanwhile, scored 177 league goals and remains the highest scorer in the FA Cup for the Magpies. Both men, however, gave the greater part of their playing career to Newcastle – spending a decade or more in a black and white jersey.

Gallacher? He hung around the Gallowgate for just five years before being sold against his will. His ratio of goals to games, therefore, was formidable. Furthermore, when he left for London he had a league championship medal tucked in his coat pocket. Shearer, Milburn and Kevin Keegan would never achieve that.

'I don't know this for sure, but I think if my father had been

English the perception of him would have been different,' says Hughie junior. 'More favourable, maybe. I'm glad he was Scottish, I regard myself as Scottish, though I was born in Derby and raised here.

'But look at Alan Shearer. They paid £15 million for him and that was enough to convince people he was a superstar. But he didn't win a championship with Newcastle did he?'

It's a justification that remains unanswerable. The case for the prosecution of Gallacher's reputation, however, would have a field-day. Exhibit one would be the lingering suggestion that he accepted illegal payments more than once. Forever railing against the modest earnings of the footballers of his era, Gallacher penned an article in 1934 stating, 'to a poor man, the wages received by a first-class footballer are not low. But I believe a footballer should be paid like all artists – according to their drawing power'.

On which basis he ought to have lived like a king. Tennis players, cricketers and baseball stars were earning relatively vast sums in the 1930s. Against that backdrop, Gallacher would admit to accepting one payment of £25 from a wealthy mill owner for overcoming Notts Forest in an FA Cup tie. Gallacher scored twice in a 3–1 win. Accepting what amounted to an ad hoc win bonus differentiated significantly, however, from those who accepted cash to throw football matches or took tax free bungs in a brown envelope. At Chelsea, unrest over wages always bubbled beneath the surface.

Adding to the woes was an expensive and delayed divorce from Annie McIlvaney. Gallacher tried three times to win a legal separation in an era when quickie divorces were anathema. Following the successful court hearing, it was revealed that the Scotland star had debts of £787, a quite phenomenal sum of money in the 1930s. Marriage at 17 cost the footballer dear and the final price was bankruptcy.

Against which backdrop, few should have been surprised to see Gallacher join Derby County. Signing-on fees were, even then, the quickest source of a buck for struggling players and County –

renowned for signing players above their standing in the game – paid £200 direct to the bankruptcy court. Many years later, an FA Commission charged Derby County manager George Jobey with illegal transfer dealings. Unsubstantiated rumours that the Midlands club had paid Gallacher £300 under the table were never proven. And yet the allegations were hugely damaging to the Scot when his playing days were over and he sought to open managerial doors closed to him by suspicious club directors.

On this issue, Hughie junior throws up a vivid memory of a smoky meeting room, recalling:

'I happened to go to the Station Hotel in Newcastle one day – I was only 11 or 12 and Dad took me there. I stood looking out the window while he spoke with Sir Stanley Rous, the chief of the FA at the time. That meeting, I think, was all about the illegal payments carry-on. It was never proven that my father took a penny. It was all nudge, nudge, wink, wink when George Jobey of Derby was done years later.

'I knew my dad and he would never have taken those payments. He might have punched the odd lad on the nose but if you ask me, he wasn't taking money. After all that, I think he felt he was a marked man. He was denied opportunities to coach for years.'

Not before time, however, he had been granted leave to marry Hannah Anderson. It was in Derby, thereafter, that Hughie junior was born, and he has no recollection of living hand to mouth in a home stricken with debt.

'It was after the bankruptcy I arrived, but I still had a nanny. I was born in a private nursing home and everything. I've got a silver spoon in the house to prove it. Dad was only earning £8 – but the average man was on 30 bob. He was earning far more than the average working man. Even if he was paying off debt he would still have a few bob left.

'I still have the contract my dad signed for Derby County. It's bona fide. I haven't read through it for bonuses, because it's fragile now and I'm loath to touch it too much.'

At Derby, Gallacher shrugged off the wicked whispers to earn a

Scotland recall well into his 30s. The ban on Anglos now lifted by the SFA, his final senior cap came in a 2–0 win over England before a crowd of 129,693.

Brief spells at Notts County and Grimsby ended with Gallacher incurring a drink-driving ban. Unimpressed, the Humber club granted their wayward veteran his greatest wish when he was allowed to return to the north-east.

This time, it was the other side of the Tyne to which he moved, Gateshead FC paying an astonishing £10,000 to take him to Third Division North football. Aware of his box office potential, Gateshead also had Gallacher's father-in-law Tot Anderson as a director. Over 6,000 fans turned out for a pre-season trial game, with 30,000 watching a Football League Jubilee clash with Newcastle. The sway of Hughie Gallacher held strong even in his final season, as his namesake young son was gradually finding out.

'Everybody knew how famous Dad was. We would go on family days out, even 50 or 60 miles away, and strangers would come up to introduce themselves. I'd be a young kid wondering how this person knew my dad. My dad never knew any of them and it got through to me after a while that he must have been something special.

'But when you are a good 'un, you don't have to go around telling people, do you? Dad didn't have to boast or justify himself. He never spoke about how good he was as a footballer to us. That's why I still feel as if I know very little about him in some ways. I remember we would kick a ball around in the street. I could see little bits and pieces of his brilliance but I was too young to appreciate it.

'I played in one charity match with him. A guy from Rangers or Celtic or Derby or somewhere pulled out and I was there and they asked me if I wanted a game. I borrowed a pair of boots and they were seven-and-a-halfs – I actually wore six-and-a-halfs – and they were flapping off me. But we beat a Colliery team and it was a joy to play beside my dad.'

A photograph of that game takes centre stage in a glossy picture card Hughie junior has produced for interested well-wishers. His pride at being in the throng of a star-packed line-up is obvious.

There may have been times when being the son of Hughie Gallacher, Tyneside superstar, has been a curse. Comparisons are inevitable and occasionally burdensome. And yet he insists,

'It was never a bind being my father's son – I was always very proud. I played football myself and there were one or two articles saying I would do this or do that because of my dad. I was with the Newcastle Ns – that's what they called the youth team in those days. I played in a cup final when we won 3–1 – I scored the first goal as a centre forward. Unknown to me, my dad was watching and he told me after I had a stinker. I hadn't actually. He and I used to go for a sly drink when I was still underage. When we walked in, my dad was thronged. He never had to put his hand in his pocket – but he still did. He would empty his pockets and no one would leave till the money was gone. He was too generous, soft even. He couldn't say no. He never touched a drop of drink before he joined Newcastle United you know.'

Gallacher was another wonderful footballer, then, who was unable to resist temptation. As the reality of football retirement beckoned, the social side of life became a crutch for the loss of his natural workplace.

The Team Valley estate was a source of employment and if it was a comedown for this great footballer to work as a non-skilled employee with firms such as Patterson Lamps, De La Rue Printers and Taylor's Metal Workers, then he rarely showed it. The flamboyance and swagger of yore was slowly diminished; the dream of a return to football in a coaching capacity never materialised.

'Dad got a job in a factory,' his son recalls, 'he had to. But he was still a superstar, make no mistake. We even worked together for a bit. He put in a word for me when I was 16 with a place called Hugh Wood Mining Machinery and he was the kingpin in there all right.'

At the end of 1942, the Gallacher family settled in a comfortable council house, with youngest son Mattie being born in April 1943. The master of the house maintained some link with the game by giving his verdict on local matches for the *Newcastle Evening*

Chronicle, even earning a ban from touchy St James' Park directors for his forthright views.

He became a regular participant in charity games, returning to Scotland often to lend his name to a worthy cause. Refereeing also became an unlikely pastime, given his previous rebellious contempt for the football authorities. There was, then, equilibrium of a sort. Until family tragedy struck.

'My mam died on the last day of 1950,' says Hughie junior. 'Things were fine when she was there because she was some lady, a rock if you like. She was a very solid companion to my father, but once she went things faded a bit. He was still invited everywhere, still asked to make presentations and do charity games. But there was just a bit of a spark missing after Mam died. She was only 43.'

Annie Mathison, Gallacher's sister-in-law, later revealed the toll of the loss, saying, 'It reached him deeply. Hughie went downhill after the death and was never the same cheery individual again.'

Gallacher's legacy lives on. Relatives of his oldest son Jackie still live in Bellshill, while Hughie junior has two grown-up children from his first marriage and two sons and a daughter with his current wife.

The ties are not close between Gallacher's sons, however. The scars of the suicide affected Hughie junior, Tommy and Matthew badly. Their relationships, prior to Tommy's death, were never quite the same. For the eldest of the three, the impact of his father's tragic ending hit home around 12 months after his passing.

'I got a letter from Buenos Aires,' Hughie recalls with a wistful grin. 'It was in Spanish, but I had it translated and it was asking my dad to submit his CV for a top coaching job in Argentina. It came from a man called Rodolfo Kralj.'

Kralj was a famous Yugoslav international of the 1930s, and of a similar age to Gallacher. He moved to Argentina, where he twice coached Club Ferrocarril Oest, a team established by an English company dedicated to exploiting the development of the railways in and around Buenos Aires.

'I held onto the letter. It was addressed to Señor Gallacher, Arsenal

Football Club, Ingleterra. I don't know why it went to Arsenal, but they sent it up to me. I still don't know where they got the address.

'Dad would have loved that. It was what he had wanted. He was very attached to his life in Gateshead and whether he would have travelled to South America, leaving us behind, I don't know. If he had considered all the options – or lack of them – he may not have taken it. I suppose it's quite sad really.'

6

Gazza

PAUL GASCOIGNE

'He is lost out there, he doesn't know what to do.
He is a lost person,'

– Mason Gascoigne on his father Paul

As Rangers prepared to face Partick Thistle in a League Cup game on 24 September 2008 Scotland's newspapers had cause to hold the front page.

A flurry of telephone calls emanated from London, demanding that enquiries be made to the local police. The story that seemed to be emerging was a desperate one. Paul Gascoigne's fragile existence, it was claimed, had ended in his death in a Glasgow hotel room and, indicative of the internet age, rumours were sweeping the UK.

Calls were made and emphatic denials received from a bewildered Strathclyde Police force. Days later, the emaciated and troubled genius emerged blinking into the Newcastle daylight to personally deny reports of his demise. The subject of tabloid fascination for most of his adult life, the 41-year-old had only just returned from a month-long bender in Portugal's Algarve and a week touring Europe with heavy metal band Iron Maiden, where unconfirmed reports of a suicide attempt entered the public domain.

Earlier in the year, Gascoigne had been sectioned twice under the Mental Health Act after spending three troubled weeks at Newcastle's Malmaison Hotel. Tabloid reports had him patrolling the lobby with plastic parrots under his arm, demanding plates of raw liver, answering his room door naked and abusing porters. Gascoigne moved on to the Hilton Hotel in Gateshead, where an arrest was made after police declared this desperately fragile individual a 'potential menace'; most of all, one suspects, to himself. Two months in rehab fighting drink and psychological problems followed, before another doomed twelve-day reconciliation with former wife Sheryl, the mother of his three children. By now, the headlines were best read by his once adoring supporters through cracks in their fingers.

The death rumour had created a sense of deep shock, yet no real surprise. The main wonder was why it had taken so long.

With vast sums of money spent and hopeless attempts to resurrect his football existence in venues as diverse as China, Boston (Lincolnshire, not Massachusetts) and Kettering Town doomed to failure, Gascoigne's life had become one of grievous turmoil.

Those who worked with one of British football's most tragic figures at his peak always feared it would be thus. Denied the discipline and the joy of playing football as a professional, Paul Gascoigne is a lost soul, a shrunken shadow of his former self.

In Walter Smith's Murray Park office the blinds are drawn. Through thin gaps, a group of Rangers first-team regulars can be spied running through set-piece drills on a heated pitch rimmed by thick snow. Inside, the manager is conjuring images of a football man-child, some warmer than others. The voice raises an octave and the speech quickens; discussing Paul Gascoigne has that effect.

Smith concedes that he always feared the consequences of the midfielder's size eights being hung on a peg for the final time.

The failure of Gascoigne's high-profile and violent marriage was very publicly relived via a tragic Channel Four documentary, *Surviving Gazza*. In it, the mental torture of his children Mason, Bianca and Regan is laid bare. The anguished phone calls, the compulsive mania, the inability of the family to wrench themselves free of this tortured genius, made for compulsive, yet deeply uncomfortable viewing. Footage was shown of a delusional Gascoigne boasting of phone calls from the late Pope John Paul II, General Gaddafi, 10 Downing Street and the White House.

On free days at Rangers, the restless energy and mania would be spent with Smith's two sons, Neil and Steven, during marathon snooker sessions. Even Mrs Ethel Smith, the Rangers manager's wife of many years, was called upon to fill the void, serving up Christmas dinner for the fidgeting guest during his second season at the club.

'Those of us that knew Paul thought it was always going to be a problem once they took away the main focal point of his life – which, of course, was football,' Smith says. 'There might have been a wee bit of messing about when it came to football. But essentially he loved playing and training. If he had been able to train for 16 to 18 hours, then come back the next day, he would have been happy. It would have fulfilled him in terms of what he needed from life. But when football left him, he could never hope to compensate for that.

'He was never somebody who could go on television and be an analyst for example. He was never going to be able to summarise football or discipline himself to go into that environment. So what happens then is that he has a void in his life he has never been able to fill.'

For Smith, managing a deeply troubled genius was both the best of times and the worst of times. He did so twice, during Gascoigne's spell at Rangers and at Everton, as the dying embers of his career fizzled out. Coping with the little boy within the maestro was at times a gentle, pleasurable pursuit brimming with indulgence; handling the schizophrenic tabloid monster known simply as Gazza was more of a challenge.

'If anybody could keep him on a tight rein then I did,' states Smith minus any hint of bombast or arrogance. 'I don't mean I was anything special; I just came closer than some did. Billy Connolly wrote a thing about Paul one day which approached it in a way I had never really thought of. He said Gascoigne's play verged on the genius sometimes and one of the problems you then have is that you have to live with the genius rather than the genius living with you. That is the opposite of how most things work in football.

'Generally you have a coach and you have a team. The team plays for you, the manager. But in Paul's case, we had to play for him; we had to live with all his foibles and his eccentricities to get that little bit of genius into our team. And if you look back, some of the goals he scored and the things he did for us were great. So I have to say that in that first two-year spell, everything we had to do was worth it. At that point, he was doing what he naturally did best – playing week in and week out.

'But as we went into the third year, that changed. The problem was that it wasn't something perceptible you could point a finger at and say, "Right, that's it – he's gone."'

At the age of 28, Gascoigne's shock move to the SPL in July 1995 had been regarded south of the border as confirmation of his effective retirement from top-level football. Smith's great friend, Sir Alex Ferguson, had tried to sign the star of Italia 90 for Manchester United at his peak; Gascoigne inexplicably snubbed the Old Trafford club for Tottenham Hotspur after promising Ferguson he was bound for the Theatre of Dreams. Smith suspects he might never have captured such a talent had Gascoigne gone to United rather than Spurs at that point. The course of the midfielder's career changed the day he damaged cruciate knee ligaments in a reckless challenge on Nottingham Forest's Gary Charles in the 1991 FA Cup Final, his last game for the Londoners. A year on the sidelines was followed by a broken leg in Italy, where he had joined Lazio. By that stage, Ferguson was no longer in the race. Few of the truly great clubs in England were.

Gascoigne was, then, regarded as an expensive gamble. His fitness, his poor discipline and his temperament rendered him unemployable for more than one manager and chairman. Seeking the extra spark which might give his tiring side something special in the push for nine-in-a-row, however, Smith had the devilment to walk where angels feared to tread.

'Managers are prepared to take the chance with that stuff. I would have thought prior to going to Italy that the best move for him would have been Manchester United. If he had come to me and asked me for advice at that time I would have told him that.

'But when he was coming back from Italy, United were a far more settled and successful team. They didn't need a player who had been injured for a large part of his time in Serie A. When I got to know Paul I realised the injuries were a large part of his problem – because he had become bored and fed up. And he had started to do things that drew attention to him, whereas if he is playing and at the top of his game, that is all the attention he needs. I know that is a simplistic analysis of a guy like that, but that is what he's like.

'So I thought, If we are prepared to take a chance injury-wise and get him back fit, then we know he's not been over-played. His injuries had largely been self-inflicted and there was an unquestionable level of football ability lurking underneath. So, yes, it was a gamble – but it was one worth taking.'

That the few interested English clubs were kept at bay owed much to a chance encounter in Florida and a snap decision on the part of the Ibrox boss. Chelsea's Glenn Hoddle had flown to Rome for talks, but found Gascoigne more transfixed by a troublesome loose tooth than he was by the prospect of a switch to Stamford Bridge. Aston Villa's aged chairman Doug Ellis had fared little better. Smith, in contrast with his rivals, had an in.

'I had been at the World Cup in America in 1994 when the family came over for a holiday,' he recalls. 'I was sitting on the beach one day, my two teenage boys kicking a ball around in the sand. The next minute, one of the boys says, "There's Paul Gascoigne."

'Sure enough, there he was; Gascoigne with Sheryl, their wee girl and her mother and father. They parked themselves just along from us and it wasn't long before, being the way he is, sunbathing became of no interest to him.

'He was up on his feet looking for a ball and he ended up playing with my two boys. It was the usual stuff, they were telling him they were Scottish and he was giving them a bit of abuse about that.

'Eventually, the boys told them I was the manager of Rangers, so he comes up to me. And the first thing he says to me is, "Rangers? I've always wanted to play for them one day." That was the very first thing he said.

'It was true Rangers and Newcastle had always had a bit of an affinity in my lifetime. I remember when there were pre-season friendlies most years between the two clubs, so that's clearly where he got this from. He didn't know me from Adam, but he knew Rangers. I started laughing, as you do when someone comes out with something like that. But we went out a few times during the rest of the holiday. He was good company, at that time he was fine.

'A year later he becomes available. I hadn't been in contact with him at all beyond Ethel sending a Christmas card and one coming back from Sheryl. But I was sitting this day feeling we needed something a wee bit different and the word was out Gascoigne was heading back to England from Lazio. So I said to the chairman David Murray, "Look, what about Gascoigne?"

'And he says to me, "Can we get him?"

'I says, "Aye, I think he can add something. I'm not sure about him and Laudrup in the one team, but . . ."

'The truth is that I wasn't entirely sure even then, but I knew we would have two terrific players. So the chairman says to me, "Okay, go for it." The problem for me was how would I go about it?

'The obvious way was to get the chairman to get in touch with his club and then talk to Mel Stein, his representative at the time. But I then thought about the advantage I already had, having met him on holiday.

'So I jumped on a plane and went to Rome to see him. Somehow or other, I got an address for his house from the club and I rolled up there out of the blue in a taxi. I felt I would rather be there doing it face-to-face.

'So I pressed the security button and Jimmy Five Bellies Gardner, his big friend – who I had never met – answered the buzzer.

'"Who's there?" he asks.

'"Walter Smith," I respond, "I'm the manager of Rangers."

'"I know who you are," he says to me. "You here to see Paul?"

'He was trying to be clever I suspect, but I resisted the temptation to say, "Well, I'm not here to see you, am I?"

'So the gate opens and the next minute a Harley Davidson motorbike is coming towards me and there he is: Paul Gascoigne. He told me I was lucky, because it was a Friday and he was getting ready to go away for a weekend with Sheryl.

'"What you here for?" he asks me.

'"I'm here because I want to sign you for Rangers," I say.

'"All right," he says to me, just like that. "I'll do it."

'I swear to you, that was all he said to me. I thought to myself, Aye right, wait till the agents and other clubs get involved.

'But we had a chat and the chairman got in touch with Mel Stein. We went down to London later to meet his representatives and then I went back to Rome to meet him. There were other English clubs interested, but throughout he kept saying, "No, Rangers are the club I want to play for." Then he signed.'

Gascoigne would later recall a schoolboy memory of a Newcastle taxi driver telling him that if the chance ever came to play in an Old Firm derby, then he should take it. Here, now, was the chance.

Some regarded the move with a wary air of trepidation. Not least Brian Laudrup, the Danish maestro already establishing himself as kingpin in the Rangers team. Urbane, cultured and multi-lingual, Laudrup was everything Gascoigne was not.

'I knew of Paul mainly because I had watched him on television,' recalls Laudrup. 'Everyone knew he was a fantastic player and a mad character; there is no other way of putting it. On the field he was a genius, but let's be honest it was well known that off the field he had his problems. I had also been in Italy before joining Rangers and I had heard a lot of rumours. But despite that I was looking forward to seeing what he had to offer as a player. I wasn't disappointed. On his day, he was up there with the very best in the world.'

Remarkably, Gascoigne and Laudrup – as different as it is possible to imagine – complemented each other magnificently. Smith's doubts over their compatibility were justified off the park, but completely unfounded on it.

'You think we were different?' laughs Laudrup. 'And I've always felt we were so similar! No, of course people recognised how different we were as people. But, very quickly after he arrived we began to look for each other with the ball and seemed to understand how the other liked to play. In football you don't have to be close friends, just good teammates. But we actually had a lot of fun and went out for meals from the start.'

From his arrival at Rangers as assistant to the combative Graeme Souness through to his own coronation, Smith had handled the likes of Terry Butcher, Chris Woods, Ray Wilkins, Trevor Francis, Trevor Steven and Gary Stevens. Gascoigne's arrival placed all of the above in a cocked hat for hype and headlines. And, some might say, natural ability.

'The Geordie psyche is not too far away from the Scottish mentality,' Smith asserts. 'Scottish people have always liked their slightly wayward footballers; there is something in us that likes that type of player. Look at wee Jimmy Johnstone or Baxter; not without their flaws, but fantastic football players.

'We seem to take to them. When I was pondering signing Paul, people kept saying to me, "Do you really want to take a chance on this?" But nobody ever said to me he wasn't a good football player. And the first two years for us were a dream. He was fine, he was outstanding, no problem. He didn't have any of those Gascoigne moments he was renowned for.'

By Gascoigne moments, Smith refers to the litany of controversies and acts of inexplicable stupidity that had littered the Geordie's career.

Such as the day he took Kevin Keegan's Gola boots home as a Newcastle apprentice to show off to friends; and lost them on a bus. Or the time Spurs teammate Steve Sedgley had the rear windscreen of his new car shot out by a 2.2 air rifle Gascoigne happened to have in his car boot. Or the day he arrived in Rome and asked for silence from local reporters before farting loudly.

Or the time England manager Graham Taylor berated Gascoigne's 'refuelling' habits before a Norway match at Wembley where, asked for a few words by a television crew, Gascoigne infamously obliged, saying, 'fuck off Norway'. For months afterwards, the hate mail from the Scandinavian country flowed freely.

At Lazio, the boredom created by serious injury problems was a dangerous state of mind for the errant star player. On his first New Year's Eve in Rome, Gascoigne visited a fish restaurant with Sheryl and ordered lobster from a huge tank in the corner. When the service proved slow, the impatient Englishman dived in fully clothed in his Versace suit and retrieved the lobster he had his eye on. 'That's the fucker I want', he announced to stunned staff as he emerged from the tank dripping wet.

Another broadcasting storm erupted when, prior to a clash with Juventus, Gascoigne belched into a television microphone, booming the burp live across Italy. Front-page news, the lead item on bulletins and described in the Italian parliament as an 'insult to Italy', Lazio frowned upon an infantile faux pas. President Sergio Cragnotti had already been stunned by Gascoigne approaching him at the club's training ground and insulting his daughter.

This, then, was the kind of character on offer to Britain's top clubs in the summer of 1995. Yet Rangers refused to blink. And initially, at least, their reward seemed total when Gascoigne captured attention in Glasgow for purely positive reasons.

Flawless control, quick feet and great vision proved that the injury woes suffered at Spurs and Lazio had not entirely blunted Gazza's abilities. Like Baxter, his finest talent was instinctive. Most coveted of all in a midfielder, he scored goals, 39 in 103 Rangers appearances proving a significant return for a record £4.3million investment and wages of £15,000 a week. In only his fourth league game, Gazza guaranteed his place in the affections of the support, slotting a quite magnificently worked breakaway goal into the Parkhead net in a 2–0 win over Celtic. Partnered by the mesmeric Laudrup, widely regarded alongside Henrik Larsson as the finest of the overseas players to grace the SPL, Gascoigne produced some stunning form. The first season culminated in the perfect climax, a memorable hat-trick in a 3–1 comeback win over Aberdeen securing eight-in-a-row for Rangers in a campaign where a thrilling Celtic side managed by Tommy Burns lost just one game.

For two untouchable years at Ibrox, the former *enfant terrible* of English football threatened to grow up under Smith's supportive tutelage. Despite the intense pressure of stretching for the nine successive titles that would equal Celtic's record set under Jock Stein, this was a player free of self-imposed injury and at his mischievous, devilish peak on the field. His was a mesmeric presence; an uncontrollable force given to tying the nation's defenders in complex knots. His loyalty was less to Rangers Football Club than it was to the avuncular Smith and his assistant Archie Knox.

The sheer joy of playing football following a year on the sidelines and an unhappy spell with Lazio was evident; the kid was back in the game.

'What always struck me about Paul at that time was that he had no great interest in looking at league tables or future games,' smiles Smith.

'I'm certain he turned up some Saturdays not knowing who he was going to be playing. He knew Manchester United and he knew when we were playing Celtic. But the boys in England would tell me the same thing; when it came to teams in the lower part of league, he wouldn't know who they were.

'The boys used to kid on to him, "Do you know who we are playing today Gazza?" But football was just football to him; it didn't matter who it was against.

'When I was naming my team before a game on a Saturday – or sometimes on a Friday the day before – you always knew that then you had his attention. He would sit there, hands clasped, staring straight at you. As soon as the name Gascoigne was read out, that was it. He was gone.

'The hands would relax and he would be elsewhere instantly. Because he always had this wee thing in his head, this wee insecurity, that you were maybe about to leave him out. Tactically, it was up to me to put him in a position in the team that best suited him – then leave him. You could not say to him, "When the ball goes here you go there." There was none of the stuff other players took for granted – that was a waste of time with Paul.'

Gascoigne was granted the keys to Ibrox, a unique form of carte blanche to perform with complete freedom of thought and movement.

It remains a life pattern of this tragi-comic individual, however, that he will always snatch defeat from the jaws of triumph.

'When Paul was on the park he was happy, it was his perfect place. But I quickly realised that off the park he was troubled,' says Laudrup. 'As a person he was restless, always on the move. He always had to be into something. He hated just sitting about. Don't get me wrong, he was a fantastic laugh much of the time and possibly the most generous person I have ever met. That was the side to him very few people ever saw. If he only had a pound in his pocket and someone asked for it, then he'd give them it – no question.

'But he felt sometimes that people didn't listen to him or take what he had to say seriously. Maybe that's what the problem was at times. He was always the funny guy, always the joker. But no one can always be funny and sometimes the jokes are hiding something underneath – there was definitely a darker side there.'

By the turn of 1998, the negative headlines began and Gascoigne would fail to complete his third season at the club. Smith and his faithful assistant Knox ran out of ploys for dealing with their wayward talent.

Discovering the precise roots of this particular footballer's mental anguish is no easy task. Inexplicable guilt caused by watching a close friend's brother, Steven Spraggon, being killed by a car before his tenth birthday prompted the onset of nervous ticks, twitches and the first signs of obsessive behaviour. Referred to a child psychiatrist, Gascoigne's visit would mark the first spell of therapy in an existence pockmarked by cries for help and abnormal levels of restless energy. The night he signed for Newcastle, the 16-year-old celebrated by heading for a pint. Within a year another friend, Steven Wilson, died on a building site after Gascoigne had persuaded him to quit Middlesbrough. Again, self-loathing became the default setting.

On a chart drawn up to catalogue his life story, Gascoigne once listed his main weaknesses as vodka, wine, beer, cocaine, Red Bull, morphine, paranoia and anxiety. But he was also battling chronic addictions, food disorders, obsessive compulsive disorder, bipolar disorder, co-dependency, gambling and an addictive personality. To that list Smith, the man who made the decision to ship this short-lived Rangers legend from the pay-roll, would surely add Attention Deficit Disorder.

'Paul had never been at a club for much longer than two years before joining Rangers,' he recalls, arms tightly folded. 'Into his third year with us, that was as long as he had played continuously for any club. And you just knew something, be it boredom or whatever, would set in. There are players like that; Maurice Johnston was another one. He was at Rangers for just over two years and that was one of his longest spells at any club.

'So in the third year he started to wander a bit. He had become used to the adulation of one group of supporters and he wanted to find an alternative. That started to become a problem.'

Towards the end of his time in Glasgow, Gascoigne ceased to be a mere 'problem' for Rangers, lurching instead towards the status of a full-blooded embarrassment. Scotland's player of the year in his first season and the star of a glorious Euro 96 tournament in England weeks later, Gascoigne's abrupt Ibrox departure in March 1998 – as Rangers chased an elusive tenth consecutive title and the Scottish Cup – caused consternation amongst a demanding support. At a time when those who had racked up nine titles under intense pressure were close to exhaustion, however, Gascoigne's indiscipline was no longer endearing. It served only to add to the increasing signs of weariness.

'It was simply the case that his level went down a bit,' says Smith. 'There were suddenly gaps in games where he wasn't so involved. He did not have the same edge as he had in the previous two years – so it took a little time for that recognition to settle in. Then you say to yourself, that's it, it's time for him to go.'

Gascoigne had never been some angelic, Horlicks-slugging innocent given to early nights and hours of sombre contemplation. But when the football was dazzling, then the eyes could be blinded to the glaring deficiencies in his lifestyle.

Some of the controversies at Rangers were trifling, some less so.

In the first category came the mock playing of an imaginary orange band flute during a pre-season game against Steaua Bucharest at the behest of mischievous teammates. Ditto the festive storm which arose when the midfielder lifted a yellow card dropped by referee Dougie Smith and pretended to book the official. His reward? A yellow card of his own.

So long as he continued to toe the line within the confines of the dressing room, the Rangers management remained supportive.

In the more serious category came a bogus rape accusation in February 1996 followed by his absence from the birth of his son Regan due to a two-week bender. Eventually, the baby brought out Gascoigne's paternal nesting instincts, the purchase of a £510,000 home in Renfrewshire and a weekend lodge at Loch Lomond signalling a new determination to settle down.

The infamous Hong Kong dentist's-chair drinking incident with England teammates prior to Euro 96 was forgotten when the Rangers star scored a quite magnificent goal against Scotland at Wembley – beating Ibrox teammate Andy Goram in the process. Proving there are human beings you can barely mark with a blowtorch, Gazza celebrated the goal by mimicking the dental-chair drinking games immortalised just weeks earlier on the front pages. But he knew better than to milk the moment with his goalkeeping club mate.

'We had already agreed to swap shirts after the game,' recalls Goram. 'He scored that goal and did his best to take the mickey out of us. As he is walking towards me, 10 yards away, with that big daft grin he had with his new teeth, I just looked at him and he got the message.'

When marriage to Sheryl finally materialised at the plush Hanbury Manor hotel in Hertfordshire it seemed that, for Paul Gascoigne, a life of contentment beckoned. Decked in a white Versace suit, 'Unchained Melody' was piped by a wind orchestra as Sheryl walked down the aisle towards him. The main marriage vow consisted of a promise that '(our) home will be a happy one'. He was playing regular football, avoiding injury, had a manager who knew what made him tick and a woman who loved him, with a young son in tow.

Yet appearances, say the cliché, can be deceptive. In *Surviving Gazza*, Sheryl admits to marrying Gascoigne in the hope that a wedding band might halt a disturbing pattern of domestic violence. Behind the scenes, however, his drinking was spiralling out of control and, as Gascoigne himself later put it, Smith 'no longer knew whether to use the carrot or the stick'.

On a family break at Gleneagles Hotel in October 1996 prior to a Champions League clash with Ajax, the Gascoigne clan went swimming and enjoyed the fresh country air. Over dinner, however, Gazza swigged a potent cocktail of whisky and champagne and the atmosphere at the table changed. Back in the room, with daughter Bianca, son Regan and the children's nanny listening next door, Gascoigne headbutted his wife and threw her to the floor, breaking a finger.

The following day, the distraught midfielder flew to Amsterdam with Rangers and lasted 10 minutes as a makeshift striker before being dismissed for an assault on Ajax opponent Winston Bogarde. As Rangers captain Richard Gough tore strips from his teammate in the dressing room at half-time, Gascoigne confessed all. In the aftermath of a thumping 4–1 defeat, there was an inevitability to the front-page exposés that followed.

Racked with guilt, Gascoigne took to stealing painkillers from the Rangers medical supplies. Even the powerful Zimovane could do nothing to dull the anguish of being taunted by ruthlessly unforgiving opposition supporters as they chanted 'wife beater'.

The manager of Rangers had done his best to smother the errant Geordie with kindness as long as possible; effectively posting his two sons as minders at the door of this tortured artist and famously inviting him for Christmas dinner. This, however, was a let-down beyond the ken of a grounded and decent family man.

Smith, though, is dismissive of the father-figure tag invariably attached to his relationship with Gascoigne. The bond between the two was always professional rather than paternal, driven by Smith's desire to draw genius from every pore of a human being in the throes of relationship torture. It was, states Smith, the path of least resistance.

'That story was never as contrived as me inviting him for Christmas dinner or taking him in,' Smith says. 'My two kids had already met him on holiday and were, by then, 17 and 18. Paul lived in a lodge at Cameron House Hotel when he wasn't with Sheryl, and my boys were members of the leisure club there. So he would phone and ask them if they wanted to come over to play snooker. Now what kids in Scotland wouldn't want to play snooker with Paul Gascoigne at that time? Neil, my eldest, would quite often beat him. So they would end up with scores of 18–16 – that was 34 frames of snooker in one night, just so Gascoigne could win some back.

'The boy would get bored a lot of the time he wasn't training or playing football. With the Christmas dinner, it was simply the case that all the players at Rangers used to take the foreign players for Christmas so they would not be on their own in an unfamiliar country.

'So [Ally] McCoist said, "What about Gazza?" He had been at Coisty's the year before – but Coisty was taking the rest of the boys this particular Christmas. So Ally asked me if I could take Paul for dinner and he would send a taxi to get him in the evening.

'I picked him up at Cameron House and took him over to our house. Brian Laudrup and Joachim Björklund stayed within a few hundred yards of me so he went up there in the evening and I told Coisty not to bother with the taxi to his place.

'People relate that story as me treating him like a son. But it wasn't like that; someone was going to be sitting on their own in Cameron House on Christmas Day. It was five minutes away from me and he was my player. It was that simple.'

Towards the end, Smith's inclination was to use Gascoigne as the stuffing for the turkey. At the aforementioned Cameron House, a midnight booze cruise ended instead in a boat crash. An impromptu drive in a four-wheel drive jeep then careered onto the hotel's lush golf course. Other times, Gascoigne would attempt to shoot his right-hand man Jimmy Five Bellies with an air rifle in the hotel grounds.

In response to the nonsense, there were times when Smith pinned his star midfielder to the wall by his garish Armani lapels, with one such episode allegedly resulting in the Englishman losing control of his bladder.

'There were elements of that, certainly,' Smith concedes. 'He would infuriate you at the same time as he would delight you. He went to his local one Friday night before a game and on the Saturday morning I found out where he had been when he turned up hungover. I threw him out and told him not to come back. He didn't play and that was the first time he ever did anything I found out about that was a clear problem.

'But he was so full of remorse and he came back three days later. Even if you are trying as a manager to be straight and stern with him, there was always a bit inside you that wanted to laugh at him. For the next month or six weeks, he was trying hard to make amends. He was so full of regret when you disciplined him for something like that; but you always knew that within weeks he would be up to something else.

'You need to put up with little bits of nonsense here and there. To get the best out of him, you have to have him on your side.'

As Rangers had thundered to eight, then the precious nine-in-a-row, there had been regular flashes of the midfielder's brilliance. The wife-beating furore was one from which Gascoigne could never expect to recover, however, the stigma of his brutal actions exposing his weaknesses to the world.

Women's groups expressed their concern and even his great friend and teammate Ally McCoist described the incident as 'inexcusable'. In a fit of self-flagellation Gascoigne told a press conference, 'I'm a disgrace.'

For Smith and so many others at Rangers, this was becoming a burden. The need to defend the indefensible and adopt the mantle of social workers was a pressure they scarcely needed. Gascoigne's state of mind was deteriorating fast.

Gascoigne admits to feeling suicidal and depressed around this time. Approaching the former Rangers doctor Professor Stewart Hillis for advice, Gascoigne asked what made people want to kill themselves? What made them flip?

'People who flip,' replied the doctor, 'don't know they've flipped.' Gascoigne was reassured, but for Rangers the alarm bells were ringing.

The final straw came at the turn of 1998, as Rangers lost to Celtic on 2 January – a rare Old Firm defeat in Smith's first tenure at the club. The defeat was bad enough, interpreted as a sign of decay and decline. The aftermath, however, was debilitating.

After two-and-a-half years in a Glasgow society where sectarian sensitivities are never far from the surface, Gascoigne inexplicably blundered into a second flute-playing folly. In contrast with the first instance in a pre-season friendly in his early days at the club, however, ignorance was no defence.

This was a city where the arrival of former Celtic striker and high-profile Catholic Maurice Johnston as a Rangers player had prompted Ibrox supporters to burn their own scarves for the television cameras in 1989.

It was a bold move by Rangers chairman David Murray and his former manager Graeme Souness to drag the club into the modern age. Against which backdrop, Gascoigne's mischief at Celtic Park was mistimed and quite spectacularly ill-judged. An impersonation of an Orange walk band member was performed before a delirious away support, but was primarily aimed at the Celtic supporters who had been chanting 'wife beater' in his direction.

Once again, Gascoigne was on the front pages rather than the back, with Rangers embarrassed that their efforts to tackle bigotry had been undermined by one of their star players. Not for the first time in his life, Gascoigne was on the cusp of a disturbing new source of anxiety.

The day after his gross miscalculation, he sat at traffic lights and was foolish enough to wind down his car window at the invitation of a random Celtic supporter.

'Gascoigne, I'm going to slit your fucking throat,' was the New Year greeting the Englishman would never forget. Laughing in response, Gazza's smile drained away as his tormentor drew a finger across his own throat.

Within days, the death threats were arriving in sacks. One letter claimed to be written on behalf of the IRA, the murderous republican terrorist organisation. Police traced the barely literate threat to an unarmed crank in Dublin they had little power to arrest. Yet they were concerned enough to show Gascoigne how to open letters and packages in such a way as to detect bombs or detonation devices. There was also a lesson in how to check for explosives under a car.

The son of a Catholic father, Gascoigne was no bigot. He was, however, a marked man and – by now – a source of humiliation to Rangers.

The Ibrox club slapped a £20,000 fine on the midfielder and resolved, privately, to accept the first acceptable bid for his services. Crystal Palace were interested, but the move finally came from Middlesbrough's Bryan Robson two months later.

Smith now admits that he should have sold the England international in the summer of 1997 – in the immediate aftermath of nine-in-a-row. He believes the legendary winger Brian Laudrup should have left then, too.

'There probably would have been merit in that,' he concedes. 'But like everything else you have an idea of what is going to happen – but you don't *know* it's going to happen. We were going into a season where we were trying to be the first Scottish club to win 10-in-a-row. And while I don't think there was ever the same edge to our team that season as there was in the previous two or three seasons getting up to nine, we were always in the hunt. What people tend to ignore when they discuss that season was the fact that we only lost the league to Wim Jansen's Celtic by two points.

'Whether Gascoigne might have made any difference to that by staying until the end of the season, I don't know. When an offer came in from Middlesbrough in March there was no guarantee a similar offer would come in the summer if they rejected it. So the decision was made to sell.'

Laudrup now agrees with his former manager that the time for goodbyes should have been the preceding summer, after the ninth title.

'It's always the hardest part, knowing when to break a team up,' states the Dane. 'You can keep a great team together for so long, but eventually the troubles start when the hunger evaporates and the desire for success drops. Maybe Gazza did lose some of his attention, more off the park than on it. Scotland is a small country and when a superstar like Paul Gascoigne arrives then the attention is bound to be too much for any man. For two or three years he was never out the papers and there were injuries to contend with. At the same time, he was getting older, we all were.

'He began to lack the discipline to show precisely what he was capable of. Personally, it had always been my intention to leave after the ninth title. I felt after that we were always going to have a very difficult time keeping the motivation levels high and when that happens you are not at your best.

'A major part of staying around for that 10-in-a-row effort was down to the fact that the players who had been through so much for Walter Smith wanted to stay with him to the last. That might have been our downfall in the end.'

Smith, who had announced his own departure at the end of the season during the club's AGM in October 1997, broke the news of Gascoigne's departure to the player in sensitive terms. Smith's replacement was to be Dutch coach Dick Advocaat and few believed the man known as the Little General would find a place in his line-up for a desperately undisciplined footballer on the edge of losing any semblance of control.

'I was leaving anyway,' Smith reflects. 'But that didn't matter, it was irrelevant to Paul Gascoigne's situation. The fact is that he had run his course at Rangers. It was time to go.'

Not everyone agrees. Andy Goram, the legendary goalkeeper of the period, also left the club that summer and believes he might have departed on a high had Gazza stayed until the end.

'If we had kept Gascoigne, I think we would have won the double. Nobody can tell me he would not have made a difference that season. Even half a Gascoigne would have made a difference.'

For Gascoigne and Walter Smith, the parting was far from final, with a brief and unexpected reunion at Everton.

Gascoigne had been freed by Middlesbrough following the death of his England career at the hands of Glenn Hoddle and various spells in rehab. A begging call to Smith proved irresistible to the man who had quit Ibrox for a club where free transfers were a necessity rather than an indulgence. In March 2002, the pair suffered an FA Cup defeat to Middlesbrough. The partnership, this time, was annulled involuntarily.

What headlines there have been since then have been unrelentingly negative. Drink and depression destroyed any prospect of a spell in China with Gansu Tianma, while ill-fated stopovers at Burnley and Boston United were mercifully brief. Kettering Town gambled on a manager lurking somewhere beneath the surface – but sacked Gascoigne after 39 days, chairman Paul Davis accusing him of being inebriated every day of his reign. In his last failed reconciliation with Sheryl, Gascoigne was displaying ever more delusional patterns of behaviour; becoming tetchy when the word 'bagel' was mentioned, developing a fixation with the number 13 and boasting of his imagined links to one of the queen's cousins. As Simon Barnes of *The Times* once put it, Paul Gascoigne's tale began in the tears of Italia 90 and will almost certainly end the same way. Ours, rather than his.

7

The Goalie
ANDY GORAM

'Two Andy Gorams, there's only two Andy Gorams . . .'

*– Scottish football supporters reacting to news of Andy Goram's mild
form of schizophrenia*

Time and the expanse of the North Sea lend Pierre van Hooijdonk some distance between his current family idyll and a colourful Celtic past.

Yet there are episodes and moments in everyone's life from which there can be no escape. During two years in Glasgow, this was a player who scored a creditable 56 goals in a green-and-white shirt. One of them, against Airdrie in the Scottish Cup Final of 1995, won the Parkhead club their first trophy in six years. When he sets his size 12 shoes down at Glasgow Airport these days, however, no one asks this outspoken figure about the winning goal at Hampden.

All they offer are recollections of the sixty-sixth minute of an enthralling Old Firm game from well over a decade ago; the split second Andy Goram identified himself as Celtic's tormentor-in-chief.

On 20 November 1995, a classic encounter unfolded in the midst of a bleak autumn. Rangers and Celtic had been rutting for supremacy at the top of an uninspiring league championship. Every now and then, however, the old rivals conjure up the kind of intensity which compels the viewer to savour the spectacle. Andreas Thom and John Collins had scored for Celtic, Brian Laudrup and Ally McCoist for Rangers when a chance arrived for the visitors.

The ball landed perfectly on van Hooijdonk's right foot and he blasted it venomously towards the top corner. It seemed, from the moment the shot left his boot, a goal. Somehow, however, Goram stretched every sinew of his stocky frame to fingertip a fizzing effort from all of 10 yards over the bar. Van Hooijdonk held his head while Goram held the world in his shovel-like hands. By common consent, it was one of the finest saves ever witnessed by a Scottish keeper; a deeply-flawed Scottish keeper at that.

Andy Goram has racked up more front pages than Madonna and come close to being kicked out of Ibrox in disgrace after boozing benders. He fielded accusations of twice turning his back on his country, racked up a string of ex-wives and gambled his way through the kind of sums usually found under the gold embossed lid of Sir Fred Goodwin's Monopoly set. He has withstood headlines concerning illicit romantic interludes in caravans and more damaging tales of alleged sectarian outbursts at supporters' nights. And yet, as he surveys the world from his Blantyre pub, he remains a survivor; a true blue hero for the Ibrox masses. There are times, indeed, when Goram seems indestructible.

'That save is still something that, whenever I am back in Scotland, people want to talk to me about,' says van Hooijdonk. 'They always remind me of it. The good thing was that eventually I did score, with a header, in that 3–3 game to get us a draw. I did beat him. But no one ever seems to remember that.

'That season, Goram was just fantastic. Not only against us, he was making fantastic saves against every team and that proved how good he was. He was a quality goalkeeper. My only question would be over how tested he truly was in the Scottish league. In Europe, Celtic and Rangers were not doing so well were they? But against us? He passed every test we gave him, yeah.'

Perhaps van Hooijdonk and Celtic should blame Pat Bonner.

As a balmy August in 1991 slithered to an end, the new Rangers goalkeeper was in a state of inner turmoil. Just weeks after becoming the first signing of the Walter Smith era, Andy Goram's Ibrox career was already in jeopardy.

He worked slavishly to meet the standards of fitness required of Scotland's champions. And it wasn't enough. Lapped by teammates in a pre-season run at Bellahouston Park, the arrival from Hibernian was joined at the rear of the pack by Smith. Why, the manager asked, was he failing to keep up with his new colleagues? 'If you wanted a runner, you should have gone for Seb Coe,' puffed the wisecracking keeper.

On return to Ibrox, a summons duly arrived. The presence of The Goalie, as he came to be simply known, was requested at the head of the impressive marble staircase that sweeps majestically up through the Bill Struth Main Stand. The message from an irate Smith was to the point: lose a stone in weight or risk an early exit, showpiece £1 million signing or not.

Shell-shocked by the bluntness of the threat, Goram took the advice and shed the pounds at the club's Il Ciocco training camp in Italy. Yet it took longer to shed the doubts over his worthiness to keep goal for Rangers as a successor to the venerable English international, Chris Woods.

In his third game, Goram lost an embarrassing goal against Hearts at Tynecastle, then another against Sparta Prague. Rangers were out of Europe and the new keeper was displaying whip marks on his rear end. Walter Smith burst into the Ibrox dressing room after the Euro defeat to deliver an unforgiving rebuke and the bleakest spell of The Goalie's career had begun. By now, even a return to Oldham held a certain appeal.

'I can remember a couple of ropey games in the early days,' says then Rangers captain Richard Gough. 'It was funny, because the gaffer asked me to room with him at the start and I was never one for sharing; I liked my own space too much. Thankfully, so did Andy, so we parted and got along just fine after that. I tried to help him as best I could. But it only really started to turn around for him after his first Old Firm game, which we won. After that, he was a more calming presence.'

Keeping a clean sheet at Celtic Park at the first time of asking would be a fillip for any Rangers goalkeeper. The real turning point came in the immediate aftermath of the game, however, with thoughtful words and valuable advice on how to handle life at the Old Firm stemming from an unlikely source.

After watching his new Ibrox opponent from the other side of the pitch, the genial Irishman Pat Bonner shook his hand in the centre circle and sought a private word in the players' lounge.

'Andy was going through a difficult time at the start,' he recalls. 'He wasn't doing so well. So I had a wee word with him on the quiet after his first Old Firm game. I wish I hadn't now, to be honest!'

As Goram grew in stature and went on to become a one-man wrecking ball for Celtic's title aspirations in the years that followed, the Parkhead club would have ample cause to rue their Irish shot-stopper's magnanimity and selfless generosity. Of all the Rangers legends who have passed into the club's Hall of Fame, few played as dramatic a role in the acquisition of nine-in-a-row than the Bury-born goalkeeper; a man whose lifestyle seemed to revolve around fish suppers and fizzy drinks, alcoholic or otherwise.

'Andy clearly listened to the advice because he went on to break our hearts for years afterwards,' smiles Bonner. 'But, you know, that's just the kind of thing goalkeepers do. We understand each other. So I took the opportunity to offer some advice on life as a goalkeeper at the Old Firm. He repaid me by saving everything we threw at him.'

That Goram liked a drink, a late night and carried a pound or two of excess in seven remarkable years at Rangers is no secret. By the admission of the man himself, he had an unerring capacity for pressing the self-destruct button. And yet as the free-flowing football of the Celtic teams constructed by Burns cut a swathe through the Scottish Premier League, it invariably collided with an insurmountable obstacle in Old Firm games. He was 5 foot 11 inches, invariably unshaven, hampered by dodgy knees and went by the name of Andrew Lewis Goram.

'That immortal quote from Tommy is always recalled, about putting Andy's name on his headstone,' adds Bonner. 'In 1995/96 particularly, Andy was the difference between us winning the league and not. As a goalkeeper you do go through those periods where everything goes for you.'

For any Rangers or Celtic player, judgement is passed before a frenetic jury of 50,000 or 60,000 diehards four times a season. Ahead of the 3–3 game at Ibrox in 1995, the team in green-and-white were edging closer to their rivals than they had for years. Van Hooijdonk and Thom had added a new thrust to the attack and under Burns collective forward strides were being taken.

'I remember that game in particular,' admits Gough, a Rangers stalwart for 11 years and captain for most of that period. 'It had everything. Great goals, good-quality players and great goalkeeping from Andy. We were very fortunate to have some strong characters in that dressing room. And because of that we managed to get some terrific results at Celtic Park. It's hard to say what drove Andy in those games in particular, we were used to seeing him play that way. Like most keepers, he was just driven by the desire to keep a clean sheet. We defended well in the face of some intense attacking and he and I had a good understanding.'

In the luminous advertising boards that lap the Ibrox pitch these days, the names of Gascoigne and Laudrup are up in lights, yet the contribution of Goram to the eighth and arguably best of the nine titles can never be overlooked. Precisely a year later, with the pressure to equal Celtic's record under Jock Stein becoming onerous and immense, Rangers travelled to Parkhead where Goram dived full length to halt van Hooijdonk's penalty kick. Not for the first time, he'd denied the old rivals at a critical juncture.

'I gave away that penalty in the dying minutes,' Gough recalls. 'He got me out of jail, that's for sure. There was just that two- or three-year period when we had very close games, nothing in them, really. But somehow we always had the upper hand.'

At the tenth time of asking, Celtic skipper Tom Boyd finally laid hands on the Scottish Premier League trophy 12 months later, in season 1997/98. Yet the scars inflicted by Goram's consistent brilliance in the preceding years remain to this day.

'Andy was one of the best shot-stoppers and reflex keepers I've ever seen,' says Boyd, a former Scotland teammate as well as an Old Firm rival. 'He could stop unbelievable shots from 10 yards out. And he could read what was about to happen and react quickly. It was heartbreaking, demoralising. You really felt it.'

In the end Goram played twenty-six Old Firm games and lost just six.

With a shake of the head Boyd admits: 'Tommy Burns, God rest his soul, spoke for us all at that time.'

Walter Smith is prone to observing in quieter moments that a manager should only ever encounter one Andy Goram in his lifetime. When the errant figure of Allan McGregor, another goalkeeper, threatened to go off the rails during Smith's second spell in charge of Rangers, it was to the manual in his head that the manager referred. He had been here before.

Goram was never anyone's idea of the textbook goalkeeper. Lev Yashin, Dino Zoff and Gordon Banks had a lithe athleticism to their build that suggested years of selfless dedication. On the short side for a keeper, Goram's penchant for the good life was never anything other than instantly evident, along with the occasional darker interlude.

At Rangers and Motherwell, Goram was accused of associating too readily with members of the Ulster Volunteer Force, to the embarrassment of his employers. Wearing a black arm band in an Old Firm game following the death of murdered terrorist Billy Wright was never his sharpest move, claiming it was a tribute to a dead auntie merely raised the eyebrows higher. And yet Goram married two Catholic women, casting the accusations of bigotry into a somewhat different light.

To this day, tales of his love life remain a staple of the red-top press, a decade since he was last playing at his prime. The ladies who encounter this former keeper with an apparently killer line in chat always seem to be readily tempted by the allure of a quick headline.

Three marriages were played out in the pages of the media. First wife Jacquie opted against a move to Scotland when her man joined Hibernian at the end of the 1980s. Second wife Tracey, meanwhile, suffered the pitfalls of Goram's fame. The two met in a casino where Tracey was the croupier, and they wed in 1991. Drinking and gambling tales simply poured forth from tabloid newspapers thereafter, some also alleging infidelity. Tracey's revenge was a demand for a £250,000 divorce settlement, allied to newspaper claims that, such was her ex-husband's behaviour, she contemplated suicide. Then came the statuesque Miriam Wylie, a fiery and formidable lady with whom Goram has enjoyed and endured tempestuous times. The relationship has been on and off so often that it never seems anything less than a tortuous affair.

The duo once kept pot-bellied pigs and two goats named Gin and Tonic whilst running a bar in Lanark. Even his ex-wives would concede that, at his best, Goram is capable of being an amusingly lovable rogue as well as a superlative keeper.

Had he avoided serious injury in his career then who can say whether Goram might have been a different character. Most of the danger times came during lengthy spells of rehabilitation, allied to boozy days of refuelling.

'With Andy, Paul Gascoigne or whoever, the question will always be one of how best you man-manage that kind of player,' states John Brown, a former Rangers teammate of both. 'Walter Smith had to fire a shot or two across his bows, but the message was always the same: so long as you did it on the park, there was no lasting problem.'

In an eventful life, the words 'drunken brawl' have always seemed to attach themselves to Goram in the way ordinary people have a postcode.

Like Paul Gascoigne, The Goalie was a player who lived his life in a very public manner, and a man Walter Smith found it difficult to remain angry with for any length of time. The childlike desire to play football for Rangers brought both players back on the path to righteousness until, finally, the first Smith era petered out with his departure in the summer of 1998.

'He was my first signing, but we had our differences,' states Smith. 'There was the famous occasion I was ready to sell him. But Andy – being Andy – reacted to the challenge that was laid in front of him and came back to play as well as ever for the team. The saves he made which won games or turned games in our favour are too many to put down on paper. His contribution towards our championship run of nine-in-a-row was both immense and immeasurable.'

The venerable boss had brought Goram on board in 1991 in the aftermath of his elevation to the managerial hot seat. Graeme Souness had quit Ibrox for Liverpool and, hampered by UEFA's restrictive three foreigner rule, Smith needed a Scottish goalkeeper. Ironically,

Goram was born in Bury, but in the kind of twist of fate that characterised his career, he escaped a life of servitude to the England national team when a call-up to the under-21 set-up ended without him making an appearance. At the time, the great man had cause to curse the waste of his talent. Later, as he earned the first of his 42 caps with a Scotland debut against East Germany in 1986 as an Oldham player, the Tartan Army would sing, 'You're not English anymore'.

There were significant hiccups along the way, most as a result of boredom and dodgy knees. Others were temperament related.

When the early yips subsided, his first season at Rangers was an outstanding success, playing 55 games as the club claimed a league and cup double. A treble the next season was accompanied by a memorable run to what effectively constituted the semi-finals of the Champions League after a pulsating Battle of Britain triumph over Leeds United.

With Mark Hateley and Ally McCoist up front and Gough and Brown at the back, Rangers were circumnavigating the old three foreigner rule by virtue of a ferocious spirit.

Nigel Spackman was one of the dwindling band of English stars left at the club and he felt the full force of Goram's will to win when he made the mistake of labelling the keeper a 'fat bastard' during a half-time bust-up at Pittodrie.

Showing the athleticism that belied his fuller frame, the goalkeeper leapt across the physio's table and thumped the midfielder twice.

'I went daft and landed a couple of right hooks,' Goram admitted later. 'We went out and won 3–1. Did Spacks get a punch in? Did he f***!'

Walter Smith allowed that incident to pass, yet as six-in-a-row beckoned, the manager could no longer turn a blind eye to acts of public folly from his keeper.

For Goram, the season of 1993/94 was a frustrating one. A knee problem necessitated an operation in California before the start of the campaign, and the recovery was lengthy. Until February, Goram was sidelined, returning to the fray for 10 games before succumbing to a new injury to his hip.

With the title won in his absence, the Scottish Cup final against

Dundee United beckoned. Walter Smith believed his first choice could play, while the keeper himself harboured grave doubts.

In a quest to improve his state of mind, Smith packed Goram off on a family holiday to Tenerife before the final.

Yet The Goalie always played as hard as he worked and a catastrophic meeting with his former Oldham teammates on their end-of-season jolly resulted in a three-day bender. As his wife and family flew home to Edinburgh, a comatose Goram lay on the floor of former colleague Mike Milligan's room, waking long after the flight had touched down on Scottish soil. Stranded without cash or a passport and with only the T-shirt and shorts he was wearing, the situation was nightmarish. And it worsened significantly when Scotland's diligent tabloids got wind of his Carry On-style romp around the Canaries.

Returning home, Goram informed an unimpressed Walter Smith that he felt unable to play against Dundee United at Hampden. Clearly of the opinion that the extra-curricular antics had done little to assist the keeper's fitness, Smith waited until the Monday after Rangers lost the final 1–0, with Ally Maxwell in goal, to place his first-choice keeper on the transfer list. Goram's Rangers career was hanging by a thread.

Flying to Toronto the next day for an Ally McCoist testimonial event, Goram was distraught.

McCoist, Ian Durrant and Brown spent the trip assuring their teammate and close friend there was still a way back.

'That trip was an opportunity for some of us to talk to Andy,' recalls Brown. 'Myself, Coisty and Durranty laid it on the line to him that if he worked hard and knuckled down, he could still get himself off the transfer list and back in the team. The thing that never changed with Andy was his desire to play for Rangers. Let's face it, we all make mistakes. But you have to remember that he was going through stuff like splitting up from wives. He got the message and never looked back.'

Ultimately, Smith never wanted to lose Goram. Lesson learned, the keeper came off the transfer list early the next season. In a proactive move to avoid a repeat, Smith took Goram's guiding light and goalkeeping guru Alan Hodgkinson to Ibrox. The former England international had been employed Joe Royle at Oldham to lend some help to a young, raw rookie with undoubted talent, overcoming a sticky start in their relationship to become the dominant force in Goram's career. Hodgkinson was also used by Scotland to take Goram and his great international rival Jim Leighton through their paces.

'Andy was always in the press for his wrong-doings off the pitch when I arrived,' states Hodgkinson. 'But he worked hard and got himself back in the team and became a top-class goalkeeper.'

Hodgkinson stops short of taking the credit for that, yet others have no such qualms.

'A lot of credit for Andy's achievement goes to Alan,' states Craig Brown, the former Scotland head coach. 'He had a fascination for goalkeeping technique which bordered on a fetish. It was simple things which could, nevertheless, make all the difference. I used to watch him training the keepers and he would always insist on a keeper having great strength in their wrists and hands. Andy took this all in and as a result his strength and technique were excellent.

'He already had the natural abilities. I remember going to watch him at Oldham prior to the 1986 World Cup. And the manager there, Joe Royle, asked me if I was there to see their keeper. I said, "Yes". He then asked me if I knew that Andy was a very good cricketer. I said, "Yes". Then he asked if I realised he was also a very good snooker player. I said I didn't but that, in any case, it was a football goalkeeper we were after anyway – not a cricketer or a snooker player. But his point was that it all tied in. Andy had great hand-to-eye co-ordination. He was strong, powerful and brave, and what he lacked in height he made up for with ability.'

Alan Hodgkinson remains a remarkable man, a sprightly worka-holic for whom retirement remains an alien concept. The former England international beams with pride at the mere mention of his two star protégés: Old Trafford legend Peter Schmeichel and Goram. When we speak, Hodgkinson is on the Oldham team bus travelling to an away game in Grimsby. Few other septuagenarians could muster either the energy or enthusiasm, let alone the athleticism, to be training men a third of their age.

'I was still working with Man United and Everton when Joe Royle kept on ringing me and saying he had the best young keeper he had ever come across,' he smiles. 'Could I spend some time taking a look at the lad and helping him along?

'I was living in Coventry at the time and very busy, but the Oldham reserves were playing Coventry one night and Joe phoned to say Andy would be playing. So I went along to Highfield Road. I sat in the director's box a row or two in front of Joe and Willie Donachie, his assistant, so I could form my own opinion.

'So here I was watching who I'd been told was the best young keeper ever. And the first goal quickly goes past him, followed by goals two, three, four and five. Then it gets to six and Joe taps me on the shoulder and says, "He's just coming back from injury Alan, this doesn't normally happen". Which is fine until he loses a seventh. So the first time I saw Andy, he lost 7–0. It was an inauspicious start.

'By then it was the end of a season and I went back to Man United. It wasn't until the next season that I agreed to take the lad a couple of afternoons a week.

'He clearly didn't take to me in the early sessions. He kicked a ball away in the huff one time and I ordered him to go and get it back. I was always a "say what I mean" man. I would tell them, "If you want to be a world-class keeper, then that's how it is." I was the same with Schmeichel.

'Eventually, Andy took it all on board and listened and appreciated all the work I did with him.'

How the two men came together is a winding tale. At the age of 14, Goram's hometown team Oldham offered him the chance to train with the youth sides. And yet, as he admits, Goram was undecided in the early days as to where his real talents lay. He would play in goal for one local amateur team on a Saturday then cricket for another on the Sunday.

Joe Royle effectively made the decision by telling the new kid he was a goalkeeper first and foremost. Flourishing at the Latics, he stayed seven years until the first major personality clash of his career.

Defender Glen Keeley arrived from Blackburn, and the two men simply operated on separate wavelengths.

With money in short supply, Royle reacted by speaking to his former Liverpool friend Peter Cormack, then managing Hibernian, about Goram. Aware that Scotland coach Andy Roxburgh was keen to see more of him, the keeper clutched the opportunity to follow in his father's footsteps and play at Easter Road. The move came as a shock to Alan Hodgkinson as he prepared for another coaching session at Oldham.

'One day I got a call from him saying, "I've gone". I said, "What do you mean you've gone? Gone where?" Eventually it was explained that he had gone to Hibernian, where his dad had been a keeper. The money Oldham got saved them to some extent, because they were in big financial trouble at that point.'

Yet the opportunity, four years later, to join Rangers was a gilt-edged chance to fulfil a lifetime of aspiration. Ironically, Hibernian won the League Cup just months after his departure along the M8. As Goram joked to new colleague Ally McCoist, a move to Rangers cost him the first trophy of his career.

By the time Goram and Hodgkinson reunited at Rangers, the goalkeeper was emerging as a force to be reckoned with. The title was retained in 1993/94 and a second League Cup winners' medal arrived the same season, with a 2–1 victory over his former club Hibernian in the final. Yet pain, worry and danger were in the post with the knee and hip injuries that threatened Goram's Ibrox future.

'Andy certainly had his injury problems with his knee,' admits Richard Gough. 'One season he missed quite a lot of the action and he showed terrific character to come back from that. When he did, we would always be in the same teams in training, even in five-a-side games. None of us liked losing a goal, even in that situation and, by God, we would get angry with each other plenty.

'But he was also a very likeable character. We shared a love of cricket – he played as an international for Scotland – and were friendly with Omar Henry, who captained the national team at that time. But ultimately it came down to getting good results for Rangers – and we did get good results.'

Those views are echoed wholeheartedly by Gough's long-term

defensive colleague John Brown, who claims emphatically: 'For me, Andy went on to prove that he was the best Rangers keeper of them all, certainly of my lifetime. In fact, he must be one of the very best Scotland has ever produced. He had a natural talent and never, ever wanted to be second best. If he lost a goal in training or in games, he was angry and he pushed himself to the limits. As a defender, he was great to play in front of because you knew if something got past you there was a great chance Andy would take care of it. It was a relationship of trust, and that's so important.

'In seven years, you can count the number of mistakes he made on one hand and that's why the supporters love him, why he still is in great demand at the after dinner talks and so on. At Rangers or wherever, people like their heroes to have human flaws – they loved Andy for that as a player and they still do.'

Trailing shredded headlines behind him like confetti at one of his three weddings, Andy Goram took poorly to the role of Scotland bridesmaid.

Engaged in the longest-running edition of the Odd Couple ever recorded, Goram jostled with Jim Leighton for international superiority for the best part of 12 years. It hardly needs saying who was the chaotic Oscar and who was the fastidious Felix.

Leighton, a quiet and taciturn man, started his career in stunning fashion at Aberdeen, then survived a brutal ending at Manchester United. He racked up 91 caps for his country, keeping 45 shut-outs, yet was left on the sidelines as Goram lorded it at Euro 96. That Leighton ended his career as the second most capped Scotland player ever is impressive. It's a sobering thought to contemplate how he might have eclipsed Kenny Dalglish's tally of 102 caps but for his great rival.

More often than not in football, the word 'rival' is an addendum to 'friend', especially in the cosseted world of the professional goalkeeper. Not this time. Down the years, both men have maintained a public air of respect, yet there has never been friendship as such. They were – and remain – too different for that.

Their relationship was made more complex still by the presence of

Hodgkinson as the Scotland goalkeeping coach. Initially, the Englishman had known Leighton in his part-time role at Manchester United. Later, his regard for Goram would usurp any lingering bonds with the implacable, if impeccably professional, Leighton. The former Aberdeen keeper always suspected Hodgkinson of pulling strings to win Goram the nod as Craig Brown's first-choice keeper. Eventually, Leighton outlasted Goram, the Rangers keeper walking out on Scotland before France 98 during a summer of near disintegration for the certainties in his life. When Wimbledon's Neil Sullivan took Goram's place, Leighton bitterly accused Hodgkinson of favouring yet another imported Englishman at his expense and prompted retired. The two men had, by then, not spoken in years.

Their enmity would spill over during an unfortunate episode in 2000 when Leighton cut short a stint coaching Scotland's under-21 keepers and flew home from San Marino when it became clear that his forthcoming autobiography was to be serialised, complete with damning criticism of Hodgkinson. To this day, the older man finds it hard to forgive or forget what was written.

'In his autobiography, Leighton said that all I ever did was praise Andy and never him. That was just untrue and an absolutely appalling thing to claim. I could have said a great number of things about Jim Leighton in response and could have revealed a number of things that would have hurt him. But that wasn't the right thing to do. As I saw it, he must have hated Andy Goram to say that stuff. A lot of the things Jim Leighton said in his autobiography were unforgivable.

'I don't think Leighton could ever quite understand the fact that Andy Goram was quite simply the best keeper in the country at that time. He worked ever so hard. I worked with Schmeichel at Man United and he was also amazing. Those two were both world class – no question.'

Neither does Craig Brown buy into the theory that he allowed his own judgement to be manipulated by a man who was, admittedly, a close friend and colleague.

'I don't think that ever happened with Alan, no. I had the highest regard for Jim as a professional. He was what I would call a gentleman of the highest integrity, so I had no beef with selecting him. The problem he had was that Alan was also Goram's club goalkeeping coach and worked with him every day. So he often felt that there were occasions when he preferred Andy Goram.'

If anything, all of this was merely the confirmation of a poorly kept secret. Leighton and Goram had little in common and when petty professional jealousies did spill over, then the only surprise was that they took so long to materialise.

Goram, gregarious and extroverted, contrasted sharply in outlook with the almost bookish introversion of Leighton. While Leighton's academic approach to keeping a football from a goalmouth was admirable, Goram was the more approachable and amiable of the two men.

But when Goram walked out on Scotland ahead of a Euro 96 qualifying match against Finland in September 1995, citing his failure to feel 'mentally attuned' for the task of representing his country, to the Tartan Army it looked as if he was acting in a treasonable manner, excusing himself to stay fresh for a lucrative Champions League clash for Rangers against Anorthosis Famagusta the following week. With a bonus of £30,000 on offer and concerns over his troublesome knee still prominent in his mind, there would appear to be solid grounds for the suspicion.

'The thing with Andy was that he was always very likeable,' states Craig Brown, 'he was a lovable rascal if you like. There was never any malice in his actions so far as I could see. So when he pulled out of the qualifier, I said to reporters that he needed his head sorted out. Of course, the headlines in the papers immediately had me saying he needed to see a shrink. That wasn't quite what I had said, but it didn't prevent McCoist and Durrant from hanging a straitjacket on his dressing-room peg when he returned to Rangers.

'I never took the view that he was turning his back on Scotland or that I should take stronger action. As I say, he was always so likeable. You could never be angry with him for long. He used to ask me why I always put him in a room next to a member of the backroom staff and I'd tell him straight: I didn't trust him. To be fair, we would laugh about it and he would accept it.'

Leighton duly performed superbly in a 1–0 win over the Finns and played a significant part in helping the Scots reach the tournament in England. How difficult it must have been, then, to see Goram – a man who had excused himself when it suited – taking a starting place for the finals.

'The hardest part was dropping Leighton,' admits Brown. 'It was so hard because his record was unbelievable. He ended up Scotland's second most-capped player with 91 caps, and amongst those he had that incredible record of 45 shut-outs. That was quite remarkable.

'At that time, I simply felt Goram's eye was in – and that was the view of Alan Hodgkinson, my goalkeeping coach. I had given them a game each on the warm-up tour in the United States and it was as difficult as any decision I ever had. I told Jim on the Saturday, 48 hours before we faced Holland in the first game on the Monday. He was shattered. He had invited his family down to England and afterwards he told me was grateful that I had given him those 48 hours of notice. Not only did it allow him to tell his family not to travel, but he also admitted that he was so mentally shattered by the news that he might have been unable to take his place on the bench with less notice.

'At training, there was a price to pay. Jim didn't speak to Hodgy for a while.'

Leighton came close to quitting the national set-up, with Craig Brown's formidable diplomatic skills averting a significant loss to the cause at a time when Scottish national teams were still regularly gracing major final tournaments.

In the event, Leighton remains the last Scottish keeper to grace a World Cup finals stage, after playing at France 98. The tournament was also the last post for Andy Goram's international career, the troubled keeper retiring from the national team just weeks before the opening game with Brazil at the Stade de France.

Who can say how onerous the pressures of reaching nine-in-a-row had been for the Rangers players? Smith had already confirmed his intention to step aside and make way for Dick Advocaat, the little Dutchman with a military bearing. Advocaat, in turn, had made it clear that the old guard would be swept aside to make way for some new infantry. Goram, like a raft of his teammates, was facing the football equivalent of a pistol at dawn.

And so it was at international level for The Goalie. It was becoming increasingly clear that Leighton was set to win the nod in France and, unwrapping the ever-present bandages from his knee, Goram took his leave of the Scotland camp with a Dear John letter to Brown before the tournament began, triggering predictable headlines of hysterical outrage.

'Andy pulled out while we were in the United States again, two or three weeks before the tournament,' Brown recalls. 'I knew he had some personal problems to deal with, but no one else did. So it was no surprise to me when he wrote a letter to the SFA saying he would like to withdraw. There is nothing you can do in that situation but be sympathetic.'

Inevitably, newspaper tales emerged of a love interest. Goram and a female companion, it was claimed, were being hounded by the media and he felt unable to give Scotland his all. That he also found himself compelled to find a new club after a glorious interlude at Rangers can scarcely have helped. In a BBC interview, Goram later claimed he had been told in the training camp he would not be playing in France and at the age of 36 felt no great desire to sit on the bench behind a 40-year-old Leighton.

'Jim Leighton did exactly the same two days before a qualifying game,' Goram observed. 'But he retired, whereas I walked out, in the eyes of the press. Whether that was because we were two different animals I don't know.

'I ended up watching it on television, and that's when you think, I wish I could have played against Brazil. But these things happen. I did what I thought was right at the time. I've no regrets.'

There would be no fond farewells, then, for either the Tartan Army or the Ibrox support. Goram played his last Rangers game in the Scottish Cup final of 1998 against Hearts, losing 2–1 in a sad end. At the time there was no confirmation that the game was up, yet few doubted it to be the case.

*

He has never claimed to be a learned man, yet Andy Goram would have done well to absorb the words of the writer Maria Robinson in the summer of 1998. 'Nobody can go back and start a new beginning,' goes the saying, 'but anyone can start today on a new ending.'

Who might have guessed, as the Rangers chapter ended with six league championships, four Scottish Cups and one League Cup, that Goram would take his tally of professional appearances above 700 games, captain Motherwell for two years and enjoy an Indian summer at Old Trafford, of all places?

A year in England with Notts County and Sheffield United ended with a return to the SPL, where former Rangers player Billy Davies was assembling a new team. James McFadden was developing in the youth team as the likes of John Spencer, Shaun Teale and Don Goodman were earning the kind of wages which would eventually drive the club into administration. The capture of Goram was the jewel in the crown, even as his fortieth birthday hurtled closer.

For two years, Goram excelled at Fir Park. With two months of his contract remaining, he was pondering whether to play on when a call from Ally McCoist one morning contained all the hallmarks of a prank. A follow-up call from Walter Smith, by now managing Everton, further heightened Goram's sense of curiosity. Ten minutes later, his antennae twitched when the phone rang and Sir Alex Ferguson's secretary claimed that the Godfather wanted a word.

It took two attempts by Scottish football's knight of the realm to convince Goram the call was for real. United had a keeper crisis due to injuries to Fabian Barthez and Raimond van der Gouw. Would Goram, he asked, be interested in filling the void for two months? The question was of the rhetorical variety.

It was a surreal turn of events made all the spicier by a blazing row with United's Celtic-supporting skipper, Roy Keane. The two spoke barely a word following a training ground bust-up and were happy to leave it that way.

For Goram, reputations had never been a driving force.

'He had a quick temper at times, certainly,' chuckles Alan Hodgkinson. 'He would react to any slight anyone aimed at him. But he never lost his lovable quality and for me he was always a great guy.

'Oh, he had his indifferent headlines and run of stuff about him off the field, but Andy always bounced back. He was probably one of the best goalkeepers ever to play with Scotland despite it all. And I don't say that lightly. As a kid I was a Ronnie Simpson nut – I modelled myself on him and would cut his picture out even though I was English. But Andy had so much ability.'

After six months at Old Trafford, Goram pitched up at Queen of the South in Scotland's First Division, winning a Challenge Cup medal to add to his cast collection. There might have been yet another spectacular comeback at the top level when officials of Rio's Botafogo expressed serious interest in signing him during a Rangers convention in Texas. It came to nothing. Instead, there was a final hoorah in Elgin, under the management of former Ibrox teammate David Robertson. Six months was enough to finally convince The Goalie that the game was up.

Brief coaching spells at Dundee, Airdrie and Clyde lasted longer than a pint of best ale in the Stonefield Tavern, Goram's current Blantyre howff, but not much.

With Rangers memorabilia plastered across the walls, regulars bask in recollections of the landlord's derring-do, not least in Old Firm games, where blood and thunder were the order of the day. To the average Joe, Andy Goram remains a living legend.

'Without doubt, Andy is the best I've seen in a Rangers jersey,' says former teammate and Ibrox midfielder Ian Ferguson. 'I've been a supporter of Rangers all my life and in that time there is no question he was the best. It's said that he was worth 15 points a season and that's certainly true. The reason for that is that he was one of the best shot-stoppers the game had seen.

'Sure he attracted some headlines, but what people do off the park has always been up to them as far as I'm concerned – it's their private life. I never read too much into what was happening with Andy – you couldn't keep up with it all anyway! I suppose folk like to read it but when you play as well as he did on the park, you can get away with anything.'

8

Jock's Boy
WILLIE HAMILTON

'Hamilton is the sad example of the brilliant individualist who doesn't conform or refuses to fit into the pattern expected by clubs.'

– Daily Record, 25 May 1964

Shortly before his death in a Welsh football stadium in September 1985, Jock Stein, the doyen of Scottish football managers, returned to the town where it all began.

In the Carnegie Hall, Dunfermline, the manager of Scotland granted a two-hour audience to his people. The night was a sell-out; a verbal romp through the games, the occasions, the joys and the bugbears of a career laced with silver linings.

Two decades earlier, at East End Park – the football stadium half a mile along Halbeath Road – Stein revealed himself to be imbued with the touch of a modern-day Midas.

Lifting the Scottish Cup in 1961 sparked a golden era for the Fifers. Decked in a white raincoat, Stein led the Pars to triumph over Celtic, the club where he would attain the status of a football immortal. Yet before a prodigal return to the East End of Glasgow, where he had over-achieved as a player and captain, there was a journey across the Forth Bridge to take on the task of transforming a mediocre Hibernian side.

Many years later, on dazzling form in Dunfermline, Stein trained his gaze above the heads of a transfixed audience and paid tribute to the professionals who had crossed his path down the years; the good, the bad and the great.

145

In the mind's eye of the first man to bring the European Cup back to the British Isles, there was also a place reserved for the unfulfilled. John Lunn of Dunfermline, who died of leukaemia in his early 20s, Alex Edwards and, most of all, Willie Hamilton.

In collating the final cast list for this book, there were those who reacted with mystification to the inclusion of this former Hibs and Hearts enigma. Hamilton was the classic under-achiever; a player of formidable talent capable of drawing out the kind of misty-eyed romanticism Stein normally eschewed. To many, he had the skill, the vision and the balance of a Baxter, and more than a few of the flaws.

As the compère in the Carnegie Hall in 1985, however, the late Bob Crampsey enjoyed unique access to Jock Stein's thought processes. A renowned and highly respected broadcaster and historian, Crampsey was regarded by younger generations as an avuncular oracle of the Scottish game. Stein, a man capable of controlling the Scottish media as if they were rabbits caught in headlights, had no qualms, however, over taking the former schoolmaster and Brain of Britain down a peg or two.

'On a quiz programme one night with Stein, I ventured the opinion that Hamilton was the most visionary player I had seen in Scotland since World War Two,' recorded Crampsey before his death at the age of 78 in 2008. 'There came a stirring from the giant at my side and a growled; "That's the first bloody sensible thing I've heard you say in your life." '

Crampsey was not a solitary witness to Stein's regard for Hamilton. With the possible exception of Jimmy Johnstone, no player gained greater regard or respect from Stein. With his strength, burst of pace over short distances – when the fancy took – marvellous passing range and shooting ability, Hamilton was Stein's golden boy.

Sports writer Mike Aitken had grown up in Edinburgh's Corstorphine, where his father – a Motherwell supporter – would take him to games at Tynecastle.

'The Hearts player who inspired my love of the game in the early '60s was Willie,' he states unequivocally. 'He was skilful, charismatic and exciting to watch. 'From the vantage point of the school end terracing, I was spellbound by Hamilton's capacity to pass, dribble and shoot. I didn't know it then, but what made Hamilton so special was that he came closer than any other Scot I can think of to epitomising the qualities that distinguish the No. 10 in international football. Because Willie was an attacking midfielder who played in the hole, opposition defenders found him impossible to mark.

'Perhaps because he played his best football in Edinburgh, Hamilton's reputation suffered from lack of recognition in the west of Scotland,' adds Aitken. 'Jock Stein thought about taking him to Celtic Park, but the move never materialised.

'It was only years later, as a sports journalist on a Scotland trip to Iceland, when I first heard Stein eulogise Hamilton. Chatting into the early hours in the foyer of a Reykjavik hotel about the great Scottish players, Stein identified Willie as the best he'd ever seen. "People such as wee Jimmy Johnstone and Jim Baxter each had that special thing they did brilliantly," ventured the Big Man. "But Willie could do it all. He could match anyone in the game with his speed, stamina and shooting power."'

Why, then, did Hamilton fall short at the top level? Why did he fail to gain the recognition of generations of football lovers in the manner of so many of Stein's charges? The reasons are many.

The physical shortcomings that dogged his career and stunted his growth as a footballer are as good a starting point as any. A stomach ulcer plagued him, yet many of the fitness issues were self-inflicted.

Here was a man with a formidable capacity for alcohol and an approach to training which occasionally bordered on the disdainful. A man alleged to have crept off for drawn-out drinking sessions at the old Longstone Bus Depot in Edinburgh with equally errant teammates in his Hearts days.

A Hibernian legend, former captain and ex-teammate of Hamilton, Pat Stanton sighs with the wistfulness of one recalling a boyhood hero as he states: 'He was a one-off, was Willie. Jock was a great admirer of his talents. He wasn't much of an admirer of his lifestyle, but it was widely acknowledged that his skill and ability were tremendous at times.

'But, you know, even today when you mention Willie to younger

147

ones, they just look at you as if to say, "Who?" When I was at Celtic towards the tail end of my career in 1977, there was one of those occasions. We'd finished training and we were sitting around the dressing room blethering and swapping tales about the various players we had known.

'I was saying to the captain Roy Aitken and the rest what a good player Willie Hamilton had been. Again, it was all, "Who's he?"'

'Bobby Lennox and one or two of the others of my era remembered him fine, but the younger lads were blank. And just at that point Jock Stein was walking across the dressing room when I said we were talking about players and mentioned Willie's name. Big Jock just said quite casually, "Think of Kenny Dalglish. If you think he is a good player, you should have seen Willie Hamilton." That was quite a tribute.'

Throughout his managerial career, Stein remained teetotal. Yet there was no hint of moral disapproval or condescension towards those who liked a drink. This son of the resolutely working-class area of Burnbank in Lanarkshire had his own vices: a love of gambling being uppermost. Surrounded by corner-boys in his younger days as a junior with Blantyre Vics, then, Stein was always willing to overlook personal foibles if they came wrapped in a cloak of outrageous talent. Late in his career, Stein took to telling people that his greatest achievement in football may have been keeping the gifted Jimmy Johnstone in the game longer than might otherwise have been the case. What psychology he applied to handling the feather-light Jinky may have been gleaned from donning the kid gloves that prodded and shaped Willie Hamilton at Hibs.

Broadcaster Archie Macpherson produced the definitive biography of Stein after years of travelling the world with the Big Man. It remains his view that Stein learned as much from Hamilton at Easter Road as the player did from Scottish football's first tracksuit manager.

'While Stein was a hard man, he was always thinking about his actions, pondering, What's in it for me and my club? Usually what was in it for both parties was success. And plenty of it.

'Willie Hamilton was a punter, a bevvy merchant of some standing. I grew up in the east end of Glasgow surrounded by Willie Hamilton types. They were the sorts with magic at their feet and beer bellies swinging to the side. Willie never had a weight problem, and he had innate talent to burn, but he was the archetypal flawed Scottish footballer.'

Macpherson credits Stein with accommodating Hamilton on a Friday night at his home in Edinburgh's Queensferry Road. The goal? To head off potential late-night indiscretions at the pass.

'Jock had to tell people about Willie Hamilton, how impressed he had been with his play. Not everyone appreciated his ability. But I also had a feeling that he left such an impression on Stein because Jock learned a lot from handling him. At Hibs, he was almost serving an apprenticeship in how to control a wayward individual. In a strange sort of way, Willie was shaping Jock Stein as much as he was shaping games. Jock learned how to get the best out of such a player and applied those lessons to great effect for the rest of his career.'

Forming a posthumous picture of an individual is a tricky affair. Unlike Hughie Gallacher and Jim Baxter, featured elsewhere in this book, there are no biographies of Hamilton to draw upon. Merely the word of those who claim his brilliance was underpinned by human idiosyncrasies. Some would say weaknesses.

A shyness bordering on the extremities of the condition made the midfielder a difficult man to know. Former teammates found nothing unpleasant in his demeanour, yet knew little or nothing about the man beneath. Hamilton appears to have been a Jekyll and Hyde individual; quiet and unremarkable, but there could be a transformation under certain circumstances. Namely when he had a ball at his feet, or a drink in his hand.

The five years he spent at his first club, Sheffield United, were amongst his most productive – delivering 21 goals in 79 appearances.

And yet, taken over a five-year period, less than eighty appearances seems a lowly total. In 16 years as a professional, Hamilton registered 253 appearances, scoring 65 goals. If the figures available are accurate, that works out at an average of a mere 15 appearances a season.

From the family home in Airdrie where the young Hamilton grew up, his sister Marion is a proud defender of her sibling. Billy, as she and all the family knew him, was neither a drunk nor a malingerer, merely an insecure, shy individual who used alcohol and football as crutches for his condition.

In an interview given to Mike Aitken in 2006, Marion states: 'Billy was a painfully shy person. The only time he looked or felt self-confident was on the football field. Even then, he was sick with nerves before every game. Billy was easily embarrassed and found it difficult when supporters approached him for an autograph or just to talk. As a footballer, he never felt he was good enough. I don't think he ever accepted how great he was. For me, his best football was played at Sheffield United.'

Born on 16 February 1938, Hamilton was the son of a colliery surface worker. He left home for Yorkshire at 16, after starting out in Coatbridge with Drumpellier Amateurs. Sheffield United manager Joe Mercer had shamelessly presented the reticent teenager with a new pair of boots during a visit to his Airdrie home. Saying no to a move to the Blades thereafter was never an option. As a young man away from home for prolonged periods, homesickness was a constant companion. Yet Hamilton earned a £12,000 move to Middlesbrough in February 1961, a switch that at least carried him back in a northerly direction. During 16 months at Ayresome Park, however, the midfielder failed to settle, scoring just one goal in 10 appearances. In the words of the gravel-voiced rocker Frankie Miller, Caledonia was calling.

At Heart of Midlothian, Tommy Walker ran a tight ship. A manager of the old school and a man considered one of the greatest players ever to wear the Hearts jersey, Walker had contemplated life as a Church of Scotland minister before becoming a footballer instead. For all Hamilton's undoubted brilliance, then, there was always likely to be a clash of perspectives between this would-be man of the cloth and a tortured soul driven by hedonism.

Under Walker, Hearts were a physical and functional team. Hamilton's direct running and dribbling were a revelation. Signed for £2,500 – much less than the £7,000 reported at the time – the new man settled incredibly quickly, scoring a wonder goal on his debut against Dundee. Hearts won only their fourth League Cup on 27 October 1962 before a crowd of 51,280, when an incisive run down the right flank from the hero of our piece teed up his friend Norrie Davidson for the only goal of the match. Hearts were also going strongly in the championship, but witnessed their aspirations placed in cold storage by a savage cold snap. A Scottish Cup game in Forfar on 12 January 1963 was their last game until a Cup defeat to Celtic in the next round on 6 March. Hamilton was absent from that game after being suspended by Tommy Walker for 14 days for an undisclosed disciplinary breach.

What the supporters didn't know was that Hamilton missed training sessions after going AWOL more than once. As teammates attest, the coach, Johnnie Harvey, tolerated his absences; Walker was less forgiving.

Striker Alan Gordon was a mere teenage prospect at the time, the thirteenth man in the League Cup final, but quickly formed a formidable alliance in a playing sense with Hamilton and future Celtic star Willie Wallace prior to the off-field infractions.

'I played with Willie only for a brief spell at Hearts over the course of 1962/63. And I must say, when I look back now, I am surprised by how few games he actually played.'

'Willie could not always be relied upon.

'He played very few games and, let's put it this way, he had quick feet and an abundance of skill, but he did not conform to what his teammates required of him on a truly consistent basis. What I do remember quite distinctly is that when Willie did turn up for training, he would always have a nervous cough. I assumed it was nervous at least, but in retrospect he never seemed to enjoy the best of health. Whether that was because he liked a drink or not I couldn't say.'

For their part, Hearts supporters were willing to forgive anything. The austerity of Walker's reign in the managerial hot seat sat uneasily with a changing climate in the 1960s. Hamilton's dynamism and maverick approach to the game chimed with the times.

As club historian David Speed recalls: 'In terms of his ability as a football player, Willie raised the bar. In the 1950s, Hearts had enjoyed some success as a passing team. But this guy would just pick up the ball in midfield and run and dribble all day. He also had a terrific long shot which he used to great effect. We had never seen the likes – he was a breath of fresh air. He was certainly the best Hearts player I had ever seen.'

After the suspension, there was a comeback of sorts – at city rivals Hibernian, rather than Hearts. To this day, moving from one club directly to the other remains something of a taboo. What frustration Tynecastle fans felt at losing their talisman for a modest £6,000 was directed at the venerable manager Walker, however.

Jock Stein was not the man who signed Willie Hamilton for Hibs in October 1963 – he was still Dunfermline manager at the time. On arrival at Easter Road six months later, however, his impact was such that the erratic quickly gave way to ecstatic.

Stein enacted revolution rather than evolution at Hibs, making remarkable progress at a team more accustomed to battling mid to lower league mediocrity; a team, indeed, where a spectator had kicked a stray ball out of the stadium under the previous manager Walter Galbraith in disgust. While police arrested the spectator in question, the Hibs chairman Harry Swann showed his agreement with the lone protestor by ordering his release and handing over a complimentary ticket for the next game.

As Stein set the heather alight on a brief stop-over in Dunfermline, winning the Scottish Cup in 1961 and scaring the life from Spanish giants Valencia in the old Fairs Cup, the writing was on the wall for the increasingly forlorn Galbraith at Easter Road.

In Edinburgh, the Big Man's impact was immediate. Not least on Hamilton, who quickly withdrew a transfer request handed in following an unhappy start to his time at the club. The midfielder would signal his renaissance under the new manager by performing in sublime fashion in the Summer Cup, the club's first trophy in 10 years. An outbreak of typhoid had quarantined final opponents Aberdeen for much of the summer and dragged the drawn out final into a third match in August, but in Leith something else was catching.

Alongside Pat Quinn in midfield, Hamilton had been under-achieving. Yet Stein placed his faith in the hands of a man he knew could return the favours where it truly mattered – on the pitch.

Jimmy O'Rourke had become a Hibs first-team player at the age of 16 years and 85 days, and would spend 12 years with the club. In his formative days under Stein, however, the striker was required to slop out the terraces with the other kids and inadvertently overheard a conversation which outlined both Hamilton's fecklessness and Stein's surprising capacity for indulgence.

'I was on the Hibs ground staff as a kid when we were paid in cash weekly on a Tuesday or a Wednesday,' says O'Rourke. 'No one depended on banks in those days. Willie was the type of guy who would be paid on a Tuesday and be skint on a Thursday. The reasons for that I don't know.

'Along with the other ground staff boys, I would have to go out and sweep the terraces of all the empty bottles and rubbish in preparation for the next game. So one day we were cleaning when we stopped to listen to Willie approaching Jock Stein for a sub of cash.

'We thought he'd get a flea in his ear. But instead Jock pulled out a note and gave it to him, no questions asked, saying something like: "You'd better bloody well pay me back for that on Saturday."

'The manager was unaware we had stopped working and were listening. When he looked up and noticed us, he shrugged and said quickly: "If you don't take chances during the week then you won't take them on a Saturday."

'That approach to life seemed to sum Willie up to me perfectly.'

Stein's biggest gamble at Hibs would be an elaborate attempt to inject a taste of European glamour into a midweek night in October 1964, persuading chairman Willie Harrower to shell out the not inconsiderable sum of £12,000 to lure Real Madrid to Leith.

A crowd of 32,000 turned up to watch the team who had won the first five European Cups, including the triumph regarded as the greatest game ever witnessed on Scottish soil – an incredible 7–3 victory over Eintracht Frankfurt in 1960. Six months before facing Hibs they had narrowly missed out on a seventh trophy, losing to Helenio Herrera's Internazionale in the final.

Despite the emergence of the Italians, Real were, without question, the most famous club side in the world, featuring remarkable talents such as Ferenc Puskás, Francisco Gento and Jose Santamaria. Yet, on a night when the football Gods shone on Leith, Hamilton dominated the game – threading pass after pass through the defence of the white-shirted aristocrats as Hibs won 2–0.

A tankard was the reward for the players who participated. They were all raising a toast to Willie Hamilton that night.

Like Hamilton, Peter Cormack arrived at Hibs after a brief spell with Hearts and was on the cusp of a decorated career with Nottingham Forest, then the first great Liverpool side of the 1970s. 'The glory of scoring the goals that night against Real went to Pat Quinn and me,' Cormack later said, 'but Willie Hamilton's performance was simply magnificent. Willie was a particular favourite of mine and to see him outshine players of that quality was something else. As if being on the same pitch as these guys wasn't enough, after the game we were all presented with a special commemorative watch by Real Madrid – the watch I received is still in good working order.'

Hamilton also received a watch, only to have the treasured memento stolen from the side of a public park when he agreed to guest in a game for a fire brigade team some years later.

'A few days after that, we finished off a memorable week by beating Rangers 4–2 at Ibrox,' Cormack adds. 'I recall that Willie had a bit of banter with Jim Baxter in the tunnel before kick-off, with each telling the other what they would do in the course of the afternoon. Well, Willie undoubtedly beat Jim at his own game, standing on the ball and controlling the pace of the game. Willie was the only player who could have done that to Jim Baxter. I was just an 18-year-old laddie at the time and I scored two goals against the Rangers to follow up my goal against Real.'

For O'Rourke, those two games also remain outstanding memories. In assessing the contribution of Hamilton, however, he regards them as not at all untypical of the displays he was producing on a regular basis. 'People say the performance against Real Madrid was exceptional,' he adds. 'Possibly because they were the former

European Champions. And maybe it was, but to me, Willie played like that every week.'

In a sense, nothing had changed. Hamilton was by now receiving recognition for his skills, yet at Hibernian – as at Hearts – he found close friends hard to come by. Not least back at Tynecastle, where he marked his return in a green-and-white jersey by scoring a superb winner in the New Year's Day meeting of the clubs. The goal, however, did nothing to build significant bridges at Easter Road. Teammates spoke of an individualist who could be demanding and utterly scathing of those of lesser ability.

'You get really top, top players who tend to be selfish in their play,' says Pat Stanton bluntly. 'They look to finish everything themselves rather than play in the teammate who has made an intelligent run. They are so sure of themselves that they don't feel they need anyone. Willie was a bit like that I suppose, but in saying that, he could do marvellous things. Over 10 yards he had fabulous pace, but after that not much happened. Things tended to fizzle out a bit, but like Dalglish, he had great balance and an ability to fend players off.'

As a man, and as a footballer, Hamilton was an enigma.

'He was very quiet,' adds Stanton. 'But there were times when he got a drink in him and when he was on the pitch when all the inhibitions would just disappear. I can remember days when results wouldn't go our way and he would just let rip at his teammates. "You're just a bunch of cowboys," he'd say. "I'm the only player here." Oddly, we didn't take it too badly, because I think a lot of us felt he had a point. For all his reserve, most of the players quite liked Willie.

'Ach, when he got drunk he could be a bit nippy, sure. There was another side to him whereby things could get a bit out of control very quickly.'

Jimmy O'Rourke confirms much of what Stanton says, adding: 'Willie was a wonderful player. He was unique in so many ways – he was a different type of player and a different type of person. He wasn't a loner exactly. He was friendly with John Parke, our left-back. They hit it off. But to my recollection that was probably the only buddy he had in the game. It wasn't that he was a bad lad. It was just difficult to get onto his wavelength.'

Hamilton played just once for Scotland. Predictably, the manager who picked him was Jock Stein. The solitary cap arrived months after Stein's departure for Celtic; the Big Man agreeing to take control of the Scotland side for two World Cup qualifiers in Finland and Poland in the spring of 1965 following the dismissal of Ian McColl. On 23 May, Hamilton was omitted from the team that drew 1–1 with the Poles, but made the cut for the second game in the double header in Finland four days later. On the eve of the game, Stein sent the new cap a telegram, stating simply show the world.

He did, but just the once. Hamilton confirmed his eccentricities by turning up at the airport for the trip with little more than a toothbrush. Perhaps he knew his stay with the Scotland national team would be short-lived, despite a creditable display in a 2–1 win in Helsinki.

The Mystery of the Silver Salver might sound like some kind of Basil Rathbone-era tale from the chronicles of Sherlock Holmes.

Within weeks of Hamilton's sole Scotland cap being doled out, however, one of the midfielder's more enduring fables would take root in the unlikely venue of Ottawa, Canada.

Hibernian had finished season 1964/65 in fourth place, overcoming the loss of Stein's services by embarking upon a gruelling close season tour of North America. The practice, at the time, was commonplace. British clubs were regarded in the homelands of basketball and ice hockey as missionary zealots for the joys of professional soccer. So it was, then, that Hibs, like a raft of other clubs, embarked upon a 20-day odyssey across America and Canada to spread the word to a doubting public. The hardest of the nine games came against fellow tourists Nottingham Forest, Hibs edging a 2–1 win over the English club. A challenge match against the Ottawa All Stars would be a somewhat different affair. In a fruitless quest to imbue some edge to a game with all the competitive spirit of a dust-up between Lennox Lewis and Ronnie Corbett, the match organisers announced plans to present a handsome silver salver to the man of the match.

As with the game itself, this would also be no contest. The Edinburgh club thumped the locals 15–0 – and Hamilton scored seven of the goals, setting up some of the others. It was, by any standards, a feat to be proud of. Teammates attest to the fact that the large plate presented to Hamilton afterwards was likewise.

'We all quite fancied this trophy and Peter Cormack scored the first goal,' recalls Jimmy O'Rourke with a laugh, 'but Willie scored the next seven. He was outstanding and his goals were recognised when he was presented with a silver salver by Carling, the beer company. It was a lovely trophy, it would have been worth $200 or $300.

'Willie shared a room on the trip with Jimmy Stevenson and Jimmy told him to look after it. Some chance. Willie couldn't get it in his holdall and to my recollection it ended up bent in an effort to get it in somehow. It was a shame, but that was just Willie.'

Pat Stanton was equally nonplussed by the casual disregard for what ought to have been a memento to show the grandkids.

'I was there when it happened,' says Stanton. 'Willie asked the trainer Tam McNiven if he could put it flat in the team hamper, because it was too big for his hand luggage. For some reason, that wasn't possible, so he just put it over his knee, bent it and got it in his bag by hook or by crook. That was just Willie. To my recollection, he hadn't even had a drink at that point, because we were moving on to another city.'

It should be pointed out that Hamilton's sister claims possession of the said trophy in her Lanarkshire home – completely unblemished. With Willie Hamilton, separating the fact from the legend is no easy task.

At the end of the tour, Hamilton returned to England unexpectedly. There was talk at the time of Stein signing his prodigal son for Celtic, Billy McNeill being sent to sound out his short-lived Scotland teammate. The reasons the move failed to materialise never emerged, yet some suspect that Celtic's rigidly straight-laced chairman of the time, Robert Kelly, took exception to the baggage such a player would bring.

'Willie had all the ability in the world,' McNeill once observed.

'Jock certainly thought about bringing him to Celtic, he was in-trigued by his ability. But the other side of it, the discipline, may have caused him to hesitate.'

Just as likely, perhaps, is a simpler explanation. At Parkhead, Stein had good players destined to win a European Cup within two years. Even without Hamilton, his Hibernian lock-picker, he already held the key to continental domination.

That decision would prove key to the disintegration of Hamilton's career; even his life as he knew it.

The playmaker joined Aston Villa instead for £24,000 in August 1965. As Stein was leading Celtic to glory, however, Hamilton was battling for his life after sustaining serious chest and facial injuries in a car accident in 1967. In the view of Hamilton's sister Marion, the car crash was a critical factor in the failure of her brother to reach his true potential. At the age of 27, Willie was released by Villa – and once again trailed back to Edinburgh to rebuild his career with Hearts.

His second debut for the Tynecastle side caught supporters by surprise. Oddly, by today's standards, they were willing to allow his past indiscretions in leaping the dyke to sign for Hibs to go unpunished.

Club historian David Speed was in Stirling the day Hamilton returned to the maroon jersey.

'He reappeared for a game at Annfield, where Stirling Albion used to play. He signed too late for his name to be in the programme, so when it was read out it took a while for the penny to drop. He didn't look as good as he had done, he had acquired a small paunch and lost a bit of hair. But even then there were still times when he reminded us of the player he had been.'

A mere 22 games in his second spell at Tynecastle suggested Hamilton's powers were waning. There were spells at Ross County, Hamilton Academicals and Ferranti Thistle, with a year in South Africa, before he called a halt to his career in the early 1970s, whilst still in his 30s.

'I honestly don't know why he didn't take the big step to play for Manchester United, Real Madrid or even just one of the Old Firm,' states Jimmy O'Rourke. 'Ability-wise there is no question that he would have made the grade wherever he went. Maybe it's just that certain players can only be controlled by certain managers.

'Stein could control him, because they had a relationship based on mutual respect. But he was so naturally gifted that he didn't necessarily have to listen to managers.

'There's no question Jock got the very best out of Willie. He could do things in a game no one else could; things that could change it in an instant. I was once dropped from the team and travelled through with my brothers to watch a game in Kilmarnock from the terraces.

'Willie had this long stride and I remember he took two steps and just thumped a 30-yard shot high into the net. It flew in. I wasn't especially surprised, because that just typified the guy. He was just a special, special talent.'

Archie Macpherson also remembers a remarkable goal, comparing it to one of the greatest ever witnessed on these shores.

'I saw Hamilton scoring a goal that highlighted one of my earliest games working for the BBC. It was a thundering shot from 30 or 35 yards and yet it never really left the ground. It was rather like that memorable effort struck by Alfredo Di Stefano at Hampden when Real Madrid won the European Cup by beating Eintracht Frankfurt 7–3.'

In these days of diminished entertainment levels in Scottish football, there seems little question that Willie Hamilton would now be a superstar. And yet, managers will indulge only so much.

Pat Stanton recalls a childlike quality to Hamilton when it came to training. Hibs coach Tom McNiven would take running sessions around the track, conveniently turning a blind eye to the fact that the star player was leaping over the perimeter fence and missing out entire laps before rejoining his teammates when the fancy took.

'You get musicians as well who are truly gifted and yet have a lesser career than they should have,' says the former Easter Road skipper. 'It's like a shooting star – they career across the sky and you're one of the lucky ones if you see it.

'There is no secret that Willie liked a drink – maybe he liked it a bit too much.'

By 1975, Hamilton had a wife, Carole, and a son, William. Seeing little future in Scotland, the Hamilton family headed for a new life in Canada. The great man returned to a life of brick-laying, the career he had trained for in his teens before full-time football intervened. Just a year after moving to North America, he died of a heart attack at the age of 38. Amongst peers and former colleagues, there remains an air of incomprehension that such a gifted player can have had so little to show for a career speckled by plaudits, if not pound notes and medals.

'Maybe he was just a guy who couldn't settle,' states O'Rourke. 'Some were like that, still are. It could have been homesickness that prevented him from reaching the very top in England or abroad.

'You can look for reasons for ever and a day. But the fact is that few folk could ever get inside Willie's mind. The one thing I do know is that he would have been worth an absolute fortune today, millions and millions.

'I was at a Hibs supporters' do up in Aberdeen where they had a question and answer session. One guy asked me how Willie would adapt to the demands of the current game. I said he would certainly have adjusted, because he had the most important thing – ability. Players are probably fitter these days because of technology and full-time training academies and so on. But the goalposts and the dimensions of the pitch are still the same and Willie Hamilton never had any problem with them.'

As former Hearts striker Donald Ford once observed: 'I came on the scene in the '60s and there were a number of wonderful players around who made me wonder what I was doing in their company. When I went into the international side, there were people like Law and Bremner. Willie had the same impact. His talent was so astounding you wondered why you were on the same pitch.

'I wasn't close to Willie as a man, but was aware of his problems. I found him hard to talk to and there was often a distance to him. That said, he could be very pleasant. He could also be quite difficult to play with because of his capacity for the unexpected. And he would look down his nose at those he didn't feel were up to it. The modern game is very predictable and nine times out of ten you know exactly what a player will do. With Willie you never knew.'

But ask the average, relatively well-informed football supporter under 40 who Willie Hamilton was, and they will cast you a look of blank incomprehension.

'The sad thing is that Willie was a player with such ability and potential to play at the highest level,' says Stanton, 'and yet very few either saw him or remember him. He doesn't get talked about the way Baxter or Johnstone do and that's a shame because he should have reached that kind of level. All that talent and nobody really got to see it.'

9

Mac the Strife
FRANK McAVENNIE

'Frankie will end up in hell, but he won't be lonely – most of his
friends will be there and it will be the best party in town.'

– Actor and West Ham fan, Ray Winstone

The phrase 'ducking and diving' might have been invented for Frank
McAvennie. Off the pitch rather than on it, where his eye for goal
has long since been replaced by a nose for trouble.

Fresh from four hours on the golf course on a chill winter's
morning, we meet in the bar of a Gateshead hotel. A glass of soda
water and lime is McAvennie's tipple of choice. The times, it seems,
are a-changin'. In the glory days, he would go on a three-day bender
and need a full day to recover. Approaching 50, he now understands
that it pays to keep a clear head.

During spells at West Ham and Celtic, Stringfellows, busty page
three blondes, the finest Moët, chat show appearances and lucrative
newspaper spreads were *de rigueur*. Since quitting football, however,
the former striker has shown an unerring knack of finding himself in
horrendous situations. The kind which, more than once, threatened
to land him in prison for a long time.

'As the wife always says, "Why me?"' ponders McAvennie with a
rueful shake of the head. 'It's always me.'

By his own admission, much of what has happened since he retired
from football is in danger of wiping out the good work done as a
quite exceptional centre forward in the Scottish and English leagues.
A tally of 136 career goals in 406 appearances represented a ratio of
a goal every three games. Celtic, St Mirren and West Ham supporters

remember a greatly under-rated player, on a par in his day with the fêted Gary Lineker.

To those who read the front pages rather than the back, however, a hard-forged reputation as a football gem has long since been undermined by his alleged misdemeanours in the eyes of the law.

Take, as evidence, the infamous sunken treasure ship scrape. The very memory is enough to prompt wry laughter, so dubious was the explanation offered for the discovery by Customs of £200,000 – half of it McAvennie's money – in the boot of a Land Rover Discovery at Dover Docks. Unwisely, the recently-retired footballer had thrown in his lot with Alan Short, a business partner with a secret shady past in drug dealing. And, despite claims the cash was an investment in a lucrative Belgium-based commercial cargo ship, Customs and Excise thought differently. They believed the money actually belonged to the infamous late Glasgow gangster Thomas the Licensee McGraw. McAvennie and Short, they alleged, were merely fronting a drug deal.

In court, Short claimed the cash had been intended all along to retrieve 'sunken treasure'. McAvennie claimed that was news to him; for the headline writers it was a gift from God.

Face turning serious for once, McAvennie grimaces, 'Don't ask me about the time I turned up at court and found out I owned a pirate ship. Honestly, I can't bring myself to go into all that again – I just can't.

'That's the problem for me now. I speak to people these days and the football is almost secondary. It's a strange one, because I created this whole image around myself. I did some stupid things, though I was blamed for a lot of things which were also nothing to do with me.'

The authorities thought otherwise. Convinced the money was intended for use in a narcotics deal, magistrates impounded it – and McAvennie, seeking to support his son and ex-partners, was declared bankrupt.

A simultaneous conviction for possession of cocaine at Glasgow Airport, allied to a summons for failure to pay a £750 fine, merely added to the ignominy of it all. The wheels had well and truly come off.

The end of his playing career, coupled with the removal of the discipline regular training and collective responsibility brought, hit McAvennie hard. Where the celebrity lifestyle had once been balanced out by non-sexual athletic pursuits, between 1995 and 2000 it was all play and precious little work.

'When I finished football, it took me five years to get over it. I went a bit wild really. I said to Paul Gascoigne when he was struggling last year that I understood what he felt. I said to him, "Why not come and stay with me in Gateshead for a bit?"

'But he has to want to help himself first and I don't know if he's there yet. I don't have to pay £1,000 a night to some psychiatrist at the Priory to tell me I'm drinking too much and taking too many drugs. I know myself. I said to Gazza I would save him money by helping him and only taking £500 a night.'

The laughter which spirals towards the hotel roof does nothing to obscure the seriousness of the situations the former Scotland star found himself in as a life of vice took a dangerous grip.

At the end of his five-year bender, there was an invitation to go to Gateshead for a few days. Whilst in the north-east, he bumped into former Celtic Boys Club buddy Michael Edward, who offered his old friend the chance to get out of London. It was, claims McAvennie, manna from heaven. If only he'd known what was to come.

Before the storm, though, there was a ray of sunshine. Through Edward he met current wife, Karen Lamberti, the woman he credits with placing his life back on an even keel. But also through Edward, he found himself on a serious drugs charge in April 2000.

McAvennie left Karen one day to accompany his old buddy on 'some business' in the city centre. It was there that Vinnie Wallace, a Glasgow publican, jumped into the car unannounced. He and Edward then headed into town while their famous friend remained in the back of the car smoking and reading a newspaper. It was a Friday afternoon and Newcastle was gearing up for a typically raucous weekend. Stag and hen parties poured their way unsteadily off trains from north and south alike. As Wallace left the duo for a train back to Glasgow, police seized McAvennie and Edward. The charge? Involvement in a drugs deal. History seemed to be repeating itself.

After pausing for respite and reflection, he says: 'Ach, it was terrible. I had gone to the train station at 4 p.m. on the Friday afternoon with Michael Edward – it was the busiest time of the week in Newcastle. There was no way anyone would be able to pass a bag of drugs. Then the cameras which were supposed to have clocked us passing plastic bags of drugs to each other were revealed to have broken down for an hour, ever so coincidentally. As I say, it was embarrassing. Embarrassing, but frightening.'

Not least when Vinnie Wallace was seized from his train in Glasgow and found to be in possession of 5,000 Ecstasy tablets and 5 kilos of amphetamine paste.

McAvennie had only a £30 overdraft in his bank account, yet was charged with conspiracy to supply Class A and Class B drugs.

'I was some drug dealer with that amount of cash in my account wasn't I? I barely knew Karen when I got caught up in that court case. I was supposed to be playing golf that morning. But it was pissing with rain and I'm not very good at going out in that weather. I had only just left her 15 minutes earlier when that all happened and police emerged from everywhere. She knew it was nonsense and couldn't believe I was there.

'To be honest, I never for one moment thought anything was going to happen to me. I was more concerned about the fact I had moved the car round the corner for a laugh while Michael was away for a few minutes. I was banned from driving at the time you see. You don't do something like that with a smile on your face if you know something dodgy is going on, do you?

'The police couldn't explain why I did it. They didn't have a clue what was going on. Michael Edward, who I was with, must have had what he was going to do all planned and didn't want to say anything to me. I was innocent.'

Even so, McAvennie was charged on the Friday afternoon and expected to be granted bail pending a trial on the Saturday morning. The English criminal justice system had other ideas.

'I ended up doing a month in remand in Durham Prison. I went for my first appearance at the court on a Saturday morning when only one magistrate was sitting. Apparently, you only get bail if three magistrates are there. I didn't know that. So I had a second bail hearing on the Monday and the lawyer never turned up till noon – he was too late.

'It had been a formality I would get bail. But this dude doesn't show and I was locked up. But I'm the type who prefers to look on the bright side of life, and if it hadn't been for him being late that day I might not have sacked him – and I might have ended up going down. The guy wasn't good enough.

'He didn't want to employ a barrister, saying he would defend me himself. Thank God I got rid of him.'

In Durham Prison, McAvennie was protected to some degree by his status as a highly successful ex-pro. He had been fortunate enough to sign the autograph book of the toughest jail warden's son years earlier. Protection, then, was never far away. Nevertheless, he was slammed away for 23 hours a day in a cell 15 feet by 10 feet with the man who had landed him in the mess in the first place – Michael Edward. The two spoke of the injustice of it all and of taking legal action against the police.

Appointing a new lawyer and a top barrister, McAvennie began to believe he might survive the ordeal. He had, he insists, thought Edward to be innocent all along. Later, in a separate trial, his fellow Glaswegian would change his plea to guilty and receive five years. McAvennie, to his enormous relief, was declared not guilty after the jury deliberated over his innocence for just under one-and-a-half hours.

'I don't know why Michael changed his stance,' he says now. 'He didn't tell me he was about to change his plea and plead guilty. It looked all along as if I was going down for nine years. All Michael had to do was tell them I had nothing to do with it, but he never did it. It shouldn't be allowed. I had done nothing.'

Emerging on the steps of the court a free man to face a barrage of media interest, McAvennie chain-smoked in sheer relief. The rehabilitation process would, however, prove laborious.

'Honestly, when I came out of Durham Prison after that it took me about a year to get back to normal. Karen and I decided to get married, but I didn't want to go out and didn't want to be in company I didn't know. I was actually shitting myself if truth be told. I knew I had done nothing and I found it hard to comprehend how I could have been put through so much when I was innocent.'

*

Adding to the immense stress of an impoverished McAvennie as he battled to save his name was the knowledge that his beloved father and guiding light, Bernard, had been diagnosed with cancer and was dying.

'If I had been found guilty, I would have been a bitter man. My dad died after that was all over and if I had gone away, I wouldn't have seen much of him before that. He was a huge influence on me. When my dad died, my mum basically died a little bit as well. I was the only one she would let in the house to stay. We were close. My niece, my sister and my brothers weren't allowed to stay. I was the only one who had a bedroom. They came down to see me when I was in prison and they wrote me a letter. They knew I was daft, but that I wasn't wrapped up in all that. It's in the past for me now.'

In the years since, he has been forced to reassess the company he keeps.

'The Glasgow police thought I was in with Tam McGraw and Paul Ferris. But I never met McGraw before he died – not once. I know Paul, but where's the crime there? I'm a Glasgow boy. What I felt was that I was deemed guilty by association. That shouldn't be right should it? You shouldn't be hauled up in court on trumped-up charges because of who you know should you? I would never walk past anyone – I don't care what they do. I don't judge a book by its cover.

'But after all that I did start to feel I was sailing too close to the wind. That's why I will never go back to Glasgow to live. I'm down here in Newcastle now and that suits me.'

There were some who feared the worst for McAvennie in his blackest hour. For the first time, those of us who believed he was essentially a rakish Jack-the-lad were forced to consider whether something blacker and more sinister resided in the soul of one of Scottish football's favourite sons. As a hard-living, free-loving footballer earning huge money in London, his moral compass had slipped off course.

Prompted and encouraged by wife Karen, the former Scotland striker set about rebuilding his life and reputation. The former, one suspects, will always be a simpler task than the latter.

'I don't go out anywhere near as much now,' he states baldly. 'I was in the Premier League when it came to drinking long after I finished playing. But I had a scare a couple of years ago when they found a wee shadow in my lung. Luckily it was just an infection, but I'll tell you what – it gives you a wake-up call. I just said, "Enough."

'If I hadn't done that, I wouldn't have lasted too much longer. My liver was gone, I was smoking too much. And that was it. I came to Gateshead to get away because I couldn't go back to Glasgow or London. They were becoming too small for me.

'Within a short time of being here, I met my current missus and that was it. I got my act together. So now I've cut out most of the drinking. I also stopped the fags three years ago. I still have the odd night out, but I could never see myself going back to the way I was.'

And yet in January 2009 another brush with the law ended in a four-month suspended sentence when a night out on the Isle of Man with teammates from a Liverpool veterans game ended in a headbutt being aimed at a local with a high nuisance value.

'I've never been a fighter or in trouble for that kind of thing before. I will talk to anyone, but there was a boy who had a go at Andy Goram, who was also over for the game.

'Then he had a go at Paul Walsh, the former Liverpool player. Six hours later, he was still hanging about and by then you don't know what he's going to do. For all we knew, he had a knife or something.

'So as soon as he came at me when words were spoken I had to be ready. Things went off a bit. He bit me and I had to be seen by a doctor – and they charged me the cost of the consultation. That hurt as much as the bite marks.

'So, the Isle of Man is a nice place and so on. But I'll never be back.

'A lot of the time, I will be somewhere and because of who I am something happens. If a fight started where we are sitting right now, I would get the blame for it, even if I was nothing to do with it. People just say, "Frank McAvennie was there", and folk nod. It's always my fault.'

Life changed irrevocably for Francis McAvennie, the boy from Milton, the night he met the king of blarney. In the 1980s, Terry Wogan was king of the chat show. BBC One at 7.30 p.m. on a

Monday, Wednesday and Friday was required viewing for the masses unwinding from a day at the coalface.

McAvennie, in the public consciousness, was a nobody. This observer can remember watching the programme in question with a curious fascination. Football followers all knew the player and admired his goalscoring talents. None of that provided an adequate explanation, however, for his appearance on *Wogan*. These were the days before the age of the celebrity footballer, flanked by the obligatory WAG. McAvennie was the top scorer in the English First Division at the time. With television and the Football League in financial dispute over highlights packages, however, the greater British public would have had more success identifying the elusive Charlie from *Charlie's Angels*. West Ham were emerging as genuine challengers to an all-conquering Liverpool team in the title race, but while McAvennie was matching his boyhood Celtic hero Kenny Dalglish in the goal charts, his beaming smile on scoring was witnessed only by the few.

As close to an accidental footballer as it's possible to find, McAvennie gained his break making up the numbers in a park game in Glasgow before being picked up by Johnstone Burgh juniors. Another of Macca's boyhood Parkhead heroes, Bertie Auld, rejected the chance to sign him for Partick Thistle. St Mirren manager Jim Clunie took advantage and a decision to train full-time on part-time wages paid generous dividends. By 1985, English clubs were taking an interest. Luton Town were the first to bite, until the condescending attitude of chairman David Evans – a Tory MP – drove the unimpressed working-class kid from north Glasgow into West Ham's arms for a fee of £340,000. It was a match forged in heaven.

'I scored twenty-nine goals in one season for West Ham,' he recalls, eyes dancing in recollection. 'You look at Fernando Torres and what he's worth and you think, I scored as many as him. I had a fantastic first season, I loved it every time I went on the park. I always felt safe, because no one could touch me there. I went out and I was all smiles. No one could ever criticise me for my effort levels. People were always taking pot shots at me from outside the game for the other stuff going on, but when I put on a pair of boots they couldn't get near me.'

Homesickness threatened to make the stay in London a brief one. McAvennie's great friend Mo Johnston had quit Elton John's Watford to return to Celtic, and this lifelong Hoops fanatic had a fancy for joining him in the early months. A team-bonding trip to Stringfellows nightclub via the Slater's Arms in Romford changed everything. Girlfriend Anita Blue moved down from Glasgow and agent Bill McMurdo negotiated incremental increases in his client's pay for every landmark reached. As the goals flowed, so did the £20 notes. Most of them into Peter Stringfellow's pockets, via an assortment of skimpy G-Strings.

It was in London's infamous club that the Frank McAvennie legend simply exploded 24 hours after his appearance on *Wogan*.

'Things changed overnight. There was no *Match of the Day* on the Beeb, so we were trying different ways to get my profile up. I did a photo shoot with Dirty Den of *Eastenders* that made all the papers.

'I was the top scorer in the country and nobody knew who I was. Saint and Greavsie took me out on the streets of London to see if anybody recognised me. Even West Ham fans were struggling.

'So I did *Wogan* with Denis Law one night. I was colour co-ordinated in all my Cartier gear and so on and he's sitting there with a pair of cords on. He turned up with a hole in his shoes and he only had one pair on him. He tried to put his leg over so nobody would see and told me to give him a nudge if the hole was showing. I said, "No problem."

'But half of Britain were watching and just before we went on he said to me, "Don't worry, wee man, there's only 20 million people watching at home."

' "Worry?" I says to him. "It's no' me that's got a hole in my shoe."

'But the following night I went to Stringfellows for a Saturday out as usual and a friend of mine called Margot Mitchell was the photographer in there. As I was dancing around pissed, bottle in hand, she came to me, tugs my arm and says, "Frank, folk want to see you outside".

'I said, "What do you mean?"

'Turns out the paparazzi were all out there muttering something about me being on *Wogan* last night. I hadn't realised the impact it had made.

'Me and Anita Blue, my girlfriend of the time, were smuggled out with coats over our head and hijacked a limousine outside waiting for an Arab sheikh or something. The driver was a bit pissed off when he learned we were going to Essex.

'But suddenly things were getting a bit silly. On the Sunday, I went to Heathrow to meet my mum, who was flying from Glasgow via London to Australia to see my brother. I said I would meet her at the airport and there were queues forming for my autograph. For two hours I was stuck there.

'But, you know, it didn't bother me. I loved the fans and I never refused an autograph. Even now I just do it, whatever I'm up to.'

The most welcome autograph hunters were generally blonde and female. In the backrooms of nightclubs, desks were cleared of paperwork by McAvennie's direct seduction technique, while even his introduction to international football proved to be a useful tool for meeting the opposite sex. Called into the Scotland squad for a 1985 World Cup play-off double-header against Australia, the striker scored in a 2–0 first-leg win at Hampden. He admits to scoring again before the return game; a visit to a dentist Down Under ending in the administration of oral treatment of a different kind from a receptionist in a white gown. By his testimony, there was little need thereafter for an anaesthetic. Later, a nightclub fracas over a woman began with McAvennie and Mo Johnston at the heart of the mayhem. Long before he became a 'Sir', caretaker manager Alex Ferguson was reduced to Anglo-Saxon language in response.

The domestic season ended with West Ham narrowly losing the title to Liverpool and Gary Lineker – a man McAvennie has precious little time for – pipping the Scot to the Golden Boot award.

A trip to the World Cup Finals in Mexico was compensation of sorts, Rod Stewart assuming the role of mine host to his fellow countrymen on social occasions. For McAvennie, however, playing for his country was an unfulfilling experience. For a man of his industry, superb scoring and crossing ability and remarkable touch, five caps and one goal were a measly return.

'I was part of a great era for Scottish strikers. We had me, Charlie Nic, Mo Johnston and Ally McCoist. Can you imagine having that now? My biggest regret is I never got more caps. I only got five – Kevin Kyle ended up getting more than me. It was just ridiculous.

'I went to a World Cup in 1986 with Fergie, but then Andy Roxburgh took over. And I wasn't one of Andy's boys – I refused to pull my socks up to my knees and all that kind of stuff.

'We went from Kenny Dalglish and Graeme Souness to that in a short space of time. I shared a room with Graeme and when he and Kenny were playing it was a joy.

'But then under Roxburgh, you started wondering to yourself, "Where is this team going?" It was starting to feel like a job playing for Scotland. It was all, "Do this and do that." There were guys like Willie Miller and big Eck McLeish at the back and we had the basis of a great team. But me and big Richard Gough finished about the same time. I played my final game in Saudi Arabia, and coming back on the plane I decided that was it. I was never any good at school, so the headmaster Roxburgh didn't much fancy me.

'Then Craig Brown came in – a man who relegated Clyde twice, and here he was as international manager. What had he done to earn that?'

At club level, the man with the distinctive peroxide hairdo had a healthier regard for his guiding lights. John Lyall at West Ham adopted an avuncular air to handling his more wayward players, of which McAvennie was commander-in-chief.

As the plates holding together his relationship with Anita Blue drifted apart, Page Three stunnas such as Maria Whittaker and Sam Fox provided platonic comfort. They also introduced McAvennie to Jenny Blyth, an ambitious celebrity wannabe. An inability to understand her football suitor's gruff Glasgow accent was no impediment to a mutually beneficial relationship. McAvennie was, by now, on £1,500 a week – yet was irked by the lack of a signing-on fee every time he signed a new deal at West Ham. The issue came to a head with a £750,000 move to Celtic. A cut in pay led to an agreement concerning a tax-free signing-on fee being drawn up on a hotel napkin.

Becoming closer to Blyth, McAvennie was torn by the move, yet vindicated his agreement by claiming a League and Cup double in

Celtic's Centenary season – though not without another of his legal interludes.

'You can't take away what we did at Celtic in that Centenary season. I do dinners with big Billy McNeill. I keep winding him up by telling him that if he'd bought me three days earlier we'd have won the treble!

'They were knocked out the League Cup on the Wednesday and went out and bought me for £750,000 on the Friday. Big Richard Gough signed for Rangers in the morning then I pitched up at Parkhead in the afternoon.

'Things just clicked that season. Wee Joe Miller arrived after me and something just happened. It was simple really, we had a good team, that was it.

'It didn't matter what else was going on off the park, it had no effect. At West Ham, John Lyall had been like a second dad to me, he was different class. He never fined me once.

'Under big Billy it was one long fine. He fined me every week. But different managers have different methods. John was great and seemed to love me, and deep down big Billy was just the same.

'The papers were never done saying I was out on a Friday night. Ach, I never went out on a Friday night. Garbage. It was all over the place one day before a game against Morton at Cappielow that I'd been living it up all night.

'I went out and scored four and big Billy turned to me afterwards and said, "Listen son, I don't care if you go out on a Friday night. Whatever you're doing you'd better keep doing it!"

'But I don't care what anyone says. I will sit here now and tell you I never went out two days before a game. Never, ever.'

He did once miss training for a whole week. At the behest of the Procurator Fiscal, however, the matter was non-negotiable.

McAvennie's Old Firm debut at Ibrox was the stuff of nightmares.

The Celtic star became involved in one of Scottish football's most preposterous spats, surviving just 17 minutes before being dismissed. Going in late on Rangers goalkeeper Chris Woods, the striker received a forearm smash and a push for his trouble. Staggering backwards he was then punched weakly by Graeme Roberts before

Ibrox skipper and England international Terry Butcher stepped in, pushing the Celtic star – who crumpled to the deck. McAvennie and Woods were instantly dismissed, while Butcher would follow later for another offence. A media frenzy resulted in Strathclyde Police seizing a tape of the incident from Scottish Television. Weeks later, the four stars were ordered to report to Govan Police Station to be charged with conduct likely to provoke a breach of the peace. Celtic had to be dragged kicking and screaming into hiring a top-class advocate to represent their star player. The move paid off when McAvennie escaped censure in a week-long charade of a trial heard by Sheriff Archibald McKay. The Rangers players were less fortunate. Butcher was found guilty and fined £250, Woods guilty and fined £500 and Graeme Roberts Not Proven.

'When Robbo got found "Not Proven" he didn't know what it meant,' laughs McAvennie. 'I said to him, "It means you got aff wi' it."

'Woodsie still says to me that I started it and got off with it. But, ach, I've never had a problem with any of those lads. We get on well.

'It was unbelievable really. How can you get a criminal record for that? It was embarrassing. Only in Scotland could that happen. It was a week off training. I turned up on the Friday when it was over and the boys were preparing to play Hearts. They gave me a round of applause when I walked back in.'

Celtic had the last laugh. A 2–1 victory on their next trip to Ibrox effectively sealed the title and the formalities were wrapped up with a 3–0 thrashing of Dundee on 23 April 1988, before a crowd of 60,000 going on 80,000. Weeks later, McAvennie confirmed his value by scoring a late double to overcome Dundee United in the Scottish Cup final. Celtic, inspired by their superb striker, had done the double.

'All the other stuff thrown at me takes away from the footballer I was,' he states with as close to a wistful expression as he will ever get. 'I don't know if that's a regret, it's not really . . .

'You look at the money the players make these days and the punters think you made the same. But what they are making is phenomenal. The most I ever made from a contract was £2,500 a week. But then I would get a lump sum signing-on fee that, in effect, made it up to £4,000 or £5,000 a week. I got that when I went to Celtic. I got a signing-on fee and just over £200,000 a year. It was great money and it helped to pay off all my ex-girlfriends.'

London continued to hold substantial sway, however. As Billy McNeill used to observe, the fastest thing he ever witnessed at Parkhead was the sight of his star striker heading for the 6.15 p.m. shuttle to Heathrow on a Saturday night after a game.

In the media, the talk was of McAvennie being desperate to return to Jenny Blyth's side in the Big Smoke. The man himself insists his ultimate gripe with Celtic was financial rather than personal. The improvised agreement drawn up to make his signing-on fee tax-free had been reneged upon. Incredibly, the former striker insists that Graeme Souness wanted to take him direct from Parkhead to Rangers in his second season – a request for a £1 million signing-on fee proving a deal breaker. Not to mention McAvennie's reluctance to play for the Ibrox club.

Arsenal also wanted to spirit Macca out of Paradise. Bizarrely, however, the striker opted to return to West Ham and became engaged to Blyth the same week. John Lyall's departure, injuries and Lou Macari's arrival as manager gave sustenance to an old adage however. In football, as in life, you should never go back.

By 1989, McAvennie had become a tabloid staple. He had also sampled cocaine for the first, if not the last, time. Lucrative topless pictures, centre spreads and invitations to the opening of an envelope; no reasonable offer was declined. In every sense, his life had become a tale of excess. Though not, he insists, when he was fit enough to kick a ball.

'Look, how could I have done what I did as a football player if I had really been up to all the stuff I was supposed to have done? I played until I was 36 – it would have been impossible if I had been as bad as they said before matches and so on.

'Sure, there were plenty of things I could and should have done differently. But I did plenty right as well.

'The biggest fault of the modern player these days is that they earn too much money and they distance themselves from the supporters.

To fans, the football is their life. I know, because I was just a fan before I stumbled into junior football. So I was privileged and I knew I was. I would go to supporters' awards dos without complaint; players don't do that now.

'When I go now I get paid for them, because I have to make a living. So I still go to a few. It's fine when you can go and get pissed for a night, how bad can that be?'

Even Rangers supporters now regard a former hate figure with some degree of warmth and affection. The animosity which used to see the striker duck from a shower of spittle and phlegm as he left the Ibrox tunnel has dissipated. As the religious barriers have broken down at UEFA's insistence, so have some of the old taboos.

'I've done after-dinner talks in Masonic halls,' he states in an eyebrow-raising admission. 'They had a toast to the queen before dinner and that was no problem to me – if someone wants to pay me I'll raise a glass to anything.

'Actually, myself and big Billy McNeill did a night in a Masonic hall with a couple of ex-Rangers players. That was last year and big Billy gave them a description of the European Cup – because none of those boys would know what it looked like. It went down well, to be fair, they were jammed in the aisles.'

Speaking engagements pay well and, he insists, play to his natural strengths.

'I've got this thing where I feel I can't do what folk would call normal work. I can't go and stack shelves in Tesco. And could you imagine me taxi driving in Glasgow? I know a lot of ex-players go down that road and I'm sure a lot of it is great. But there are all sorts of reasons why I couldn't do it. I'd be getting a slap every night and constant attention from folk coming into the car drunk and so on. It would be all, "I was a better player than you McAvennie." So I have to keep doing something else.'

For McAvennie, however, some constants remain. The fidgeting is relentless, while an ability to laugh through thick and thin has been integral to this uproarious Glaswegian's sanity. When the bulk of Scots are sniggering at your fictional antics on national television every New Year's Eve, an appreciation for the absurdities of life helps.

When comedian Jonathan Watson attributed the 'Wherez the Burdz?' catchphrase to one of football's most lovable rogues on *Only An Excuse*, the man himself was bewildered, yet quietly flattered. His mother Jean invariably spent Hogmanays behind the sofa, while the former Scotland striker could only ponder how much money Watson was making from lampooning a lady-killer reputation honed to perfection.

That the character remains integral to the show's popularity some 14 years since McAvennie last kicked a ball in competitive anger is testament to his staying power. These days, confused onlookers wonder just who is the real Frank McAvennie – and who is the parody?

'Jonny Watson has helped to keep me in the limelight,' he says with a grin. 'He goes to dinners as me and charges them £5,000. I go to dinners and take between £500 and £1,000. But, ach, I don't grudge him it. I enjoy *Only An Excuse*. Jonny just seems to love doing it, he can't get away from it now.

'One of the papers had a pop at him, saying the kids these days don't know who Frank McAvennie is. Well, that's just nonsense. Let's face it, there are times that I've kept myself in the papers without anyone else's help.'

Not always, it should be said, for the best reasons.

'I took my young son to the Time Capsule in Coatbridge,' he recalls, 'and, honestly, it was like a tsunami wave in the pool as folk came at me. I was becoming claustrophobic. And that was all kids.'

Also dipping his toe back into the world of football agency work, McAvennie admits that restless energy has always been his gravest enemy. Sticking at the one pursuit has never been a strong point.

'I was involved in a company which looks after football players once before, but the guy I was working with quit, telling everyone he was off to be a millionaire. It just didn't work. I can find them like no one else can't I?

'But I'm enjoying it now. We've a few good young Celtic and Rangers players in the company I'm working with and hopefully they will make it. We also have about five internationals from the Scotland team so we are doing all right.

'I'm playing a bit of golf, spending more time with the wife and I'm enjoying life. It's good at the moment.'

Son Jake is a regular visitor to the couple's Gateshead home and the little boy's father remains inordinately proud of his child from the marriage to Laura McArthur.

'My boy did two weeks on the front page of the *Daily Record*, posing for publicity for a Panini football cards promotion they had on the go. He's doing the modelling for that stuff now. He's a looker, but I don't know where he gets it – it's certainly not from me. He will be all right when he gets over his shyness . . . that's one thing he has got from me. But he's a well-mannered kid and I'm proud of him. Considering who his dad is, he's turning out well.'

Young Jake can still see his old fella kicking a ball in his fiftieth year. McAvennie adopts a policy of 'have boots will travel' to all of those who covet his services.

The Masters series for legendary former stars has become a semi-lucrative business, enjoying annual coverage on Sky Sports and beyond. The Scot has graced the colours of clubs he never played for, so keen is he to relive former glories.

It's the green-and-white of Celtic that remains his first love, however, and the players from the Centenary season remain close.

'A group of us are going over to Ireland after St Patrick's Day for a veterans game against Liverpool. I'll have to get myself fit for that. Wee Joe Miller has also been on the phone because he wants me to go over for a game in Dundalk. It's great fun and the boys get paid for it; plus they all love a night out.'

His still-slender figure may not move with the same industry or guile of yore, yet Frank McAvennie has little option but to remain quick on his feet; keeping out of trouble is a pursuit which requires some fast footwork. The Isle of Man scrape, he insists, was the last brush with the law. And he means it.

'I did a lot of daft things and made a lot of mistakes. But I think I've come out a better person. I pick my friends these days – they no longer pick me. There will always be someone willing to take a pop, but I think I'm wiser for them now.'

10

The Idle Idol
ANDY RITCHIE

'Jock Stein took us out to the field where there was a
practice match between two teams of 14–16 year olds. He
nudged me, "What do you think of that striker?" – a big
fellow called Ritchie who is on the ground staff, he is 15
and stands an impressive 6ft 1in. Already at this age he is
John Charles, gentle in his play, accurate and creative in
his passing and on the run his great stride devours
ground.'

– John Rafferty, the *Observer*, 14 May 1972

Andy Ritchie is in a cavernous bar, leaning forward on a brown
leather sofa, pondering the price of vice.

Unlike George Best, there are no Miss Worlds or drained champagne bottles by way of consolation or explanation. Only empty
dreams and a hatful of regrets over the drinking, gambling, loose
words and psychological flaws that plagued a career less decorated
than it might have been.

When people ask, he makes no attempt to apply what he describes
as 'two coats of white paint' to his shortcomings.

'I read the books and some players do that,' he says. 'What you see
with me is what you get. I don't suffer regrets every day any longer,'
he states, before pausing for effect. 'Only every second day.'

In the aftermath of the disastrous World Cup odyssey of Argentina 1978, Scottish football was cast into a vast reservoir of doubt
and depression. This unlikely Morton cult hero had the ball placed at
his feet.

He could make it sing, dance and jump through hoops. Caressing and commanding a football was never the problem. It was controlling himself which posed the gravest challenge to a potentially dazzling career.

The top scorer in Scotland at 22, his reward was a Player of the Year accolade in 1979. To put the feat in context, Morton players don't win such awards. They do not even win such awards in Greenock, where a fleet of Celtic and Rangers buses head for Glasgow every Saturday. Scottish football was, for a time, enthralled by Ritchie's repertoire of free-kicks, languid creativity and close control.

Yet within four years, burgeoning resentment at the £1 million transfer fee on his head manifested itself in rampant indiscipline. By 1985, at the age of 28, Ritchie was finished with playing football.

Spells as a scout at Celtic, Aston Villa and Derby County recreated a spark, yet when the work dried up the personal problems multiplied. In 2006, his life torn asunder by divorce, financial difficulties and family strife, Ritchie was effectively homeless, turning to residential help following a breakdown.

'My career and my life have been a major let-down,' he says frankly between cigarette breaks and pints. 'Not only to me, but to many others as well.

'By allowing my career to end so soon, I failed my family, especially my two sons, Mark and Stephen. I was never living the life of a professional athlete; I was never leading by example.

'I knew two years after I finished playing – some time around 1985 – and had gone to London to work as assistant secretary in the Barbican Centre what I had done. It was office and leisure work, a good steady job with a solid income.

'But it wasn't scoring goals. I woke up one morning and started suffering one of the panic attacks I've taken all my adult life. The game was up, I couldn't do it anymore. I knew there and then I wouldn't kick a ball as a professional again.'

In the years after his playing career ended, this exponent of the Brazilian free-kick and toothy grin reinvented himself. Successful spells coaching the kids at Hamilton and St Mirren resulted in a return to his first club Celtic at the dawn of the Tommy Burns era. Burns and Ritchie had been close colleagues and friends since the age of 15, yet allowed their relationship to cool significantly prior to the former's death at the age of 51 in May 2008. A final failure to paper over their differences remains another of Ritchie's litany of regrets.

Also a servant to Wim Jansen and Dr Jo Venglos, the subsequent Celtic managers, before falling foul of the Kenny Dalglish regime, Ritchie was prone to bouts of depression. In contrast with his early years in football, life has never been easy for this most likeable of characters.

Born in Calderbank, Lanarkshire on 23 February 1956, older brother Liam and younger sister Jan completed a respectable working-class family who, like most in the west of Scotland, holidayed doon the watter in resorts such as Saltcoats and Rothesay. His father, Andrew senior, worked for Rolls-Royce and took his sons to watch Motherwell. There was nothing in his upbringing, Ritchie insists, which would explain the self-destructive traits of later years.

These days, he's remembered through a sepia-tinted haze as an overweight and lazy individual, prone to brilliance on regular occasions. It sounds harsh, yet the reminiscences are fond and accompanied by laughter lines around the eyes. Few, however, realised that behind the permed hair and loose-cannon demeanour lay a man wrestling a variety of demons.

'I was a sick young pup,' he concedes now with startling frankness. 'I suppose I have always had what you might describe as an addictive personality.

'When I was at the top of my game I didn't handle it all properly. I socialised, I partied, I had a good crack at the whip. Too much for my own good.

'I not only cheated myself, I also cheated a lot of other good people as well. I drank too much, I smoked too much and I liked a blow of hash on the odd occasion. It wouldn't be uncommon for me to be blind drunk on a Friday night before a game against

Rangers or Celtic, nursing a raging hangover as kick-off approached.

'I kept bad time, I was cheeky, I didn't try terribly hard. We were always told at Morton to report to the Tontine Hotel in Greenock on a match day for our pre-match meal. The manager Benny Rooney would stand at the top of the steps waiting for me.

'Meanwhile I'd be sneaking in a window at the back of the building, taking my seat and waiting for him coming back to the table where I'd protest my innocence. He would fine me, but on the Monday I would just go to the chairman Hal Stewart and threaten to leave if there was a penny missing from my wages the next week.

'I played the emotional blackmail card shamelessly.'

For much of his married life with ex-wife Rena, Ritchie lived in Viewpark, Uddingston. His house was a mile or so from the home of the late Jimmy Johnstone, a senior teammate in his ground staff days as the next big thing at Celtic. In contrast with Jinky, any chance Jock Stein had of prolonging Ritchie's career beyond its natural shelf life disappeared when his young protégé inexplicably rejected a four-year contract to join Morton in October 1976. Even now he asks himself why.

'Before he died in 1996, my father said often that I could have done more in the game. In my younger days he would come home from watching the game I had played and the conversation would always go the same way.

' "How did he do today, Dad?" my mother would ask.

' "Ach," was the standard reply, "He never moved about and he was hopeless."

'My old maw would come back with, "Aye, but how many did he score?"

'And with a scowl my dad would say, "Just the two."

' "Just the two?" she would exclaim, "he must have done something right."

' "Aye," my old man would say, "but he could have done mair."

'My dad was a man of few words, but he had a talent for nailing the truth to the wall with one line.'

Encouraged by his father to attend a Middlesbrough open trial on a Sunday afternoon in Cumbernauld at the age of 14, Ritchie turned up with two friends and was hauled off after 20 minutes.

Not until later did he learn that 'Boro coach Harold Sheperdson had been trying to stop scouts from other clubs muscling in on this young talent.

He failed. By the Tuesday of that week, Rangers, Celtic, Manchester United, Coventry and 'Boro all declared an interest.

By his own admission, Ritchie had given precious little thought to becoming a professional footballer. All of that changed in the course of a March week that had his father checking the calendar to make sure it wasn't 1 April.

Training with Rangers on a Tuesday and Celtic on a Thursday, Ritchie signed an S-form with Jock Stein's Celtic and joined the Boys' Club in 1971.

Lifelong friend Tommy Burns was on a ground staff of five, and before his untimely death from cancer at the age of 51, Burns went on to manage Celtic, employing his erstwhile teenage colleague as the chief scout. Yet in the 1970s, Ritchie was the older and more regarded of the duo. Where he went the shorter, thinner Burns would go also. The duo would clean boots and changing rooms in the morning before running along London Road to Tommy's grandmother's house in Calton's Soho Street. Raised in the shadow of his beloved Celtic Park, Burns would lead the way, the two teenagers running, sweating and hungry, past the local dairy to a warm welcome, where tea and jam sandwiches would always await. Tending to the needs of his ailing grandfather, the young Burns showed the sensitivity that would be his trademark in later years.

'The old fella would see imaginary spiders and rats in the bed and would cry out, "Thomas, Thomas!" And Tommy would pull back the cover, lift his old legs carefully and remove the imagined rat to make his grandpa feel that bit better about things,' Ritchie recalls.

Lunch over, the pair would race back along London Road in their green training gear and white socks where reserve coach Willie Fernie would administer the afternoon's tasks.

One of the jobs was always to play table tennis with the legendary manager, Jock Stein. Burns and Ritchie would take advantage of Stein's pronounced limp to play sneaky low shots they believed the heavier set man could never hope to reach.

'The big face would glower at you if you beat him. He was a tippy-tappy fancy sort of player who tried to hide the ball. He'd have the jacket off, with his big braces showing over his shirt, and Sean Fallon, his assistant, would come in to watch.

'If he won a game it was all, "Next! Come on Tommy, your turn to take a hammering, son." It was all roaring and laughing, great fun.'

If defeat was never compulsory, then it was occasionally advisable. Those who confronted Stein's insatiable will to win would be hauled back at the end of the afternoon for a rematch. Only the foolhardy dared to win twice.

Ritchie won his share of ping-pong challenges but always believed, nevertheless, that he was being groomed for stardom.

Few players, not even the famous Quality Street Gang of gifted reserve team stars who preceded his emergence, were handed first-team debuts at 17.

Over time, however, the relationship changed and progress slowed.

'If truth be told, the real problems for me began when I made the Celtic first team,' he recalls. 'I was named on the bench for the last game of 1973 against Dunfermline. What the manager hadn't told me was that I would come on as a substitute for Billy McNeill. I never realised Jock Stein would take off the captain of the Lisbon Lions to put me on.

'People thought, "Geez, this must be some player, this kid." The minute the substitute's board went up, I could virtually hear a collective intake of breath. After it the big man simply said, "Well done." Nothing more. But that was enough for me.'

Prior to our meeting, Ritchie had been reminded by his brother Liam of the day football ceased to be an easy ascent. An ageing Bobby Charlton humiliated his younger opponent as player-manager of Preston North End for 70 minutes in a pre-season friendly.

There were highlights, including the winner in a 2–1 victory over Aberdeen at Pittodrie. Yet Ritchie's Old Firm debut would prove a pivotal moment in curtailing his Celtic appearances to just 10 starts. A golden chance presented itself to beat Rangers keeper Peter McCloy with the Ibrox side winning 2–1. The ball stuck fortuitously between the towering goalie's legs.

'My problems started before then,' states Ritchie, 'the moment Jock signed a guy by the name of Atholl Henderson from St Johnstone for a fee of £35,000. He started to play this guy in the reserve team before me. And that was when I developed an attitude; a distinctly bad attitude.

'Atholl Henderson was a lovely fella – but he wasn't a tenth of the player I was. Atholl played no more than two games for the first team by my recollection. But one thing became clear; he had quickly gone beyond me in the pecking order and I didn't like it.

'"How could they do that to me?" became my mantra. What I should have been saying was, "Excuse me, Atholl, you're on my turf", whilst elbowing him aside.

'Morton had come in for me in October 1976 for a few thousand quid and a drop in wages. I had developed the bad attitude with bells on by then. How can I put this? I was a cheeky, arrogant idiot.

'I remember the day Jock phoned me to tell me Morton had come in for me. It was a Wednesday and I was on a day off at home in the flat Rena and I had in Cumbernauld.

'It was before 9 a.m. and I picked up the phone. It was Jock Stein growling at me.

'"You not out your fucking bed yet? Get your big fat arse into Celtic Park," he said, without so much as a hello first. "You said the other day you wanted to move. I might be able to help you."'

Ritchie arrived to find Hal Stewart, chairman of Morton, sitting beside Cappielow goalkeeper Roy Baines, a makeweight in a proposed player-plus-cash deal. Astonishingly, Celtic would actually pay money for Baines, rather than the reverse.

Ritchie retired to the legendary Joe's Kitchen greasy spoon cafe in London Road, close to Celtic Park, to talk the deal over with the Morton chairman and his wife.

'Hal gave the same chat to everybody. A good salesman gives the same pitch time after time with the same degree of enthusiasm. So I don't think he saw anything in me to any great degree. I was just another body he could get in for a few quid and sell on for a few more. It wouldn't have mattered if I was Andy Ritchie the footballer or Hercules the Bear.

'If Hal saw a couple of quid in you, the world was your oyster. He would have been the ultimate Scottish agent, had there been such a thing at the time. But there was Rena drawing me daggers. Her views on the matter were clear. "You don't have to go," she was saying, kicking me under the table. "Stay at Celtic, we'll sort it out."

'So I went back to give Jock my answer and he surprised me.

' "I'll tell you what I'll do," he said to me. "There's a new four-year contract on the table here. If you sign it we'll start all over again fresh. All the stuff that's gone before will be in the past. You can get yourself back in and get fit and we'll say no more about it."

'There would have been no pay-rise in it for me. I'd still be on £40 a week – though if I got in the first team there would be more for me. They would sort out the bonuses and I would receive a £1,000 signing-on fee.

'But we never got to that stage. I wanted to play every week, score goals, make a name for myself and resurrect my career. I didn't want to sign up again and find myself in exactly the same position 12 months later. My mind was made up.

'Big Jock couldn't believe it. "Do you really want to go to that elephant's graveyard?" he asked me.

'But Haldane Y Stewart could sell sand to the Arabs and he'd convinced me I was the best player since Pele.'

Stewart may not actually have believed that much. Within two seasons, however, there were plenty around Greenock who did. Initially, the reception and first impressions were underwhelming. A leaking gas fire created the impression of a gas chamber in the old Cappielow main stand when the new signing arrived on the morning of his debut against a Clydebank side featuring the late Davie Cooper. An air of decay hung over Cappielow and circulated the corridors.

'I remember meeting my great boyhood hero, the former Mother-well striker John Goldthorpe, as I walked in.

' "Andy, what you doing down here?" he asked me.

' "I'm playing against Clydebank tonight, John," I replied.

' "You're whit?" he asked me. "What? Are you down on loan?"

' "Naw," I said, "I signed for Morton this afternoon."

' "What the f*** did you sign down here for?" he asked me. That wasn't the best of starts.

'But the real culture shock arrived on the Saturday, when we went to Love Street to play St Mirren, our greatest rivals. We lost 5–1 to a team managed by a certain Alex Ferguson. That Saturday night, I drove home saying to myself, You'd better get your finger out; you don't want to be hanging about here too blinkin' long.'

Yet when the goals started flowing with a double against Montrose the following Wednesday, including a trademark free-kick, Ritchie settled. So well, indeed, that within weeks Celtic – unbeknown to the great man himself – tried to take him back for £170,000.

'Had I known at the time, I would have created merry hell to secure my return to full-time football. It was only many years after I had finished as a football player that I even learned of the bid from Sean Fallon, Jock's old assistant.

'As part of the deal, Morton would be duty bound to clarify that I had only ever been on loan. It's difficult to explain in words how I felt about it years later. I just wish to Christ I had known at the time.

'I quickly realised at Morton that I had never really wanted to leave Celtic. But things had gone so far, relations had soured so badly, that I had to. I was putting pressure on myself to succeed and I had to get away, to reinvent myself.'

To a large extent, he succeeded brilliantly. After scoring the goals which took Morton to the Premier League in a season-and-a-half, Ritchie became that rarest of entities: a Player of the Year plying his trade outwith the Old Firm.

When he earned his accolade from the Scottish Football Writers' Association in the Albany Hotel, Glasgow on an April night in 1979, he was just 22. The pride he took from having his father and grandfather in the grand room that evening was palpable. By his own admission, however, the award prompted a downward spiral rather than an unstoppable ascent.

In the days before footballers enjoyed rock star status, the celebrity that followed was difficult for a young working-class man with an attitude and a healthy slice of self-conceit to absorb.

'Things began to change after that,' he recalls. 'I parked my car outside a primary school in Greenock one day and young boys were playing football in the playground. One of the lads scored a screamer past the obligatory fat kid in goals. And as I turned the lock in my car door, I heard the shout, "And Ritchie scores!" I thought he was taking the piss. He wasn't, the kid hadn't even seen me. But at that time my reputation was growing all over the place. I was being recognised everywhere I went, from Laurencekirk to Lochee.'

What had also changed was Ritchie's attitude. The good habits bred at Celtic had flown out of the window to be replaced by heavy drinking, major gambling and a 40-a-day nicotine addiction. By his own admission, he played many of his best – and worst – games nursing a hangover. Friday night sessions in the Windmill Tavern in Lanarkshire would be followed on Saturday morning by a panicked search for the family car, a missing wallet and a phone call to an obliging teammate to get him to Greenock for the pre-match meal, where manager Benny Rooney would be pacing around a hotel foyer checking his watch.

'I always remember Johnny Goldthorpe driving me to training at Morton one evening in our promotion season in 1978.

'Johnny was 32, had been a good pro and knew a thing or two. I had always looked up to him until the day he turned to me in the car and said, "You'll not last until you're 27 in this game."

'I was angry, furious in fact. I wasn't having that, not even from Johnny Goldthorpe. I was only in my early twenties at that time and I was flying. I was scoring goals, winning rave write-ups and was the best player in the country. What did this old fella know? Well, one thing he did know was the smell of drink – and I was in that car passenger seat steaming drunk. I'd been drinking all afternoon, and some of the morning as well. And that wasn't especially unusual for me. I'd still be stinking of drink when I played games. And somehow I was still scoring goals.

' "I'll do whatever the f*** I want," summed up my attitude best.

'Big Jock Stein had told me towards the end of my time at Parkhead – because I had begun to develop an opinion – that the best thing I could do was take the cotton wool out of my ears and shove it in my f****** mouth.

'Don't get me wrong, I enjoyed every minute of all that. I didn't do it to blot out any pain or any crap like that. But I saw no need to change. I had been boozing, gambling and doing whatever and we had still gone to the top of the league.'

Morton finished seventh in the Premier League that season, after leading before Christmas. Part-time football remained a constant despite promises from the chairman, Hal Stewart, to go full-time. To the more ambitious members of the playing staff, it was a betrayal.

Desperate to play for Scotland and increase basic earnings of £50 a week bolstered by a new contract and an afternoon job as a Morton Lottery Ticket salesman, however, Ritchie wanted out. With his gambling now out of control, he needed out.

'I bought a house in Mossend to celebrate signing a four-year deal. I was asked by the future Celtic director Brian Dempsey to open the show home. The homes were worth £25,000 – a king's ransom at the time. And Rena loved them, the soft furnishings and plush shag pile carpets were high fashion. There was cheese and wine and all that stuff. That day, Brian offered to sell me the house next door, fully fitted out with white goods and carpets and curtains, for a discounted price.

'I still put quite a substantial sum of money down on the house. But within 18 months we had to sell it to pay off my gambling debts. We moved back in with my mother-in-law.

'I also bought a Mercedes from the former Radio Clyde disc jockey and entertainer Mr Abie some years earlier. I remember getting a decent deal on it, it was a beautiful car.

'But I sold it six months later to a guy in Stirling for more money. I got there, collected the cash and was skint 24 hours later. I punted the lot. We were talking £6,000 – a lot of money at that time.

'I went for some help for it. So much so, that I was off the gambling for five years. But that was then.

'Hal made me chief sales agent with the Morton lottery. They upped my part-time playing salary by around £100 a week – but that incorporated afternoon work, taking lottery tickets to newsagents and working on the commercial side of the club. They had also given me £2,000 to sign a new four-year deal.

'There would be adverts in the local press urging locals to "Give Andy a Hand". But that was never enough. I wanted full-time football.'

If Stewart was an indulgent, avuncular figure to his most temperamentally challenged star player, then the paternalism was motivated to a large extent by self-interest.

The Morton chairman decided that he would accept not a penny less than £1 million for his prolific striker. Hearts, Sheffield Wednesday, Liverpool, Atlético Madrid, Leeds and Brian Clough's Nottingham Forest were all credited with an interest. The era of rising transfer fees was beginning in earnest and Clough would pay £1 million for Birmingham's Trevor Francis. All of which hardened Morton's resolve to hold firm when Ritchie was one of the nation's most coveted properties.

'I felt good when I won Player of the Year because Morton people who had never been invited to the dinner in their lives suddenly had a front row table,' Ritchie recalls. 'It changed my life in a sense, raising my profile to a new level. But I had no need to feel unworthy in any way. I *was* the best player in Scotland that season.

'I kept one of my mother's old maxims in mind at all times. Like the nose on front of your face, it's always in front of you. I believed something would happen for me that summer. Someone was eventually going to come along and take a chance on me. They had to.

'The worst thing that could have happened had precious little to do with me. The day Raymond Stewart became the most expensive teenager in British football, leaving Dundee United for West Ham for nearly half a million quid, was the day the pupils in Hal Stewart's eyes were replaced by pound signs.

'And Hal was quoted soon after as saying, "How can I sell a guy scoring 30 goals a season to an English club for less than that? This guy can entertain people and score goals. You can buy a full-back anywhere." Until they decided they wanted to move you on, you were their player. It was tantamount to slave labour.'

Inevitably, the chains which bound Ritchie to Morton bred resentment. In general, however, he has never sought to shift the blame for his demise onto the shoulders of others. Ritchie describes the aftermath of his award-winning feats as his lost 'Smirnoff Summer', when the drink flowed freely with the celebrity endorsements and invitations.

There were invitations to play darts with Jocky Wilson on television at the behest of his new personal sponsors, Tennent Caledonian Breweries. Opening shops and fêtes became a more acceptable pursuit between drinking sessions. To get to the events, Alexander's the Ford dealers in Greenock granted Morton's top player the use of a free car.

Billy Smart also asked Scottish football's new poster boy to open the Kelvin Hall Circus by kicking the ball to a performing elephant. The BBC, much to Ritchie's lingering embarrassment, captured the moment for posterity.

'I was being recognised wherever I went,' he laughs now with a bewildered shake of the head. 'The most bizarre example came in the 1980/81 season, a year or so after I'd reached my peak. Morton entered the old Anglo-Scottish Cup and were drawn against Notts County, a decent team at the time.

'I remember lying in my room in the Central Hotel in Nottingham waiting for the game that afternoon when I took a call from a friend of mine by the name of Bobby Galbraith.

'He came from Bellshill but had moved to the Nottingham area many years previous. I thought it was the usual, an old buddy crawling out the woodwork in the search for a match ticket.

'"Andy, how are you?" he asks.

' "Bobby," I replied, "I'm in my bed waiting for the game."

' "Aye, sorry, I won't keep you. What you doing after the game?"

'Now he was talking. We were staying down there after the match and travelling back up the next morning. If Bobby wanted to come round for a beer or something to eat, then great. "I'm bringing a pal with me Andy, he wants to meet you."

' "Not a problem, Bobby, I'll get you a couple of tickets sorted out for the game and then I'll see you back here."

'So we played the game and I was having one of those wild and wonderful evenings I seemed to specialise in at that time. Everything was coming off for me, every flick, every pass. Afterwards, I showered and changed and went to meet Bobby at the main reception where this guy was standing beside him with crêpe-soled shoes, luminous socks, a long Teddy-boy jacket and a frilly shirt with a bootlace tie.

'Turns out it was Dave Bartram, the lead singer of Showwaddy-waddy, who spent every week in the Top 10 at the end of the 1970s. Dave was Bobby's pal and was desperate to meet me.

'I struggled to get my head round this. All right, the guy wasn't Rod Stewart or Bowie, but this fella was never off *Top of the Pops*. They were big-time. And yet here was the lead singer standing waiting to meet me like an autograph hunter. I felt it should have been the other way round.

'We drove from Nottingham to Leicester to get a curry, had a drink, had a laugh and smoked a bit of dope. Eventually, Dave took me back to the team hotel at 6 a.m. We had a great night and he was all over me like a cheap suit. He told me how he had heard all about my reputation up the road and had seen my goals and read all about me. As this pop star told me all this, I remember thinking to myself, You've cracked it now, big boy!'

The father of Radio Clyde DJ George Bowie, an impresario and promoter called Ross Bowie, had also been in touch concerning some showbiz engagements. Comedian Andy Cameron and DJ Mr Abie were on his books and his acts dominated the bill at Glasgow's Pavilion Theatre.

'I came from a background where that kind of thing was regarded as a bit poncey. But I took on the odd gig or two when I was hot in publicity terms. Red Rum came up to officially open the Tote Bookmakers in Port Glasgow and Greenock. For winning the Grand National three times, the horse's owners were being paid £500 appearance money. I was getting £400 for appearing alongside – three times my weekly wage at the time.

'Another thing I took on was when the Radio Clyde DJ Tiger Tim Stevens and me would go to local schools where he would play music and I would tell the kids how to behave. At that time, I'm not certain I was the best example to anyone.'

Ritchie was by now drinking more than ever. A three-month bender would result in a frantic Morton chairman rushing his new superstar to Stobo Castle spa resort in the Scottish Borders in order to shift a stone-and-a-half in weight before the new season's opener against Celtic at Parkhead.

'I had ballooned up to 16-and-a-half stones by the time pre-season weigh-ins were taken. I couldn't lose a pound due to my extra-curricular activities. I had two weeks to get in shape, and I was in distinguished company. Lulu was staying there at the time. And so was Joan Collins with her husband Ron Kass, the president of Apple Records during the heyday of the Beatles.

'The German physio I was assigned had been a champion sprinter. He would hammer me every afternoon and evening in training and see to it that I dieted and had all the appropriate treatments. From jacuzzis to foot scrubs, I had the lot. If I threw a pair of underpants down on the floor, they would be returned to me washed and ironed before I had the chance to pick them up.

'I had been on what might best be described as a bender that summer. I went on holiday a few times and spent some time down at a caravan in Girvan on the Ayrshire coast we would use from time to time. All the while I was drinking heavily. The word would go out that Andy Ritchie was coming along to a session and suddenly folk would be on the phone. And their friends would come out to be there to be in my company. And they'd want to buy me a drink as well.

'I fell just short of my original target for weight loss after the first two weeks. But Stobo Castle worked in so much as I lost 17 pounds and returned to Cappielow in time to face Celtic at Parkhead.

'They looked at me when I walked into the dressing room as if I was ill. I looked gaunt. I should have scored a hat-trick at Parkhead that day. But to celebrate my freedom, I had a couple of glasses of red wine and a steak and salad in an Italian restaurant in Glasgow that night before being driven back to Stobo Castle in Hal's car to finish my course.

'Did it change me? Did it make me see the error of my ways or rethink my lifestyle? Naw, I just kept thinking, I'll go back to Stobo next season. And Morton will pay again. I drank too much because I enjoyed it. The circumstances of the time were that I was in demand for nights out and there were people more than happy to give me the booze for nothing. And when I had a good drink, the other vices followed.'

Remarkably, none of this dimmed Ritchie's scoring prowess. The Cappielow side improved on their inaugural placing in the Premier League, finishing sixth. They also reached the League Cup semi-final against a star-laden Aberdeen.

'In the semi-final, we prepared confidently enough, but we just froze.'

There was some measure of revenge for that defeat in the fourth round of the Cup in 1980/81, when Ritchie scored one of his best ever goals, turning Willie Miller and Alex McLeish – Scotland's central defensive partnership – this way and that before chipping the ball nonchalantly into the net beyond goalkeeper Jim Leighton.

After knocking out Scotland's most progressive team, managed by Alex Ferguson, it seemed that a trophy might be in the offing. When they reached the semi-final against Rangers, however, the lights were effectively switched off on Andy Ritchie's career.

To this day the pain of being excluded from the showpiece match by manager Benny Rooney visibly pains this one-time gentle giant of the game. It was, he concedes, an event which prompted an inexorable downward spiral.

'I remember us going to Largs a few days before the big game to prepare and escape the clamour for tickets. It hadn't been a great season. I had been up and down, performing at certain times and not at all at others. If I'm being blunt, then I have to admit that I kept my best performances for the television cameras coming.

'My drinking and gambling were as bad as ever. But I always seemed to be able to produce a big performance when the stakes were high. I thought and assumed I would be playing. When we came back to Greenock on the Friday, 24 hours before kick-off, we headed to Cappielow for a final training session.

'And down at the far side before the wee Dublin end, as they called one of the terraces, wee Benny called me over for a word.

' "You're not playing," were his exact words to me.

'I honestly thought he was taking the piss. "You're what?" I asked him.

' "I'm not going to play you," he said again. "I'm leaving you out and you're on the bench."

'Because the rest of the boys were there, I went back to training and decided against a scene. But when I got home in a black daze I told Rena and she was as shocked as me. None of us could take it in. Somehow I felt that he would see sense, that I would get the call in the morning and everything would be okay.

'I thought Benny was trying to provoke a reaction, trying to make me pull the finger out. I went to bed convinced it was a managerial masterstroke to make big Andy a Cup hero.

'But it wasn't. I got to Celtic Park where the semi-final was being played and nothing had changed. I was out. I felt like some form of pariah. Before the game I thought to myself that, even though I hadn't always been fair with Benny, even though I had been a complete prick, this was unforgivable.

'How could he forget where we had come from? When I arrived, Morton were second bottom of the First Division. I had averaged twenty-seven goals over four years and yet it had come to this.

'Benny said he wanted a more physical edge to our play and as time goes on he will probably tell people that he left me out for this reason or that reason. The bottom line was that he felt I wasn't doing enough. And if he had just come to me and said that man-to-man we could have discussed it.

'I suppose in my heart of hearts, I knew that the real problem lay with me and not Benny. I had problems I wasn't facing up to. Benny wouldn't have left me out the team if I had been behaving myself and playing well every week. From then on it was a downward spiral.'

Morton had been punching above their weight. The first provincial club to challenge the dominance of Glasgow's behemoths, they were in time overtaken by Aberdeen and Dundee United – led by the inimitable duo of Alex Ferguson and Jim McLean.

Under McLean, an acerbic character, the Tayside club won the league in 1983, the year Morton were relegated and Ritchie was finally released from his purgatory. Aberdeen, meanwhile, were storming to the European Cup Winners' Cup, overcoming Real Madrid on a rain-lashed night in Gothenburg.

Morton, by now, were a busted flush trying to figure out a way to break the news of Ritchie's departure to join his boyhood idols Motherwell without damaging season ticket sales.

A sense of disillusionment among both parties had become wholly mutual. In his final season, Ritchie's efforts were as sporadic as his goals. Former Rangers manager Jock Wallace, back in Scotland after a spell at Leicester City, figured that he might coax the old Idol back into life. With Wallace, a former Burmese jungle fighter, players knew precisely where they stood.

'I remember a pre-season game up north against a Highland League team. I played half an hour and was at the bar having a shandy with my teammate, Ian McLeod. Suddenly big Jock swept in, craned around the room and spotted my drinking buddy.

' "You were hopeless tonight, son," he says. Then Jock stuck the head on him. Just like that. Call it a Glasgow kiss, a headbutt, a stookie, whatever you like. Either way it was a hell of a blow straight to the bridge of Ian's nose. I had been at the club just four weeks and had never witnessed anything like it in my life. I checked if Ian was all right and as he raised his head he looked unshaken.

' "Ach, he's done it before," he told me. And we drank on as if nothing had happened.'

For Ritchie, there was also the classic Wallace pre-season initiation ceremony. Gullane Sands in East Lothian had been a traditional torture chamber for Rangers players ordered to run up and down Scotland's steepest dunes until vomiting was no longer avoidable. Pictures of prostrate players bent over double became commonplace in Scotland's newspapers.

'Bizarrely, I enjoyed the experience,' laughs Ritchie. 'I didn't feel terribly good afterwards. But it was always a PR exercise as much as a serious training stint. When I got there the photographers were already waiting for me.

'From Jock it was all, "Look who I've got here coming to Gullane with me, Scotland's laziest player." The gimmick value was obvious. We only went the once and never returned. The snappers got their pictures and that was that.'

Incredibly for a player held against his will for a ransom of £1 million by Hal Stewart in the halcyon days, an illuminating article in a Motherwell programme revealed his eventual transfer fee: £27,000.

At one point, Liverpool had been just £50,000 short of the fee Morton would have accepted for his transfer. When Ritchie finally did head for new pastures, therefore, everyone was a loser.

Not least the player himself, when Wallace returned to his first love, Rangers, for a second spell in charge.

The new Motherwell manager, Bobby Watson, ended one of his first training sessions by conducting a conversation with Ritchie that went thus.

Watson: 'Do you have a career outside the game?'

Ritchie: 'Naw, why?'

Watson: 'Because you won't play at this club for me. You are not the type of player I want here.'

As Ritchie recalls now, 'That was one hell of an opening gambit. Which prompted me to tell him he wasn't exactly my type of f****** manager.'

Watson, a successful businessman outside football, seemed to crave the attention of life as a frontline football manager.

To that end, Christmas 1985 brought a three-line whip from the manager, ordering players to bring their children to the club party, where he would be playing Santa.

Feeling less than assimilated with life at Fir Park, Ritchie left his sons Mark and Stephen at home. It would prove a costly decision, Watson withholding two weeks' wages in an act entirely devoid of festive goodwill. A final parting of the ways became inevitable and desirable for both parties.

After months of drinking binges and precious little training, Ritchie agreed to a request from Benny Rooney and Mick Jackson to play for Albion Rovers for a £40 fee. With unemployment in Margaret Thatcher's Britain sky high and work at a premium, there was little in the way of a decision to make.

'I was working in pubs, building sites, roads, whatever. For the family, it was a hand-to-mouth existence,' Ritchie recalls.

He scored on his debut and, when Rooney and Jackson left for Partick Thistle, was offered the job as manager whilst still in his mid-20s. Aside from handing a young Bernie Slaven his sea legs, however, here was a man unsuited to the discipline and demands of management.

By the age of 28, Ritchie was in London embarking upon a business diploma and working as a car park attendant to support his young family. The rewards came with an administration post in the Barbican Centre, and served as a relief from a game Ritchie had fallen out of love with.

Of all the regrets, his failure to earn senior recognition in a Scotland jersey remains amongst the most painful. It was a close call more than once, with his hopes being raised towards the end of the 1977/78 season prior to the World Cup finals in Argentina.

Ritchie was scoring regularly in the First Division with Morton. And one night the phone rang, with the irrepressible Scotland manager Ally MacLeod on the other end of the line.

'He said to me quite bluntly that he would love to include me in the squad. He asked me how I felt about it and I told him I wouldn't let him down, that I would turn up and do my best.

'Ally made no bones about it. He told me it was going to be a hard process convincing people that a part-timer playing outside the Premier League could play for Scotland. But he was looking at what I was doing from set-piece situations as much as anything else.'

MacLeod's phone call came to nothing when the SFA committee men vetoed Ritchie's inclusion in the squad, with the equally prolific Rangers striker Derek Johnstone becoming the beneficiary.

Not until his former Celtic manager Jock Stein was installed at the helm in the aftermath of a disastrous campaign in Argentina did the call finally come. Even then, it was an act of tokenism tinged with arsenic.

Informed by Morton chairman Hal Stewart that he was to be named in the squad for a European Championship qualifier with Belgium in November 1979, Ritchie was shopping when the news arrived that he had been listed as the solitary over-age player in the under-21 team.

'I remember thinking big Jock was taking the piss again. And then my dad took me aside, sat me down and had a word. "You go and do what you need to do and play for your country," he told me. "It doesn't matter what happens after that, no one can take that away from you."

'He was right. So I played. But when we flew back, I didn't give a toss whether I sampled the experience again. I remember on that flight home John Robertson of Nottingham Forest crawling up the plane on his hands and knees to scrounge a fag from me.

'In those days, smoking on a flight was still permitted and there was I sitting near the front having a cigarette and a bottle of beer. I didn't care any longer.'

Andy Ritchie never played by normal rules, although in recent years he has been forced to do so by the law of the land.

A savage betrayal by a former acquaintance worsened an already scarred life to a near-unbearable degree. Legal restrictions prevent disclosure of the circumstances in these pages. Yet the knowledge of what happened dominates his waking hours to an onerous degree. In 2006, the burden of hopelessness became too much.

His mental health deteriorating as a succession of jobs fell by the wayside, Ritchie suffered a breakdown, seeking help from the Professional Footballers Association Scotland for his myriad problems. His marriage of three decades had disintegrated and another home had been lost.

'I maintain I have never been an alcoholic, but I would concede this much: I've had my problems with alcohol. A pal of mine, Bobby McLaughlin, saw the signs when I rolled up to spend three weeks living on his couch.

'Bobby eventually phoned a gem of a man in Tony Higgins, the former Secretary of the old Scottish Professional Footballers' Association.

'Tony came out to Uddingston and left promising to see what he could do. Three days later, Bobby took me to see some people in Paisley from the Renfrewshire Council on Addictions (RCA).

'I went in to confront my issues one day in November and ended up spending 15 months under the umbrella of the experts in Barrhead.

'In March 2008, when I came to the end of the course, I had to move out. With the apron strings of the RCA cut, I had little option but to declare myself homeless to East Renfrewshire Council.

'If I said that was easy then I'd be lying. As a result of swallowing my pride, I lived in a homeless unit in Barrhead for a time. But I'm facing up to rebuilding my life now.'

Now scouting for Stockport, a role as an SPL delegate keeps Ritchie involved in the Scottish game. Charged with representing the league in an inspection capacity, the whys and wherefores of the backroom action are no substitute for the halcyon days. There are ample hours outwith this weekend, part-time role to reflect on how badly wrong things became. Others share his frustration.

As Morton legend Allan McGraw observed, 'There are not many things that make me angry, but that's one of them. What a player, what a talent, what a waste. He could do things with the ball that even Maradona couldn't. He could have been a superstar. And that makes me angry. He wasted his talent, but that was Andy. He just didn't want it enough.'

Through it all, few could have retained the sense of humour that covers a multitude of sins. The toothless grin is far from forced when he says: 'Tony Higgins uses a great line on the after dinner speaking circuit, saying that the year he spent with George Best at Hibs was the equivalent of spending a fortnight with Andy Ritchie at Morton. I think he means it in a kind of nice way . . .'

11

The Three Amigos
PAOLO DI CANIO, JORGE CADETE, PIERRE VAN HOOIJDONK

'We used to call them the Three Amigos. I'm not surprised
by what happened to any of them. What does surprise
me is that someone is willing to pay to take trouble
off your hands.'

– former Celtic managing director Fergus McCann, November 1998

On a Thursday morning in September 1996, watery clouds hung low over Celtic Park. A small band of autograph hunters and car park dwellers sheltered from a light drizzle. Inside, a Vesuvian fire was erupting to rival the carnage which flattened Pompeii.

Paolo Di Canio, Celtic's explosive summer signing from AC Milan, was in full flow. And in the firing line was the club's first ever German striker, Andreas Thom. A quiet and sombre former East Germany international, Thom had joined the Dutchman Pierre van Hooijdonk in 1995 in the first wave of continental Celtic imports shipped in by manager Tommy Burns. Neither man had succeeded, however, in halting a Rangers side on their march to an eighth successive league championship.

In the spring of 1996, the capture of the Portuguese international striker Jorge Cadete from Sporting Lisbon had come as close as any to breaking the monopoly. A quiet, frizzy-haired loner, Cadete spoke fractured English and conversed with his teammates on a needs-must basis. His arrival had been shrouded in a registration scandal which would cost Jim Farry, the secretary of the SFA, his job. His goals towards the end of a dramatic 1995/96 season had also come close to shattering the dominance of a star-studded Ibrox team. Close, but not close enough.

Now, under debilitating pressure to prevent Walter Smith's side from equalling Jock Stein's Celtic world record of nine-in-a-row, Burns added another unpredictable southern European to his squad.

Di Canio, an undecorated playmaker in Serie A, arrived for a knockdown £650,000. In his first days at the club, he pursued room-mate Peter Grant around a hotel room brandishing a fish and boasted of shaving every hair on his body. Amongst teammates, then, his madness was merely confirmed – rather than revealed – in the aftermath of a Coca-Cola League Cup defeat to Heart of Midlothian. In a bust-up which serves as a summary of the turmoil and internal mayhem wrought by the destructive forces later dubbed the 'Three Amigos' by managing director Fergus McCann, even a helpless female translator would be dragged into the maelstrom.

The Italian had been one of five senior players sent to meet with managing director Fergus McCann over a bonus dispute. The majority shareholder had, in typically brusque fashion, refused to entertain a delegation concerned by the withdrawal of win bonuses for unused substitutes allied to the imposition of a ban on agents in the players' lounge. As so often in the Fergus McCann years, Celtic were stricken by tribal infighting. And an extra-time defeat at Tynecastle blew the fuse in the midst of a combustible atmosphere.

During the game, Thom had a clear opportunity to pass to Di Canio. Had he done so, the enigmatic winger would have been through on goal. Rightly fearing an offside flag, however, Thom failed to make it. For Di Canio, this was the latest in a series of perceived slights allied to growing frustration with an imploding club. Ambushed by Di Canio's demand for a team meeting, the manager Tommy Burns agreed, calling the players together after training.

As other players, including captain Paul McStay, John Collins and a raft of Scots looked on, Di Canio took a verbal cutlass to Thom's reputation in Italian, a translator faithfully conveying the litany of abuse in English. It should have been a frank exchange of views, with little in the way of collateral damage. Until, that is, the towering van Hooijdonk – an ally of Thom's – decided the outburst was unwarranted. Van Hooijdonk used every inch of his 6 foot 4 inch frame to shout down his southern European teammate. All of which made Di Canio angrier still. Casting around teammates as most shuffled their feet, the former Juventus star duly found backing for his grievance in the form of the mouse-like Cadete.

And so ensued a thoroughly cosmopolitan verbal battle, with fingers being pointed and long-forgotten grievances resurrected, much to the bemusement of the watching teammates and the chagrin of the management.

'There was a clear-the-air meeting after that one,' admits Billy Stark, Burns's assistant. 'It was a situation Tommy felt had to be dealt with at a time when foreign talent was flooding into the Scottish game. This was fairly new to us and Paolo demanded a meeting in the players' lounge, which Tommy agreed to.

'Paolo thought Andy Thom and Pierre van Hooijdonk were teaming up together with their northern European outlook and that clashed a bit with how he and Jorge Cadete saw things. It was a temperament thing and words were spoken.

'As the team management, it was the job of Tommy and I to confront the situation and deal with it. It wasn't an easy one. But Paolo was never the sort to bottle things up and allow his frustrations to fester. He had to deal with the differences there and then and get them out in the open and Tommy agreed that was the best course of action.

'Of course, it was difficult to manage. There were things you just didn't see coming round the corner and at all times we had to try and deal with things quickly and efficiently – and in my opinion Tommy always succeeded in doing that.

'You can't just bring overseas players in with a different outlook and culture and impose rules and regulations upon them. Saying "This is how we do things here" wasn't the way to deal with it.'

In Di Canio, van Hooijdonk and Cadete, Burns had gathered together three marvellously flawed individuals. On the field, they flowed in a pleasing if imperfect symmetry. Off it, they simmered and raged with perceived injustices over pay and conditions. All of this at a time when Celtic needed minds focused on the troublesome task in hand.

It was this unpredictable and morale-shattering influence that led McCann to dream up the bizarre, yet memorable, Three Amigos tag. And which contrived to cost a forlorn Burns his job at the end of the 1996/97 season.

Confirming the events of that day for the first time, Andreas Thom remains nonplussed by what unfolded in the midst of one of Celtic's most infamous periods.

'I don't think Paolo was a difficult player to play with exactly,' he says. 'But how can I put this? Everybody is a little difficult in their own way. Paolo was a good player, a great talent. I had no idea that he wanted a team meeting to discuss the situation. It was a little embarrassing in the end.'

For Burns and Stark, poached from Kilmarnock as a young and relatively inexperienced management team, this was new and un-charted territory. The previous season, the flame-haired, bespec-tacled Glaswegian and his foreign legion, ably assisted by gifted stalwarts such as McStay and Collins, had been crippled by a perpetual inability to overcome an Ibrox juggernaut featuring Paul Gascoigne, Ally McCoist and Brian Laudrup. They had lost just one game in the league, but predictably and tellingly, the defeat was to Walter Smith's team.

Early in the new 1996/97 season, matters were deteriorating further. Audible dressing-room grumbles concerning McCann's running of the club were increasing in volume. The League Cup defeat at Tynecastle brought matters rearing wickedly to a head.

Malky Mackay had arrived at Celtic as a young defender follow-ing a spell as a bank clerk in Glasgow city centre. Dovetailing the normality of a day job with playing for Queens Park on a part-time basis – his father still serves on the Hampden committee – his sturdy Glaswegian upbringing had barely prepared him for this.

'That was a bizarre episode,' he laughs. 'When Paolo first came to Celtic, he had one of the girls at the club interpreting for him. He hadn't been at Celtic all that long and his English was still patchy. So we all convened in the players' lounge wondering what's going on when Paolo points at Andy Thom and gets the translator to accuse him of all sorts. He then goes off on one in typically Italian fashion until the girl stops him and they start to have a bit of an argument aside from the main argument. By this point, we're all asking her what's going on and she says, "I'm not saying what he wants me to say."

'It turned out Paolo was cursing and swearing in Italian and making all these accusations about Andy.

'Meantime the other guys got involved and it's a scene of mayhem. But that was just typical Paolo, he definitely had half a marble loose.'

Pressure can do strange things to a man. Van Hooijdonk had evolved from a quiet, polite and unassuming striker into one with a healthy conceit of himself in his third season at the club, and was close to rejecting the kind of money supporters can but dream of to sign a new contract.

Di Canio, meanwhile, had previously stormed out of the club's Barrowfield training ground to walk the half-mile back to the stadium in a raging fit of temper after a bust-up with goalkeeper Gordon Marshall. Scoring a penalty against Hearts, he had also contrived to earn himself a red card before the restart. And Cadete appeared to be in the grip of some form of breakdown, silently slinking deeper into an introverted persona. In Fergus McCann's words, he was a debt-ridden 'financial basket case'.

And yet the manner in which they played their football – then expertly manipulated their release from Celtic in search of more cash – suggests these were players who amounted to far more than a motley collection of chancers and ne'er-do-wells.

With typical prescience, McCann had warned Tommy Burns – with whom he shared a fractious working relationship – that if he granted the three an inch, they would take the whole nine yards. He was right.

Intriguingly, however, time has been kind to the trio in the mindsets of the supporters, many of whom long for their flowing, dashing style of football. The Three Amigos description was intended as an insult, but became a term of endearment. For all their faults and mid-season contractual fluctuations, they could play football the fabled Celtic way. There have been times in recent years when some might have exchanged success with silverware under Gordon Strachan for the failure with a flourish of the Burns years, so thrilling was the football to watch. When all three returned for a Tommy Burns memorial game at the end of the 2008/09 season, the supporters hailed them as lost sons returning to the homestead. In that regard, then, the Three Amigos have become only mildly tainted Celtic legends.

In football, as in life, context is everything. How Tommy Burns came to sign three charismatic, yet inwardly flawed, footballers owes much to circumstance. In March 1994, Celtic had been close to extinction. The old board of directors had been a collective of family custodians. The dynasties of the Kellys, the Whites and the Grants had run their course. With debts running to hitherto unimaginable levels and Fergus McCann cleverly providing the bullets for the energetic and highly mobilised Celts for Change supporters' group, the Bank of Scotland took fright. Supporter boycotts had provoked the desired effect and, with the bailiffs lurking at the door, McCann was called back to his native Glasgow to put up the £9 million required to save the club, with minutes to spare.

Off the pitch, Celtic were financially stricken. On it, they were little better. Lou Macari, a former member of the famous Quality Street Gang, had been a fine Celtic striker, a decorated Scotland international and an articulate manager hired in the club's darkest hour. He was ill-equipped, however, to weather the storm of change blowing through the club. The abrasive, forthright and mildly eccentric McCann knew only one way by which to operate – his way. And so it was that the young Kilmarnock management team of Burns and Stark was approached to take over at Parkhead.

From the off the new manager, a former Celtic midfielder with a quick temper, was fire to the owner's oil. Within three weeks, Burns and McCann had arrived at virtual breakdown point in their relationship.

Burns wanted immediate and expensive remedial surgery on the team. With Rangers chairman David Murray famously determined to throw a tenner into the pot for every fiver McCann sacrificed, however, the battle for supremacy on the park was never likely to be straightforward. Determined to push ahead with the rebuilding of a crumbling stadium, McCann replaced the old shoebox and biscuit tin economics of the past with a new professional approach. Throwing money at the team without fear of consequence was never an option. Under McCann, good housekeeping was an imperative.

Against this backdrop, then, there would be no competition with Rangers for the Laudrups or Gascoignes of this world. Spending was always on a more modest level.

Playing their home games at a rented Hampden, Celtic entered the 1994/95 season under Burns and without a trophy since 1989. They had lost the League Cup final in humiliating fashion to First Division Raith Rovers and inspiration for change was required from somewhere, anywhere. In the event, Burns and Stark turned to Holland for the first of the Unholy Trinity.

'We had to gamble at that point,' Stark concedes. 'If someone has great ability like Pierre van Hooijdonk or Paolo Di Canio, they should be at a higher level. You then ask yourself, why are they coming here if they are so good?

'Are they manageable? Are they a gamble worth taking? You have to assess the pros and cons and we decided on balance that these guys were well worth it.'

On the scouting side of the club, Burns had promoted his old ground staff chum Andy Ritchie to assist Davie Hay with searching for first-team players.

And Ritchie recalls: 'We needed charisma. The club needed a lift, Tommy demanded it. He had a vision of passing football which embraced temperamental genius, whatever the baggage attached.

'I was desperate to sign Georgi Kinkladze from Manchester City for £5.5 million. That was a king's ransom to Celtic. We needed to break the bank to excite the crowd and fill a new 60,000 stadium. There was too much negativity around the place and the guys we needed weren't to be found in the Scottish Premier League.

'We knew Fergus McCann was reluctant to spend big. But we still needed players like Kinkladze from somewhere. Which meant we had to gamble on the slightly flawed maestros of this world.

'We weren't shopping in Harrods, we were shopping in the Clearance Warehouse for the slightly frayed items others didn't have to gamble on.'

When moving Ritchie from a job in youth development to scouting, Burns had handed his old friend a video featuring the Dutch club NAC Breda. The instruction was to have a look at the American international Ernie Stewart and provide an assessment of his potential worth to Celtic.

'I went with the Breda video Tommy had given me to a back room with a television off the tunnel,' Ritchie recalls. 'It was a Friday and the videos had started rolling in at a frightening rate. Most of them would end up in a plastic supermarket bag in a cabinet.

'But the most productive viewing still came from that first video. We made a pot of tea, dug out the Jaffa Cakes and invited Packie Bonner [the former Celtic goalkeeper] in to join us.

'But every time Stewart threw in a cross, this giant of a striker was getting on the end of it. I got to imagining this giant in a hoops jersey bullying Richard Gough and the Rangers defence.'

Petrus Ferdinandus Johannes Stevenson van Hooijdonk was born in Steenbergen, in the Netherlands, on 29 November 1969. He impressed scouts from NAC Breda at the age of 11 at a youth trial and joined the club, ostensibly as a right midfielder. At 14, on being rejected by NAC, he joined VV Steenbergen, where he became a striker, eventually joining RBC Roosendaal. Within two years, he rejoined his boyhood idols at Breda and, with a remarkable 81 goals in 115 appearances over 4 seasons, attracted Celtic's attention.

From the off, van Hooijdonk was captivated by the passion and personality of the manager Tommy Burns. For van Hooijdonk the move would be life-changing and, for a time at least, his single-minded streak was obscured by gratitude at Celtic's willingness to take a chance on his talents.

'Pierre just naturally latched on to some of us,' states Malky Mackay. 'The young ones who were unmarried like myself would all go out on a Saturday night and Pierre would come along. As a result of that, he became a good friend of mine and with a number of players. We even ended up going on holiday together at one point.

'Whatever they ended up saying about Pierre when he went south later in his career, he was always a really nice fellow to me. He had a great sense of humour and was shrewd; a sharp guy who always had a twinkle in his eye. He would join in all the dressing-room humour and understand it. Of course he was also a typical Dutchman; put two Dutch players in one room and you'll have three different arguments raging at the same time. That became apparent when things went a bit awry with Fergus McCann and then at Nottingham Forest later, what with going on strike over pay and stuff.'

Van Hooijdonk made an immediate impact, scoring a superb goal on his debut against Hearts. At the end of his first season, he rose to head the only goal of the Scottish Cup Final against Airdrie as Celtic ended a desperate six-year trophy drought.

Yet the Dutchman had been disappointed by what he had found at Celtic on his arrival.

'I wasn't surprised we were playing our games at Hampden,' van Hooijdonk admits, 'they had warned me they were building both a new stadium and a new club. But I was more than a bit disappointed with the standards at Celtic. I was expecting something better because of the name of Celtic across Europe. Now I can see why people felt that the arrival of new signings like me and Di Canio was the start of a new era – but at the time I didn't know that was the case. I was just looking at the standard of people I was playing with and thinking I had expected more.

'It was a major thing for me to move to Celtic because I was just 25 and it was my first move abroad. Now guys move much younger and have their satellite television with all the stations from their home country – I didn't have anything like that. I had to stay in my house in East Kilbride and one time I was even spat on in my car around a mile from the stadium as I stopped at traffic lights. Wherever I went I was recognised, because I was tall and dark, so it wasn't as if I could go quietly unnoticed in Glasgow. It was hard.'

Glasgow was, then, sealing a tight vacuum around this gentle giant.

'By the end of Pierre's time, there were unsettling influences clinging to his coat-tails in Glasgow,' adds Andy Ritchie. 'The adoration and attention had gone to his head. He was a young man and he changed.

'By the time he moved to Nottingham Forest, he was in the big league. He had always had great aspirations and as a kid adopted at a young age, perhaps that was understandable.

'But that was a different Pierre from the one who had arrived at Celtic. From the outset he was a lovely boy, big, quiet and soft, polite to a fault. He appreciated the opportunity he had been given to come to a club like Celtic. He needed a step up and Celtic badly needed him to return the favour.'

Aided by the arrival of Thom on an unprecedented £10,000 a week later that summer, van Hooijdonk scored an impressive 32 goals as Celtic launched a concerted title challenge. The revitalised Parkhead team lost just one league game all season – to Rangers in a 2–0 defeat at Parkhead in September.

There were, however, draws – too many for Tommy Burns to countenance. Aware that the strike force lacked genuine pace, efforts were made at the turn of 1996 to bring in a reinforcement.

Jorge Paulo Cadete Santos Reis was better known as Jorge Cadete. A Portuguese international striker who forged his reputation with Sporting Lisbon, where he scored 68 goals in 169 appearances, Cadete had become embroiled in a contract wrangle with the Portuguese club and was 27 when he arrived in Glasgow. He had played at Parkhead once before, when Celtic overcame Sporting 1–0 in a UEFA Cup first leg tie. His manager had been Bobby Robson – a man Fergus McCann would later seek to recruit as Burns' managerial replacement.

Andy Ritchie takes up the story, explaining: 'Tommy had seen Cadete rout Scotland in a 5–0 thrashing against Portugal in Lisbon. But it wasn't until Bobby Robson moved to Barcelona and brought them to play a friendly at Parkhead that we gave serious thought to bringing him in. Robert Prosinecki and Ivan De La Pena dazzled folk that night before we retreated to the coaches' room afterwards.

'Bobby had Jorge under his wing during a successful spell at Sporting Lisbon and when we said we were looking for a striker to play last man on the shoulders of the defenders, Jorge's name came up. We learned he might be available and how much money it might take to sign him.

'Typically, he also had his problems. Like van Hooijdonk and Di Canio, he had an erratic streak and arrived at a time when he might best be described as a sick pup. He had problems in his marriage, deep-ranging personal problems and a cash-flow problem. But what a player Celtic got for £650,000. Sure it was a gamble, but gambles don't always go against you.'

Cadete would claim later that he had, in fact, paid his own fee to secure a release from Sporting after a protracted wrangle. There was, he claims, a 'verbal agreement' for the fee to be repaid by Celtic. Against that backdrop, his introduction to the crowd at half-time of a game against Partick Thistle on 24 February 1996 was rapturous. Yet thanks to a highly controversial administration irregularity the Portuguese striker failed to make his debut until 1 April, scoring in a 5–0 rout of Aberdeen. The reason, Celtic suspected, was a deliberate quest by the SFA chief executive Jim Farry to delay Cadete's registration until it was too late to include him in a Scottish Cup semi-final against Rangers – a game Celtic lost 2–1. Ordinarily, such talk would be dismissed as paranoid ramblings. Yet, not for the first time, McCann's suspicions would be vindicated three years later when an independent commission found in Celtic's favour. On 8 March 1999, the Scottish Football Association sacked Farry for gross misconduct.

By then, Cadete had long since departed. In the remaining games of the 1995/96 season, the striker claimed a further five goals. The next season, he continued in prolific form, assisted by Di Canio's addition to the squad. In all, Cadete claimed a remarkable 39 goals in 41 starts for Celtic, a record of Henrik Larsson-esque proportions.

And yet in contrast with the Swede's legendary composure and aloofness, Cadete was a fragile creature, beset by anger over his alleged treatment from McCann.

'I would have loved to play with Henrik Larsson at Celtic and to have been as successful,' states Cadete, 'but Fergus made sure I could not do that. Remember, I had paid my own transfer to Celtic and when I signed I made sure it was in my contract to have the fee repaid. Fergus gave me his word – and then said a year later that he knew nothing about it. I never asked him for more wages but, after scoring 33 goals, I thought I was at least due what I was still owed. My agent spoke to them nine times in a year about it and yet he would not budge – so that's why I had to ask for a transfer.

'I only ever speak the truth – and when you consider that Pierre and Paolo also had problems with Fergus McCann, you know who to believe.'

At the end of season 1996/97, Cadete left and was expected to return for the following campaign. He never did. A troubled personal life allied to deep discontent with the Celtic regime ended in a £3 million move to Celta Vigo. Among teammates left to pick up the pieces, there were mixed feelings.

'Jorge started in a blaze of glory and it ended in tears,' admits Malky Mackay. 'Most of them his, but he had some problems. His English was less fluent than the other foreign lads and he had some issues going on. He was okay to talk to in the dressing room, but he was very different from all the other players. He was never one who would want to be involved in what was happening around the club. In essence he was a real loner.

'The guys who get to know the Scottish ways will inevitably fare better than the others. Di Canio embraced life in Scotland – albeit briefly – but I don't think you could ever have said the same of Jorge. He was certainly never an unpleasant person. There was just always the sense that he was a fleeting star, that he was passing through.'

Cadete would never recapture the success he enjoyed at Celtic. Spells at Vigo, Benfica and Bradford produced a trifling number of appearances. Then, at the age of 35, the striker arrived at Partick Thistle for a high-profile four-month soirée. Expressing regrets for an opportunity lost at Celtic, Cadete was a pale reflection of his former self. In the intervening years he had won the Portuguese version of *Celebrity Big Brother* and acquired a popstar girlfriend by the name of Nicole. A pet canary called Fergus showed a sense of humour too often posted missing at Celtic.

Like most of the Dutch players who would pass through the Old Firm, van Hooijdonk adapted a little more easily to the damp, northern European landscape of industrial Glasgow.

Yet he too had his problems with McCann. A lengthy contract renegotiation ended acrimoniously when van Hooijdonk claimed that an offer of £7,000 was 'good for a homeless person, but not good enough for a top-class forward'. In a city with proud socialist roots, it was a crass, insensitive and deeply out of touch remark. Yet to this day, van Hooijdonk claims his statement was taken out of context, insisting:

'I remember everything that I said in Glasgow and I can still remember the journalist who wrote that. To me, he used a quote without context. It's a bad quote if you read that and that alone, but no one really wanted to read my full view. It was blown up out of proportion. The fact is this; you come and you go as a football player. Some stay a little longer, some don't. The media had a relationship with the club to keep up – they didn't have to think about me.'

Tommy Burns, like Fergus McCann, was by now tiring of a player who had become a problem. Accused of refusing to warm up before a UEFA Cup tie with Hamburg UEFA, refusing to do promotional or charity visits and of demanding £20,000 a week to stay at Celtic, van Hooijdonk was axed for a 2–0 defeat at Ibrox. Before the death of Burns in May 2008, van Hooijdonk returned to Glasgow with his twelve-year-old son and the two men shared a dinner in Glasgow, reminiscing over old times. Years earlier in October 1996, however, their relationship had become precarious.

'I remember Tommy Burns with great memories. Tommy was always surrounded by love. Wherever he went, I never heard anybody say something bad about him – not even one guy. That is something unusual. Even in my own situation, Tommy left me out of the team at one stage, and I did not agree of course, but I kept my respect for him. Because of the way he behaved as a human being.

'The only person I didn't get on with at Celtic was Fergus McCann. Emotion plays an important part in the football business, but he dealt with every situation without emotion – neither negatively nor positively. He never showed the slightest bit of warmth to any player at the club.

'I remember after a pre-season game against Arsenal when Di Canio arrived, we were standing in the Celtic foyer with our partners talking when McCann walked through. Paolo saw the man who had signed his contract just weeks before and stepped forward to shake his hand. McCann just ignored him, completely ignored him. To him it had just been another deal, not a human being. He lacked all the qualities that Tommy Burns had in abundance.'

In 12 months at Celtic, Paolo Di Canio was a vibrant, entertaining and flamboyant footballer, not to mention a highly troublesome individual. To those who like their football played in the fabled Celtic way, he was a ball-juggling messiah, the antidote to the mediocrity that dogged the club prior to Fergus McCann's financial salvage job.

That he was, however, deeply flawed in a temperamental sense is undeniable. That much was evident long before the infamous incident when Di Canio incurred the wrath of the English FA and earned penalties totalling £90,000 and an 11-game ban for pushing premiership referee Paul Alcock to the ground during a Sheffield Wednesday v Arsenal game at Hillsborough in 1998.

'Di Canio was the classic man-child,' recalls Andrew Smith, who was then the *Celtic View* editor. 'There was a game against Rangers at Parkhead and his family were coming over from Italy. There were around twelve of them flying over and Di Canio had only six tickets to go round from the allocation granted to players. He literally started jumping up and down on the spot demanding more tickets.

'He was screaming, "I'm not playing! I'm not playing!" in much the same way as a two-year-old might throw a tantrum. They eventually said, "Okay, okay" and found him more tickets. But it was like watching a child – the club would try anything just to calm him down.'

That Tommy Burns somehow managed to channel the creative madness of his new signing for what seemed to be the greater good was, then, one of his greater feats as Celtic manager. He did so by granting Di Canio his head, by accepting that the star of the show should enjoy the right to ad lib. Whether or not Di Canio, who was signed from Italy for a knockdown price, was blameless or highly complicit in the failure to stop Rangers winning a ninth title remains a matter of subjective opinion.

Yet the bitter end to this football conductor's time at Celtic stood in stark contrast to beginnings sparkling with hope and expectation as he scored on his debut against Kilmarnock in a 3–1 win.

'How Paolo came to be the first major Italian to play for Celtic can be explained by events which began a few months before he signed a contract,' states his biographer, Gabriele Marcotti. 'He was at AC Milan, and on a tour of Beijing he was little more than a fringe player. He asked his agent Moreno Roggi to see if he could find him a new home and the link with Celtic came from Joe Jordan, a former Milan striker and ex-Celtic coach under Liam Brady.

'There was a dinner to discuss his future in a Brazilian restaurant and Jordan told Paolo by phone Celtic wanted him. The minute he got home, he went to look at an atlas to see precisely where Scotland was. Glasgow was near the top of the map but he moved anyway.

'Celtic then asked him to take a pay cut. He was on a very good deal at Milan and he was offered £650,000 a year by Fergus McCann, who told him it would be worth the gamble to play his part in reviving Celtic.

'At that time, Paolo believed that he was told to accept that and then see how things were going after a year. He was under the impression they would review things the next summer.'

Like Cadete before him, then, Di Canio placed great store in alleged verbal promises. Yet if Di Canio was taking a pay cut, then Celtic were taking a gamble. In Scotland, few had heard of this Latin firebrand, his background with Lazio, Juventus and Milan serving as the only evidence of a pedigree.

'Tommy had heard that Di Canio was available in the summer of 1996 and he asked me one day if I knew anything about him,' Andy

Ritchie recalls. 'I was honest. I didn't know a great deal, but I knew a man who did. I phoned a guy called Pierro Esposto. He was very close to Juventus, Di Canio's former club. I also knew he was an excellent judge of a player. To me, he was an Italian with a Scottish mentality. If anyone knew whether this guy was cut out for life in Glasgow, this guy did.

'His words to me were: "Paolo Di Canio is a major talent, Andy. And I mean a major talent. He will excite the fans and have them in raptures, standing on their seats. But he will make your manager an old man in 12 months. He will have everyone around the club in turmoil." I have never heard a more accurate player assessment in all my many years in professional football.'

If truth be told, Celtic had little real concept of the volcanic emotions that drove this unpredictable and highly flammable football player.

'Initially, we looked at his ability and quite simply it was as good as I had ever seen,' says Billy Stark. 'We looked at the big clubs that had taken Paolo on, who had taken a chance on him. You were talking Milan, Juventus and Lazio, and we thought to ourselves, if those clubs have taken a chance on him, then he must have something.'

To make amends for the wage cut which left their new arrival and wife Betta to survive on a mere £12,500 a week, Celtic also agreed to shell out a lump sum of £365,000 in image rights to the new bhoy. In return, the club would be granted the rights to utilise the winger's image in commercial ventures.

There was, however, a problem. After banking the cash and signing the papers, Di Canio steadfastly refused to co-operate with a single request made by the club's marketing department in the months that followed.

On Boxing Day 1996, there came a tantalising taste of a marketing man's dream. Di Canio scored a quite majestic last-minute winner against Aberdeen at Pittodrie in a 2–1 triumph. And he did so wearing a flamboyant pair of Pantafola d'Oro boots made in Italy of gold leather. For Celtic, this was a truly glittering opportunity to market replicas of these highly distinctive boots to impressionable young supporters as the Paolo Di Canio range. Yet Di Canio, in an unquestionably generous gesture, gifted the boots the next day to Radio Clyde's annual Cash for Kids charity Christmas fundraising appeal, and sports retail tycoon Tom Hunter – Scotland's richest man – paid £30,000 to pip lottery millionaire John McGuinness to the punch. Any hopes Celtic had of Di Canio fishing out a new pair the next week were quickly dashed. The boots were a one–off – and the star player never wore them again.

'Paolo was as good a trainer as I've ever witnessed,' Billy Stark adds. 'He was a beast and I don't just mean with a ball at his feet. He would lead the way in the long runs in the pouring rain or do anything asked of him. He had a superb physique – and that was one of the main factors in his brilliance. He would also bring his own personal trainer on occasion to work on things long after everyone else had gone. So there was nothing flawed about him in a physical or professional sense, it was purely that mental side of things which held him back.

'He was always convinced he was right. He had that stubborn Italian streak that characterises so many players from that country and he believed that if he was creating goals and scoring goals by beating players at will, then he should be allowed licence to do as he pleased.'

A love of artistic creativity extended beyond the football pitch. In an illuminating tale of the contradictions that drove this unpredictable character, Di Canio made one of the more unusual demands Celtic received from a player.

'The only request I ever received for tickets to go and see *La Bohème*, the opera, came from Paolo,' recalls the then Celtic PR manager, Peter McLean. 'The production was on at Glasgow's Theatre Royal and I managed to get four tickets – so Paolo asked if my girlfriend and I might like to join him and his wife. We were happy to accept and the experience was enhanced when Scottish Opera looked after us exceptionally well, placing us in the VIP room before and after the show.

'It was certainly unusual for an Old Firm footballer to be in there,

I would imagine. And on seeing Paolo, a very middle-class woman from what I guessed to be Edinburgh couldn't resist coming over to speak to him.

' "You are a footballer are you not?" she asked.

' "Yes, madam, I am," said Paolo.

' "Well, what does a footballer know about opera?" she asked a bit sniffily, with her friends now listening in and giggling.

' "Probably not very much compared to you, madam," replied Paolo with perfect politeness.

' "But what, may I ask, prompted your footballer's interest in opera?" she asked again.

' "Well, madam," says Paolo quietly. "When I played with Juventus in Italy, a man who sang opera used to call me up to ask for tickets. You may have heard of him, his name is Luciano Pavarotti . . ."

'But he didn't stop there. He then started belting out passages of his favourite operas at the top of his voice in the VIP room to his new audience.'

Those, then, who underestimated this most unpredictable of music lovers did so at their own peril. Behind the apparently irrepressible extrovert behaviour, however, was a contradictory – almost child-like – quality.

'We were taken afterwards to meet the English lead tenor Ian Storey,' adds McLean. 'In opera circles he's quite a name and this brought about an amazing change in Paolo. Suddenly he was a nervous wreck. His shirt was sweaty, he was pacing from foot to foot and he kept telling Ian Storey what an enormous honour it was to meet him, how he respected his work so very much.'

For Di Canio, the art and culture of an operatic performance chimed closely with his own concept of how football should be played. The game, he believed, was artistic entertainment first and foremost and in that respect he and Tommy Burns shared an ideology.

'Paolo told me that he and Tommy Burns ended many of their conversations with an embrace close to tears,' claims Gabrielle Marcotti. 'He always felt Tommy had a raw deal from Celtic. He is a blood-and-guts kind of guy who embraces the whole warrior ethos. And when he arrived, Tommy and he had trouble communicating on the inaugural stadium tour because of Paolo's lack of English and the accent of the Glaswegians. But whenever there was a breakdown in communication, Tommy would start pounding his chest and say, "Heart, heart". That really resonated with Paolo and his way of thinking.'

And yet impatience with teammates – and their unwillingness to give him the ball either quickly or often enough – would spill over into acts of petulance. Not least the day the wayward winger stormed from the Barrowfield training pitch in protest at a slight more imagined than real.

'Big Gordon Marshall was in goals at training that day and he didn't throw the ball to Paolo when he was screaming for it,' Stark remembers. 'Well, that was it. Paolo marched straight off the Barrowfield training pitch and traipsed all the way back to Celtic Park by foot in disgust. All because he was in a massive huff about the fact Gordon hadn't given him the ball when he wanted it.'

A plea from manager Tommy Burns to calm down and stay at the club soothed troubled waters. And, according to Stark at least, there was no lasting damage where team morale was concerned.

And yet one man was, for the first time in Celtic's illustrious history, coming close to regarding his own needs as greater than those of the club.

'He got involved in things which diluted his effectiveness as a player,' claims Andrew Smith, a Celtic employee through nine largely barren years during the 1990s. 'He was an undeniably talented player, but they ended up with a situation where everybody started deferring to him. Di Canio dominated the club with the sheer force of his personality and as a result, he diminished some of the players around him. Some almost seemed to shrink in his presence. And that may have impacted on the failure to win the league that season.'

Di Canio's brilliance was recognised by his fellow pros when they voted him their player of the year in 1997. And the idea that such a performer may have done more harm than good to the collective effort appears, at first glance, to be absurd. Not for the last time in his meandering career, however, Di Canio would leave a club without a winners' medal.

The final Old Firm league game of the season came within close proximity of a Scottish Cup quarter-final against Walter Smith's side. Celtic won the Cup game, Di Canio scoring a nineteenth minute penalty after Malky Mackay had headed Celtic into the lead with a header in a 2–0 win. In the league, however, Rangers had developed a remarkable knack of absorbing all the pressure this multi-talented Celtic team could throw at them – then breaking up the field to score the winner. They had won all three Old Firm league games played that season without losing a goal.

On 16 March, with the pressure to stop nine-in-a-row intense, the Ibrox side did it again. Celtic's preparations had not been ideal, with van Hooijdonk jumping ship in a switch to Nottingham Forest.

Already five points adrift, another 1–0 Parkhead defeat destroyed any lingering hopes Celtic had of winning the league. Di Canio became embroiled in a spat with Rangers midfielder Ian Ferguson three minutes from time. Mark Hateley of Rangers and Celtic's Mackay had already been sent off in a game pre-ordained to be tempestuous. And as Rangers moved closer to a critical win at the home of their ancient rivals, Celtic's talisman snapped, becoming embroiled in a verbal altercation with the Ibrox player and making a gesture which suggested he intended to break his opponent's leg. As time up arrived, Di Canio aimed a slap at his Rangers rival as they resumed their feud, with Celtic goalkeeper Stewart Kerr and physio Brian Scott trying in vain to push Di Canio down the tunnel.

Years later, the Italian accused the Ibrox midfielder of yelling: 'F**k off you bastard' in his ear. And yet, at the time, Di Canio claimed the Rangers midfielder included a vile sectarian term of abuse – a charge that prompted Ferguson to make an unprecedented phone call to Parkhead the next day.

'That was a nasty allegation, a low and vindictive claim that still annoys, and that was why I phoned Tommy Burns at Parkhead the next day to let him know the truth,' says Ferguson. 'I had total and utter respect for every Celtic player I ever faced – Paul and Willie McStay, Peter Grant, Tommy himself. Ask any of them and they'll tell you I'd never have uttered what Di Canio claimed I said. We were heading up the tunnel afterwards to get it sorted and were pulled apart. Let's just say it came as no surprise to me that the only player not to appear afterwards for a post-match drink, from both clubs, was Di Canio.'

As legendary Rangers nine-in-a-row skipper Richard Gough admits now, the Ibrox pre-match game plan worked perfectly.

'Di Canio was a special player, but we always knew that we had to try and wind him up. We just niggled at him the whole game, we tugged him, swore at him, noised him up – and it worked.' Laughing, Gough adds: 'It's funny, because I met him later when we played in an Everton v West Ham game and we were on opposite sides again. But he came to me after the game and said, "El Capitano, theez is a piece of cake compared to the Old Firm, no?"'

With the league lost, the Scottish Cup represented Celtic's final chance of silverware for the season and defeat to First Division Falkirk after a replay sounded the last bell for the Burns era.

No Old Firm manager in the modern era can hope to withstand a clean sweep of league defeats to their city rivals in one season. Had Celtic won even two of the games they largely dominated against Rangers, it might have been different. The wily Walter Smith had, however, gained the measure of Burns – a man whose coffin he would help to carry into St Mary's Church many years later.

Andy Ritchie had been on the Celtic ground staff with Burns when the two were 15-year-olds and, as chief scout, knew better than most the tensions that underlay the manager's relationship with his managing director.

'Fergus and Thomas had never had a great relationship and every defeat towards the end exacerbated the level of tension. Every time Tommy went upstairs to speak to Fergus, he would return in a worse mood. Towards the end of his time in charge, he would be angry, bitter and frustrated. There was never abuse, never any bad language, that wasn't Thomas. But he and Fergus were in a state of permanent conflict.'

McCann, in truth, was fighting fires on a number of fronts. Van Hooijdonk had gone in acrimony and Di Canio was now hell-bent on following him. Cadete, meanwhile, had also begun agitating for a move. The twin failures to stop Rangers winning yet another title or to capture the Scottish Cup hit Celtic hard. Di Canio still believes that Celtic were 'cheated' by referees and the authorities. Others were able to adopt a more sanguine and less emotive approach.

Tommy Burns died in May 2008 after a battle with melanoma, prompting a vast outpouring of grief for a loyal servant to the club. He is no longer here to say whether, in retrospect, he might have handled the Three Amigos with a firmer hand.

'Tommy was a young manager and he was unfortunate because the Rangers team of that eight-in-a-row season had never been better,' observes Andrew Smith. 'That Celtic team would have comfortably beaten the four-in-a-row Rangers incarnation. But it was a horrible freak of timing that Tommy assembled such a team at a time when Rangers were so strong.'

The sacking of Burns by Fergus McCann prompted an escalation of the events which ended in an unsavoury parting of the ways between Celtic and Di Canio, who boycotted a pre-season trip to Holland and cut short a jaunt to Ireland. For the club's newly appointed general manager, Jock Brown, this was an early test of his formidable legal skills. At one meeting with Di Canio, tea and biscuits were produced and attempts made to conjure up an atmosphere of bonhomie. Brown was met, however, by monosyllabic responses, Di Canio's by now well-developed English suddenly deserting him.

'The bottom line was he believed he had been promised a pay hike by Fergus – or so he said. I heard Di Canio was upset about Tommy Burns leaving the club,' recalls Brown. 'But there was never a word to me about that in my meetings with him. Di Canio was working his ticket, no question.'

When Di Canio was infamously 'traded' to Sheffield Wednesday for Regi Blinker, supporters bemoaned the loss of another star player at the behest of the acerbic McCann.

In retrospect, Pierre van Hooijdonk, Jorge Cadete and Paolo Di Canio played fine football. But they never played winning football. And at Celtic, success is non-negotiable.

'You could argue that there were times when Pierre, Jorge and Paolo together with Andy Thom shouldn't all have been on the same pitch at the same time,' says Malky Mackay. 'The benefits in an attacking sense were being cancelled out by the defensive side of things.

'It is sad, because Tommy gave his heart and soul to Celtic and wanted nothing more than to bring the league championship back to the club, but it wasn't to be. Did we under-achieve as a team? Undoubtedly. There should have been at least one title in there. At times it felt like we had a dream team.'

For Parkhead legend Davie Hay, integral in recommending all three players, their legacy lives on in the mindset of a support that has always adored flawed maestros.

'Those three players embodied some exceptional talent,' says Hay. 'Just how talented we never found out, because they were only there for a short time. What you have to remember is that we were up against an exceptional Rangers team. But in a sense I'm not the best man to ask about those players and that team – ask the fans. There lies the answer to how any Celtic team is perceived. And I think the fact that people still talk about them today tells you everything.'

12

The Gaffer
STEVE PATERSON

'In 34 years, I reckon I've given the bookies more than
£1 million, it's horrifying. I have created havoc with my lifestyle.'

– Steve Paterson

Choosing the definitive headline for Steve Paterson's troubled life is no easy task. The *Sun* splash that sketched out the greatest high set new standards for tabloid genius. Who will forget 'Super Caley Go Ballistic Celtic Are Atrocious' in a hurry? Certainly not Kenny Dalglish or John Barnes.

The February night in 2000 when the former England winger's fledgling managerial career was strangled in Paradise also marked the emergence of a quietly spoken, introverted tactician in the Inverness Caledonian Thistle dugout. Steve Paterson had none of the flamboyance of Barnes, or the sustained career success of the Liverpool legend Dalglish, who was director of football at Parkhead the night the Highlanders humbled Celtic from the Scottish Cup. His appearances in a technical area were so low-key as to be almost invisible. His rise to the upper levels of Scottish football was almost without trace. Nothing, then, could have prepared the world for the day he created a sensation.

'Paterson Reveals Drink Problem' read the news banners when the then manager of Aberdeen failed to show for a league game against Dundee at Pittodrie after an all-night session. Even Mary Poppins and her umbrella could hardly have lifted the cloud which descended upon the Highlander on an infamous afternoon in March 2003.

'The night before, we had been at a centenary dinner for Aberdeen

organised by the city council,' recalls former Dons chief executive
Keith Wyness. 'It was a glittering event to mark 100 years for the
club and it passed off without incident. It was a good night and I
remember seeing Steve there behaving in a perfectly acceptable way.
There was nothing untoward to report at all. I began to get a clue of
what happened later in the evening the next day, when someone told
me he had been seen out very late.

'That made me a little apprehensive and that was accentuated at
2 p.m. when Duncan Shearer, the assistant manager, came and
dragged me out of the boardroom and told me Steve wasn't going
to make the game against Dundee.

'Naturally we were pretty shocked by this, these things just don't
happen at that level. On the Sunday morning, he was hauled round
to the home of the club chairman, Stewart Milne, for a meeting I was
in on. He told us what had happened and about the problems he had.
As I say, Steve was always a very deep character and it was almost
impossible to get far enough into his head to know how best to help
him.

'But as human beings we felt sympathy for the man and we felt we
had to help him first and foremost. He had some pretty huge issues
and the scale of those shocked us. But we felt that such was the public
embarrassment and humiliation of what was happening to him in the
media and the city, that it would surely get him back on the straight
and narrow. He had suffered enough; it was front page news in
papers across the land. Unfortunately, that didn't prove to be the
case.'

Since that fateful day, the headlines have become more lurid, the
problems more pressing. Paterson lasted another 14 months at
Pittodrie before stumbling into a downward spiral. When Aberdeen
dispensed with his services, he chose to be smuggled from the ground
in the boot of Duncan Shearer's car rather than face a barrage of
flashbulbs. And yet his problems were only really beginning. Shying
from the spotlight has been rendered impossible ever since.

His Aberdeen pay-off went to bookmakers, money for a family
holiday was cast down the drain, the drinking escalated, his marriage disintegrated and his career crumbled. Brief spells at Forres

Mechanics and Peterhead failed to obscure a basic truth and ultimately he referred himself for treatment at the Sporting Chance Clinic. The events which preceded his absence from the dugout against Dundee were not the cause of the malaise, merely the public confirmation.

Now a social worker in a care home in the north of Scotland, Paterson continues to battle his demons. Fighting crippling debts estimated at tens of thousands of pounds is, however, a heavyweight contest. Every time he comes off the ropes, it seems, this is a man who succumbs to another knockout blow.

Aberdeen are no longer the club who proved themselves the equal of any in Europe in the aftermath of winning the European Cup Winners' Cup on a sodden night in Gothenburg in 1983. Successive managers have failed to cope with the extravagant expectations created by Alex Ferguson's achievements. And yet Paterson's problems began long before he accepted a poisoned chalice as successor to Ebbe Skovdahl at Pittodrie in December 2002. Ironically, the laconic Dane had endured years of speculation concerning his own alleged love of the demon drink in the Granite City. Paterson, a popular choice with the supporters following his achievements with Inverness, placed all of that in the proverbial cocked hat.

'Steve had done so well at Inverness Caledonian Thistle, taking them to the greatest result of their history, so he was as much a fan appointment as anything,' states Wyness. 'But that was fine, because we wanted to find a younger manager than Ebbe Skovdahl had been at the time. It helped that he was a resident of the north of Scotland, so while he wasn't exactly local, his appointment made a lot of sense.

'Of course, the gossip concerning his drinking had gone round and we had heard some tales. But, how can I put this? In professional football that's not especially surprising. So I met him and we discussed things and he convinced me that he had the drinking under control. It was an awkward thing to discuss at a first meeting, of course it was. But it was evident to me that it was something we had to address if we were going to make him the manager of Aberdeen.

'Though I was aware of stories that gambling was one of his favoured pursuits, I have to say that it didn't manifest itself at all.

Let's face it, a gambling addiction is a hard thing to check on – even if you knew about it, which we didn't.'

Paterson's appointment was no straightforward affair. For a time, the deal hung in the balance, recalls Wyness. Dundee United had also actively pursued the Inverness manager's services just weeks earlier and suffered disappointment. Paterson and his assistant Duncan Shearer had all but agreed new, extended five-year contracts with the Highland club on better terms and resigned themselves to staying put – until Aberdeen came calling.

'I read in his actions at the time that he was playing hard to get,' states Wyness. 'Now I think something else. Looking back, it's clear that he was terrified at the prospect of exposing himself to the position of managing Aberdeen. He was a deep guy, Steve. But at the time I thought it was best to regard that as a positive. He was a thinker, unlike some in football, and he needed to be convinced that we needed him.'

Paterson has admitted, however, that he should not have moved to Pittodrie. His gambling and drinking were already rocketing out of control, his debts were growing and self-doubt was gnawing at his consciousness. His marriage to former model Mandy had fallen apart and he was in the throes of personal and professional chaos. For his ageing mother Margaret and two daughters, Jessica and Emily, none of this could have been easy.

'Steve actually settled in fairly well at first,' says Wyness. 'It was a big step up for him and the attention that was lavished on the manager of Aberdeen was a bit different from the demands at Inverness or the Highland League.

'One thing he didn't do was move into the city itself. The reasons for that are obvious: Aberdeen is a one-club city where everyone knows your every move and he couldn't hide his deep-rooted problems living there. He was originally from Moray and lived in Fochaber with one of his daughters and that suited him fine, I always felt, because he kept himself well and truly off the radar. What we didn't know at the time, however, were the true reasons that he wanted to keep it that way, which only became clear later.

'Aberdeen fans are everywhere and being in the spotlight really bothered him. He was essentially an introvert and he truly hated the attention from supporters and press. Add the fact that internet supporter messageboards were carrying stories about him all the time and it was tough for him. One story was so persistent on one of the forums that I had to confront him about it and he just flew off the handle. We had to be very careful and dance around the whole issue. It wasn't purely because of the employment law aspects, which you have to be very aware of, it was also because we just wanted to do the right thing. In hindsight, the fact that he was undergoing all this public humiliation purely exacerbated the problem. Rather than embarrassing him into changing his behaviour, it served to make it worse. Being found out was the worse thing that could happen.

'He had been in denial about his problems for so long, I don't think it dawned on him initially just how serious the Dundee incident was – it took time, and the chickens finally came home to roost when he realised people were pointing at him in the street because he was the manager who missed his own team's game.'

In the end, Paterson survived 18 months in the Granite City. From an incident as grave as skipping a game there could be no way back, however anxious the club were to treat a troubled employee in an appropriate fashion. For Aberdeen, this was another disastrous managerial appointment – with a twist.

'It wasn't so much a case of us having mutual trust issues in the end,' claims Wyness, 'it was more that he simply didn't trust himself – he couldn't. We referred him for treatment for his problems and he missed a couple of appointments.

'Meanwhile, the reports about his activities on the websites kept going on. Results were never brilliant, but things had improved and they weren't too bad. But there was no doubt that a lot of the players never seemed to take to him. There was always a distance to Steve, and in management that didn't always help.

'It was horrendous when we eventually sacked him, because it was as if we were piling another layer of pressure and problems on him. But by that stage, we had little choice. We had gone to second bottom in the table and there were all these issues.

'The people I really felt for, Steve aside, were his assistants,

Duncan Shearer and Oshor Williams. Oshor, in particular, had given up a good job at the FA to join us at Aberdeen and now here he was, out as well.

'I've been at Everton in the Premiership since then, so I've had some big situations to deal with. But that was up there with the hardest.'

For Paterson, the situation was far from a simple setback either. Humiliated, he dealt with the sacking by blowing his £100,000 compensation pay-off on bets. Later he would blow a promise to take his daughters on holiday with £2,000 he had saved up – losing all but £90 of the cash on a gambling spree.

'Outsiders might look at me and think I've led a charmed life,' stated Paterson about his career, which included moving to Manchester United when he was 17. 'But I have been a tortured soul all these years.'

In the world of professional football, he has been in some remarkably good company.

Conclusion

'And all the stars that never were, are parking cars and
pumping gas . . .'
– lyric from Burt Bacharach's 'Do You Know the Way to San José'.

In writing this book, the same question recurred in my head. What, if
anything, can be learned from the experiences of the footballers
featured here? The truth is this: no 'one size fits all' cloak can be
thrown over our wayward warriors. Each had their own problems
and each had their own reasons for resorting to self-destructive
behaviour and under-achieving as a result.

To those who covet the lifestyle of a sporting idol – and who
doesn't? – there is bewilderment at how or why these men failed to
deal with the trappings of success, or with the creeping onset of
failure.

My initial conclusion was that most of the footballers featured
here were incapable of saying 'no'. Look at the most ruthlessly
disciplined and successful players in British football, such as David
Beckham, Alan Shearer and Henrik Larsson in recent years, and they
were the types to shut out the world when that focus was necessary.

The same could hardly be said of many of our heroes here. Had
they learned to lock the front door and place the phone off the hook,
then many would have avoided the problems that blighted their
careers and lives.

And yet to simplify the matter to that degree is to assume they
were capable of saying 'no'. Some were no more in control of their
own lives than they were their bank accounts.

Why? Because they had deep-rooted issues which transcended their choice of career, their fame or their brilliance. They had character flaws, addictions, the kind of problems you, me and the man next door suffer in everyday life. They were, in short, normal human beings. And as history proves, we don't always learn the lessons of those who have gone before, however long we may survive in this mortal coil.

Whether any man ever truly relinquishes the demons which drive him on is open to question. The advancing years were no cure-all for the woes of Best, Baxter, Gallacher or Ritchie. The likes of Charnley and McAvennie may claim to be better people now than they were 15 years ago, but what all of the above have in common is that growing older caused many of their problems, because it removed their ability to play football. Robbed of the discipline and routine of the professional athlete, they lost meaning and purpose in their mid 30s or sooner. Suddenly, they struggled to make sense of the anti-climax and perhaps began to believe their faculties were failing and that their lives ceased to have meaning.

And, as professional counsellors will attest, it is the fear of failure that causes most angst in a driven and otherwise privileged sportsman.

Peter Kay of the Sporting Chance Clinic – established by former Arsenal and England defender Tony Adams to help troubled sportsmen – explains it thus:

'Scoring a goal or crossing the line is the most natural buzz known to man. When 40,000 people are chanting your name, the buzz heightens the effect of the cocktail further. It's the same chemical effect as someone taking cocaine. The brain reacts in the same way.

'Not everyone can deal with its effects. Many of the men and women I have worked with in the world of sport have fear as their driving force. It's a fear of the success turning to failure, the fear of being found out. It's hard for successful people to admit to or confront their shortcomings. They grow up achieving everything they ever dreamed of through self-will and selfless determination and dedication. Along the way, so many of these individuals develop a stage persona for the TV, the fans, the club officials. And it's far removed from the real person who lurks beneath. They keep people at bay for fear that they will be seen for who they really are, that the mask will be torn off. Being emotionally articulate or emotionally vulnerable in a changing room is not really heard of. It's not the done thing. Professional sport, in my opinion, can be a very lonely place.

'And yet still people don't quite see why footballers or athletes have problems. We often look at the wealth of sports people and make the assumption that life is perfect. You hear the question, "What do they have to worry about?"

'Wealth does not preclude an individual from addiction. It might stave off the ramifications for a time, but that's all. Footballers and athletes are human beings, like you or me, and addiction is a human condition. Often, sports people have pressure trying to live up to the hype, the back page image and the public perception.

'The real problems occur when they are not playing, or coping with injury. They find diversions and the problems begin. And it matters little what their background is.'

Here lies an important distinction. In this book, the phrase 'wrong side of the tracks' finds a lazy and easy resting place, being attached to many of our working-class heroes. And yet Kay insists it matters little whether a sportsman is born in the ghetto or reared with a silver spoon, black or white, illiterate or equipped with a first from Oxford.

'Certain professions have a higher propensity to difficulties. Journalists, catering workers, airline pilots, lawyers and top-class athletes often share the same characteristics as addicts.

'Often, it's the intelligent ones who are the hardest to treat. They are usually more cerebral and think deeply, sometimes too deeply. And yet it's hard to understand addiction logically. Most people just think, "Cut down, don't drink as much, don't gamble as much."

'If only it were that straightforward. In order to get better from addiction, you need to admit that you have a problem. It's the only disease known to man which gnaws away at the brain telling you everything is fine.'

As Andy Ritchie told me early in this project, he believed he was drinking heavily as a player for one reason: because he enjoyed it.

Perhaps, for some, it really was that simple. Baxter died at the age of 61 with no discernible regrets; he lived his life to the full and accepted the consequences of his hedonism.

It may be no coincidence that most of the players featured here were strikers or attacking midfielders. Only Goram and George Connelly played any kind of defensive role. Perhaps the men who make things happen are adrenaline junkies, who are then desperate to replace the thrill of seeing the ball hit the net with alternative highs off the field.

Perhaps, in fact, there is a danger of over-analysing it all. If there had been no joy in these flawed maestros, I would never have written about them. Let us celebrate these marvellously gifted men who lit up our lives with their brilliance, however fleeting.

To the troubled stars everywhere, from Maradona to Macca, we can but salute them for the memories and paraphrase Robert Preston's sign-off in *Hellraisers*, an affectionate examination of the life and times of Hollywood stars Richard Burton, Peter O'Toole, Richard Harris and Olly Reed. Soak up the lives and wayward times of these flawed geniuses and enjoy them; chances are they bloody well did.

Further Reading

Best, B. *Our George: A Family Memoir* (Sidgwick & Jackson 2007)

Best, G. and Collins, R. *Blessed* (Ebury Press 2002)

Connelly, G. and Cooney, B. *Celtic's Lost Legend* (B&W 2007)

Crerand, P. *Never Turn the Other Cheek* (Harper Sport 2007)

Di Canio, Paolo *The Autobiography* (Collins Willow 2000)

Gallacher, K. *Slim Jim Baxter* (Virgin 2002)

Gascoigne, P. *Being Gazza* (Headline 2006)

Gascoigne, P. with Davies, H. *My Story: Gazza* (Headline 2004)

Goram A. and Gallacher, K. *My Life* (Virgin 1997)

Hilton, C. and Cole, I. *Memories of George Best* (Sportsbooks 2007)

Joannou, P. *The Hughie Gallacher Story* (Breedon Books 1989)

Macpherson, A. *Jock Stein: The Definitive Biography* (Highdown)

McAvennie, F. *Scoring: An Expert's Guide* (Canongate 2003)

McColl, G. *'78: How a Nation Lost the World Cup* (Headline 2006)

Paterson, S. with Gilfeather, F. *Steve 'Pele' Paterson: Confessions of a Highland Hero* (Birlinn 2009)

Ross, G. *Morton Greats* (Breedon Books 2004)

Scottish Football Historian No. 107, Autumn 2008

Turnbull, E. with Hannan, M. *Having A Ball* (Mainstream 2006)